WITHDRAWN

D0074923

Current Issues in Applied
Memory Research

Current Issues in Memory

Series Editor: Robert Logie

Professor of Human Cognitive Neuroscience, University of Edinburgh, UK

Current Issues in Memory is a series of edited books that reflect the state-of-the-art in areas of current and emerging interest in the psychological study of memory. Each volume is tightly focused on a particular topic and consists of seven to ten chapters contributed by international experts. The editors of individual volumes are leading figures in their areas and provide an introductory overview. Example topics include: binding in working memory, prospective memory, memory and ageing, autobiographical memory, visual memory, implicit memory, amnesia, retrieval, memory development.

Other titles in this series:

The Visual World in Memory
Edited by James R. Brockmole

Current Issues in Applied Memory Research

Edited by Graham M. Davies &
Daniel B. Wright

CALVIN T. RYAN LIBRARY
U. OF NEBRASKA AT KEARNEY

Psychology Press
Taylor & Francis Group
HOVE AND NEW YORK

First published 2010
by Psychology Press
27 Church Road, Hove, East Sussex, BN3 2FA

Simultaneously published in the USA and Canada
by Psychology Press
270 Madison Avenue, New York, NY 10016

*Psychology Press is an imprint of the Taylor & Francis Group, an
Informa business*

© 2010 Psychology Press

Typeset in Times by RefineCatch Limited, Bungay, Suffolk
Printed and bound in Great Britain by
TJ International Ltd, Padstow, Cornwall
Cover design by Lisa Dynan

All rights reserved. No part of this book may be reprinted or
reproduced or utilised in any form or by any electronic,
mechanical, or other means, now known or hereafter
invented, including photocopying and recording, or in any
information storage or retrieval system, without permission in
writing from the publishers.

The publisher makes no representation, express or implied, with regard
to the accuracy of the information contained in this book and cannot
accept any legal responsibility or liability for any errors or omissions
that may be made.

The publication has been produced with paper manufactured to strict
environmental standards and with pulp derived from sustainable
forests.

British Library Cataloguing in Publication Data
A catalogue record for this book is available from the British Library

Library of Congress Cataloging-in-Publication Data
Current issues in applied memory research / edited by Graham M.
Davies & Daniel B. Wright.
    p. cm.
  Includes index.
  1. Memory—Research.   2. Cognitive psychology.   I. Davies,
    Graham, 1943–   II. Wright, Daniel B.
  BF375.C87 2009
  153.1′2—dc22

                                                    2009011537

ISBN: 978–1–84169–727–7 (hbk only)

To our mentors, Alan and Ann Clarke (GMD) and George Gaskell (DBW) who first aroused our interest in taking psychology out of the lab and applying it to real-world issues.

Contents

Figures

Tables

Contributors

Pooja K. Agarwal, Department of Psychology, Washington University, One Brookings Drive, Campus Box 1125, St Louis, MO 63130–4899, United States

Laura Chalmers, School of Psychology, University of St Andrews, St Andrews KY16 9AJ, United Kingdom

Dr Patrick Chauvel, Inserm U 751, Laboratoire de Neurophysiologie et Neuropsychologie, Aix-Marseille University, Marseille F-13000, France

Dr Stephen D. Christman, Department of Psychology, 2801 West Bancroft Avenue, University of Toledo, Toledo, Ohio 43606–3390, United States

Dr Graham M. Davies, School of Psychology, University of Leicester, Lancaster Road, Leicester LE1 9HN, United Kingdom

Dr Elke Geraerts, School of Psychology, Erasmus University Rotterdam, PO Box 1738, 3000 DR Rotterdam, The Netherlands

Dr Sean H. K. Kang, Department of Psychology, Washington University, One Brookings Drive, Campus Box 1125, St Louis, MO 63130–4899, United States

Marissa H. Kiepert, College of Education, Ritter Hall, Temple University, 1301 Cecil B. Moore Avenue, Philadelphia, PA 19122–6091, United States

Dr Sarah Kulkofsky, Human Development and Family Studies, Texas Tech University, P.O. Box 41162, Lubbock, TX 79409–1230, United States

Dr Cara Laney, Forensic Psychology, University of Leicester, 106 New Walk, Leicester LE1 7EA, United Kingdom

Darren S. Levin, College of Education, Ritter Hall, Temple University, 1301 Cecil B. Moore Avenue, Philadelphia, PA 19122–6091, United States

Dr Elizabeth F. Loftus, Psychology & Social Behavior, University of California, Irvine CA 92697–7085, United States

Dr Kamala London, Department of Psychology, Mail Stop # 948, 2801 West

Bancroft St., University of Toledo, Toledo, Ohio 43606–3390, United States

Dr Malcolm D. Macleod, School of Psychology, University of St Andrews, St Andrews KY16 9AJ, United Kingdom

Dr Elizabeth J. Marsh, Psychology & Neuroscience, Duke University, 9 Flowers Drive, Box 90086, Durham, NC 27708–0086, United States

Dr Harald Merckelbach, Department of Clinical Psychological Science, Maastricht University, Maastricht, 6200MD, The Netherlands

Dr Chris J. A. Moulin, Institute of Psychological Sciences, University of Leeds, Leeds LS2 9JT, United Kingdom

Dr Ruth E. Propper, Psychology Department, 315 Turnpike Street, Merrimack College, North Andover, Massachusetts 01845, United States

Dr Linsey Raymaekers, Department of Clinical Psychological Science, Maastricht University, Maastricht, 6200MD, The Netherlands

Dr Henry L. Roediger, III, Department of Psychology, Washington University, One Brookings Drive, Campus Box 1125, St Louis, MO 63130–4899, United States

Dr Jo Saunders, School of Psychology, University of Swansea, Singleton Park, Swansea SA2 8PP, United Kingdom

Dr S. Kenneth Thurman, College of Education, Ritter Hall 350, Temple University, 1301 Cecil B. Moore Avenue, Philadelphia, PA 19122–6091, United States

Dr Michael Wang, School of Psychology, University of Leicester, Lancaster Road, Leicester LE1 9HN, United Kingdom

Dr Daniel B. Wright, Psychology, Florida International University, 11200 S.W. 8th Street, Miami, FL 33199, United States

Preface

This book arose from an invitation from Robert Logie, Professor of Psychology at Edinburgh University, who is editor of the 'Current Issues in Memory' series for Psychology Press. GMD was the Founding Editor of *Applied Cognitive Psychology* and has seen into print many outstanding examples of the application of theories and ideas derived from laboratory research to memory issues in the real world. The book offered the opportunity to illustrate and describe some of these applications for a wider audience and to discuss their implications in a way that is normally impossible within the confines of a journal article. DBW, himself a former Associate Editor of *Applied Cognitive Psychology* with a distinguished record in research on applied memory issues, was an obvious and willing co-editor.

Applied memory research is a growing area and we could have easily approached enough names to fill a series, let alone a single book. We decided to focus on three particularly interesting and productive areas of research: applications to education, the law and neuroscience. We are grateful to the busy professionals who have taken time out to write for a non-specialist audience about research to which they have all made such important contributions. We are also grateful to Rebekah Waldron, our editor at Psychology Press for her patience and encouragement, to Emily Davies for technical assistance in producing the typescript, to Nick James who undertook the indexing and finally, to Robert Logie for his careful reading of the original manuscript and helpful comments.

Graham M. Davies
Daniel B. Wright

Introduction

Graham M. Davies and Daniel B. Wright

Research on applied memory is one of the most active, interesting and vibrant areas in cognitive psychology today. Findings from the best applied research enhance not just practice but also theoretical knowledge of how memory functions, highlighting the strengths and shortcomings of this vital faculty. Memory is central to everyday cognition; it allows us to use past experience to interpret the seemingly chaotic perceptual world of the present and to plan for the future, enabling us to pass fluidly and seamlessly through our busy environment. Why, then, is so much research on practical aspects of memory of recent vintage? The answer lies in the history of psychology on the two sides of the Atlantic.

AN OVERVIEW OF APPLIED MEMORY RESEARCH

From 'dustbowl empiricism' to cognitive psychology

Most conventional histories of memory in psychology begin with the research of Hermann Ebbinghaus (1885/1913) and his two-year study of his own memory, using a standardized method of his own invention: the learning and re-learning of serial lists of nonsense syllables (randomly generated consonant–vowel–consonant combinations) to the rapid beat of a metronome. Initially, Ebbinghaus's work was not widely influential for the *Zeitgeist* of memory research in Britain or North America. In the period prior to the First World War, there were many studies of everyday memory dealing with such issues as eyewitness testimony (Munsterburg, 1908) and memory for advertisements (Strong, 1914); research and practice in applied memory enjoyed a settled relationship. However, subsequent to the First World War, this picture changed in the United States.

The emergence of behaviorism as the dominant school of psychology in American universities led to a greater focus on basic processes of learning in animals and humans and the neglect of anything as overtly mentalistic as everyday memory (Mills, 1998). For many researchers, the royal road to understanding human memory (later re-branded as 'verbal learning') lay not through the analysis of everyday experience, but rather through an extension of the rigorous research methods developed by Ebbinghaus, now available in translation from the original German. Nonsense syllables, unlike familiar words, were assumed to ensure learning divorced from the learner's previous knowledge (termed 'extra-experimental associations'). To Ebbinghaus's serial learning was added paired associate learning, a technique seen as paralleling instrumental conditioning in animals. In the next half-century, influential United States textbooks, such as Charles Osgood's *Method and theory in experimental psychology* (1953), contained virtually no mention of memory as an area of study, let alone its applied aspects. This new approach was termed 'functionalism' by its proponents and undoubtedly led to major advances in research methodology and control, but its contribution to understanding everyday memory experiences was, at best, limited. So limited, in fact, that the approach came to be labeled as 'dustbowl empiricism' by its detractors (Baddeley, 1997).

In the first half of the twentieth century, an emphasis on the application of psychology to practical problems within education, national defense and industry shielded British psychology from the worst excesses of behaviorism. Memory issues continued to preoccupy some of the leading researchers of their day. Sir Frederic Bartlett in his book *Remembering* (1932) rejected the rote learning of nonsense syllables exemplified by the Ebbinghaus approach in favor of exploring memory for folk tales and newspaper articles. The characteristic omissions and distortions which he observed in reproductions of this material led him to conclude that memory involved not passive reproduction, but rather active reconstruction based on knowledge structures derived from past experience which he termed 'schema'. Bartlett saw schema as a critical determinant of first remembering and later recalling meaningful material. However, these ideas were dismissed as nebulous and his research methods as anecdotal by his critics. It was left to a new generation of psycholinguists and cognitive scientists to rediscover the importance of Bartlett's concept of schema. Theories which postulate the existence of 'frames' (Minsky, 1975) and 'scripts' (Schank & Abelson, 1977) captured in a language and terminology unavailable to Bartlett the central importance of knowledge and understanding to effective cognition.

As in so many areas of culture, the 1960s brought change and a renewed interest in mental processes among psychologists on both sides of the Atlantic. In 1956, an American psychologist George Miller, drawing on his background in applied memory research, drew psychology's attention back to the concept of short-term memory (first proposed by William James) through his classic paper 'The magical number seven, plus or minus two' (Miller, 1956). Later, Miller spent a sabbatical at Stanford with Eugene Galanter, a psychologist with a background in engineering and mathematical psychology, and Karl Pribram, a brain scientist and practicing surgeon, which resulted in a manifesto for a new approach to human cognition: *Plans and the structure of behavior* (Miller, Galanter, & Pribram, 1960). This called for a more active conception of the learner as one who acts on his or her environment using past knowledge to formulate plans to anticipate future events.

Miller et al. (1960) sought a model for human behavior less primitive and constrained than conditioning and proposed the TOTE (test-operate; test-exit) model of feedback as the basic building block of human cognition. This idea was borrowed from engineering science and represented alongside Broadbent's work (see below) some of the earliest attempts to think of the brain as a complex machine. This strand of thinking, coupled with advances in computing and information processing, led psychologists to draw insightful analogies between the hardware/software distinction in computing and the structure and function of memory. One important outcome of this strand of research was the so-called 'modal model' of memory proposed by Atkinson and Shiffrin (1968) with its concept of 'control processes' or strategies which the learner mobilizes to relate incoming information to knowledge already available in long-term memory.

Miller et al. (1960) had already foreshadowed the importance of memory strategies through drawing attention to the effectiveness of imagery-based mnemonics for learning large numbers of arbitrary noun word pairs in a single exposure, a startling refutation of the view that such learning was necessarily slow and incremental as posited by behaviorist models. Paivio and colleagues went on to demonstrate that the imagery evoked by a word in a rote learning task was a powerful determinant of its ease of learning (Paivio, 1969). Work on so-called 'natural language mediators' demonstrated that nonsense syllables, far from being so drained of meaning that they must inevitably be learned by simple rehearsal, were regularly re-coded by learners into familiar words or phrases with a startling impact on speed of learning (Prytulac, 1971). Research on the recall of word lists showed serial learning played but a limited role compared to the learner's search for meaning and relationships among the items in the list (Mandler, 1967; Bower, 1970). Finally, the process of recall had been treated by functionalist models as a semi-automatic process of little theoretical interest, but now recall emerged as a complex search and retrieval process central to effective remembering (Tulving & Pearlstone, 1966). This new approach permeated Ulric Neisser's *Cognitive psychology* (1967), the title of which rapidly became synonymous with this emerging area of study.

In the UK, Bartlett's ideas continued to influence the direction of research on memory issues. He had always affirmed that there was no useful distinction to be drawn between pure and applied research and that the two types of research enjoyed a symbiotic relationship. He was instrumental in creating the Applied Psychology Unit at Cambridge in 1944, which spearheaded research on practical problems involving memory and attention, with particular reference to the armed forces and industry. Successive Directors of the APU, particularly Donald Broadbent and Alan Baddeley, shared Bartlett's view of the interdependence of theory and application, but linked it to a strong concern for methodology and control, one of the positive features of behaviorism. In *Perception and communication* Broadbent (1958) set out an information-processing model of attention and memory, while colleagues explored the properties of short-term memory, a by-product of research begun originally to explore errors made by telephonists (Conrad & Hull, 1964). Baddeley moved easily between the worlds of pure and applied research, reflected in the title of his influential text *Human memory: Theory and practice* (1997). Baddeley (1979) coined the term 'Applied Cognitive Psychology' to describe the application of concepts and theories derived from laboratory research to understand and address practical problems in the real world, an area which has grown rapidly in the ensuing years.

The 'everyday memory' movement

Academic interest in applied memory sparked a series of successful international conferences given over to practical aspects of memory, at the opening of the first of which Ulric Neisser gave a rousing address in which he condemned much of the psychology of the last half-century for its neglect of the really interesting aspects of memory in favor of pedestrian paradigm juggling (Neisser, 1978). The sheer range of topics on which research was presented rather belied Neisser's gloomy assessment, as his speech acknowledged at the second congress held a decade later (Neisser, 1988). At the third meeting in 1994, a new grouping, the Society for Applied Research on Memory and Cognition or SARMAC, was founded, bringing together scholars in the area, and this body continues to hold regular conferences (SARMAC, n.d.). A host of new journals emerged to publish the results in this burgeoning area, including *Applied Cognitive Psychology* (founded 1987), which is linked to SARMAC, *Memory* (founded 1992) and the *Journal of Experimental Psychology: Applied* (founded 1995) published by the American Psychological Association.

Neisser's onslaught on mainstream memory research provoked an inevitable counterblast. Banaji and Crowder (1989) in their provocatively entitled paper 'On the bankruptcy of everyday memory' appeared to condemn these new trends in favor of the traditional ways of studying memory. However, once the combative tone of their article was set aside, the powerful and important message of their paper remained: just because a topic is interesting does not mean the findings will necessarily contribute to science. In evaluating research, the methods employed to study a phenomenon are as important as the choice of what is studied. Banaji and Crowder noted some pieces of applied research that they applauded as well as others that they thought less worthy. It was clear from the subsequent debate (Conway, 1991; Roediger, 1991) that those applied memory studies which met with universal praise were those which married methodological rigor to issues and problems that concern people in the everyday world. The range and variety of contemporary contributions is reflected in Frank Durso's *Handbook of applied cognition* (2007), which describes the contributions of applied memory research to understanding such everyday preoccupations as the media, consumer psychology, the environment, driving, aviation and human–computer interaction.

AN OVERVIEW OF THE BOOK

As the historical overview demonstrates, applied memory research has matured into a distinct and significant area of study. In this book we selected three broad topic areas – education, law and neuroscience – to illustrate how researchers in applied memory can illuminate real issues of importance in contemporary life. Each of these sections is preceded by a brief overview to provide a conceptual and historical context for the contributions it contains.

- The section devoted to *education* highlights recent research on the consequences of testing and of examinations on students' memory and representation of information and on the application of the working memory model of memory derived from laboratory research into acquisition of 'the three R's' – reading, writing and 'rithmetic.
- The section concerned with the *law* looks at recent research in three critical areas where the authenticity and accuracy of memory is an issue for the courts: the reliability of memories of childhood trauma recovered after long delays; the likelihood that children will readily disclose the full extent of any abuse they may have suffered when questioned by an investigator; and new research which reveals the startling inability of witnesses to identify strangers to whom they have been talking only seconds previously: change blindness.
- The section on applications to *neuroscience* begins by exploring every patient's worst nightmare – waking up in the middle of an operation but being unable to tell the surgeons involved – and describes new techniques for communicating between doctor and patient, which have shed fresh light on the relationship between explicit and implicit memory. It moves on to describe studies of handedness and eye movements which reveal how different parts of the brain deal with different forms of memory, including everyday memory. Finally, the sensation of déjà vu: recent studies of patients who repeatedly believe they have 'been here before' appear to suffer from a special form of memory error linked in turn to disturbed electrical activity in the brain.

A final chapter by the editors provides an overview of the contributions and offers some speculations as to where the next challenges for applied memory researchers are likely to come from within our complex, changing world. We hope this account of recent research on applied memory will interest students who wish to extend their reading beyond the core material of cognitive psychology, graduates on more specialized courses in educational, forensic and neuropsychology, academics and indeed all those who wish to enrich their knowledge of the contemporary frontiers of applied memory research.

References

Applied Cognitive Psychology (n.d.). *Applied Cognitive Psychology* Homepage. Retrieved from http://www3.interscience.wiley.com/journal/4438/home?CRE TRY=1&SRETRY=0

Atkinson, R. C., & Shiffrin, R. M. (1968). Human memory: A proposed system and its control processes. In K. W. Spence and J. T. Spence (Eds.), *The psychology of learning and motivation* (Vol. 2, pp. 89–195). London: Academic Press.

Baddeley, A. D. (1979). Applied cognitive and cognitive applied psychology: The case of face recognition. In L.-G. Nilsson (Ed.), *Perspectives in memory research* (pp. 367–388). Hillsdale, NJ: Lawrence Erlbaum Associates, Inc.

Baddeley, A. (1997). *Human memory: Theory and practice*. Exeter, UK: Psychology Press.

Bartlett, F. C. (1932). *Remembering. A study in experimental and social psychology.* Cambridge: Cambridge University Press.

Banaji, M. R., & Crowder, R. G. (1989). The bankruptcy of everyday memory. *American Psychologist, 44*, 1185–1193.

Bower, G. H. (1970). Organizational factors in memory. *Cognitive Psychology, 1*, 18–46.

Broadbent, D. E. (1958). *Perception and communication.* London: Pergamon Press.

Conrad, R., & Hull, A. J. (1964). Information, acoustic confusion and memory span. *British Journal of Psychology, 55*, 429–432.

Conway, M. (1991). In defense of everyday memory. *American Psychologist, 46*, 19–26.

Durso, F. T. (with Nickerson, R. S., Dumais, S. T., Lewandowsky, S., & Perfect, T. J) (Eds.) (2007). *Handbook of applied cognition* (2nd ed). Chichester: Wiley.

Ebbinghaus, H. (1913). *Memory. A contribution to experimental psychology* (H. A. Ruger and C. E. Bussenues, Trans.). New York: Teachers College, Columbia University (Original work published 1885).

Journal of Experimental Psychology–Applied (n.d.). *Journal of Experimental Psychology Applied* Homepage. Retrieved from http://www.apa.org/journals/xap/

Mandler, G. (1967). Organization and memory. In K. W. Spence and J. T. Spence (Eds.), *The psychology of learning and motivation* (Vol. 1, pp. 328–372). New York: Academic Press.

Memory (n.d.). *Memory* Homepage. Retrieved from http://www.tandf.co.uk/journals/pp/09658211.html

Miller, G. A. (1956). The magical number seven, plus or minus two: Some limits on our capacity for processing information. *Psychological Review, 63*, 81–97.

Miller, G. A., Gallanter, E., & Pribram, K. (1960). *Plans and the structure of behavior.* New York: Holt, Rinehart and Winston.

Mills, J. A. (1998). *Control: A history of behavioral psychology.* New York: New York University Press.

Minsky, M. (1975). A framework for representing knowledge. In P. H. Winston (Ed.), *The psychology of computer vision* (pp. 211–277). New York: McGraw-Hill.

Munsterberg, H. (1908). *On the witness stand: Essays on psychology and crime.* New York: McClure.

Neisser, U. (1967). *Cognitive psychology*. New York: Appleton Century.

Neisser, U. (1978). Memory: What are the important questions? In M. M. Gruneberg, P. E. Morris, & R. N. Sykes (Eds.), *Practical aspects of memory* (pp. 3–24). London: Academic Press.

Neisser, U. (1988). Time present and time past. In M. M. Gruneberg, P. M. Morris, & R. N. Sykes (Eds.), *Practical aspects of memory: Current research and issues* (Vol. 1, pp. 459–465). Chichester: Wiley.

Osgood, C. E. (1953). *Method and theory in experimental psychology*. New York: Oxford University Press.

Paivio A. (1969). Mental imagery in associative learning and memory. *Psychological Review, 76*, 241–263.

Prytulak, L. S. (1971). Natural language mediation. *Cognitive Psychology, 2*, 1–56.

Roediger, H. (1991). They read an article? Commentary on the everyday memory controversy. *American Psychologist, 46*, 37–40.

SARMAC (n.d.). The Society for Applied Research on Memory and Cognition Homepage. Retrieved from http://www.sarmac.org/about.htm

Schank, R. C., & Abelson, R. P. (1977). *Scripts, plans, goals, and understanding: An inquiry into human knowledge*. Hillsdale, NJ: Lawrence Erlbaum Associates, Inc.

Strong, E. K. (1914). The effect of size of advertisements and frequency of their presentation. *Psychological Review, 21*, 136–152.

Tulving, E., & Pearlstone, Z. (1966). Availability versus accessibility of information in memory for words. *Journal of Verbal Learning and Verbal Behavior, 5*, 381–391.

Applications to education

Implicit in theories of teaching and learning are ideas as to how material can best be remembered and later recalled. Piaget (Flavell, 1963) pioneered the study of learning processes in childhood, emphasizing the role of progression and stages of development: a child cannot be expected to master new material until they have reached the developmental stage appropriate to the task in question. In Russia, the work of Vygotsky (1962) had also posited developmental stages, but linked progression specifically to social and cultural factors, particularly language, rather than age. In the United States, the long hegemony of learning theory produced some limited practical applications to classroom learning. Skinner's analysis of classroom learning had produced an intense but short-lived interest in teaching machines based on operant conditioning principles (1958). Such mechanical devices led directly to the current generation of computer-assisted learning and E-learning systems (Garrison & Anderson, 2002), which still incorporate features derived from Skinner's original behavioural analysis.

However, other learning theorists were influenced by the ideas of Piaget and Vygotsky as reliable translations of their key works became more widely available. Gagné (1985), for instance, also offered an interpretation of classroom learning founded on conditioning, but contrary to Skinner, saw such forms of learning as only the lowest rung of a hierarchy of increasingly sophisticated learning techniques necessary for the mastery of such basic skills as reading and spelling. It was Bruner, however, who led the cognitive revolution in education. His early studies of thinking (Bruner, Goodnow, & Austin, 1956) led him to the conclusion that high-level cognition involved a hierarchy of complex skills such as hypothesis testing, which did not readily lend themselves to a reductive analysis in terms of stimulus and response. These ideas fed through into a more general theory of education and teaching which emphasized the importance for effective learning of discovering principles in the classroom, rather than their passive assimilation from a textbook or teacher (Bruner, 1966). The debate which Bruner inspired on the relative value of discovery learning versus didactic teaching continues to reverberate in education (Mayer, 2004).

The relevance of the verbal learning tradition to education was extensively explored by Ausubel (1963), who could find little evidence for the operation of associative interference in classroom learning tasks and concluded that the acquisition of meaningful material required the formulation of rather different rules of learning. Two of the three contributions to this section suggest that the reaction to verbal learning may have been overdone and that there are facets of that research tradition which may have high relevance to basic educational processes.

One such application is to testing and assessment. In most educational settings, tests and exams are considered relatively neutral events, intended to measure students' knowledge but with little thought about how the tests may affect and alter that knowledge. Multiple-choice and short answer tests are popular in that they can be quickly and objectively marked, but what is the impact of testing on the learner? Henry Roediger, Pooja Agarwal, Sean Kang and Elizabeth Marsh describe studies that demonstrate the circumstances under which testing can actually facilitate learning more than further study and review. They also consider certain situations where testing may have a detrimental effect. It appears that concepts and procedures derived from the laboratory tradition of studying human memory can have application to real-world problems.

The other example concerns the processes of forgetting. For the student, forgetting is traditionally seen as a vexatious process, an enemy of effective learning in the classroom and in life. Recently, a new approach to forgetting – retrieval-induced forgetting – has emphasized the positive virtues as well as the negative consequences of forgetting. Retrieving information from memory inhibits other competing and incorrect information linked to the target item, making it less accessible. Malcolm MacLeod, Jo Saunders and Laura Chalmers demonstrate how this insight into the nature of remembering and forgetting has powerful implications for such everyday tasks as examination performance and eyewitness memory.

In the United Kingdom, the working memory model, originally developed by Baddeley and Hitch (1974), has been highly influential in memory research and has proved to be one of the most robust and applicable models for understanding learning processes in the classroom. Restrictions on the content and capacity of working memory have been shown to be powerful factors in learning simple mathematical operations and progress in reading and spelling. However, as Darren Levin, Kenneth Thurman and Marissa Kiepert emphasize, such research has highlighted concerns over how working memory is defined and measured. Levin et al. review a range of studies drawn from educational and clinical settings and question whether existing findings from practical settings require further refinement of the original theory, illustrating the classic reciprocal relationship between theory and practice.

References

Ausubel, D. P. (1963). *The psychology of meaningful verbal learning.* New York: Grune & Stratton.

Baddeley, A. D., & Hitch, G. (1974). Working memory. In G. Bower (Ed.), *The psychology of learning and motivation* (Vol. *8*, pp. 47–90). New York: Academic Press.

Bruner, J. S. (1966). *Toward a theory of instruction.* Cambridge, MA: Harvard University Press.

Bruner, J. S., Goodnow, J., & Austin, A. (1956) *A study of thinking.* New York: Wiley.

Flavell, J. H. (1963). *The developmental psychology of Jean Piaget.* Princeton: Van Nostrand.

Gagné, R. M. (1985). *The conditions of learning* (4th ed.). New York: Holt, Rinehart & Winston.

Garrison, D. R., & Anderson, T. (2002). *E-learning in the 21st century – A framework for research and practice.* London: Routledge.

Mayer, R. (2004). Should there be a three-strikes rule against pure discovery learning? The case for guided methods of instruction. *American Psychologist, 59,* 14–19.

Skinner, B. F. (1958). Teaching machines. *Science, 128,* 969–977.

Vygotsky, L. S. (1962). *Thought and language* (E. Hanfmann and G. Vakar, Trans.). Cambridge, MA: MIT Press. (Original work published 1934.)

1 Benefits of testing memory

Best practices and boundary conditions

Henry L. Roediger, III,
Pooja K. Agarwal, Sean H. K. Kang
and Elizabeth J. Marsh

The idea of a memory test or of a test of academic achievement is often circumscribed. Tests within the classroom are recognized as important for the assignment of grades, and tests given for academic assessment or achievement have increasingly come to determine the course of children's lives: score well on such tests and you advance, are placed in more challenging classes, and attend better schools. Against this widely acknowledged backdrop of the importance of testing in educational life (not just in the US, but all over the world), it would be difficult to justify the claim that testing is not used enough in educational practice. In fact, such a claim may seem to be ludicrous on the face of it. However, this is just the claim we will make in this chapter: Education in schools would greatly benefit from additional testing, and the need for increased testing probably increases with advancement in the educational system. In addition, students should use self-testing as a study strategy in preparing for their classes.

Now, having begun with an inflammatory claim – we need more testing in education – let us explain what we mean and back up our claims. First, we are not recommending increased use of standardized tests in education, which is usually what people think of when they hear the words "testing in education." Rather, we have in mind the types of assessments (tests, essays, exercises) given in the classroom or assigned for homework. The reason we advocate testing is that it requires students to retrieve information effortfully from memory, and such effortful retrieval turns out to be a wonderfully powerful mnemonic device in many circumstances.

Tests have both indirect and direct effects on learning (Roediger & Karpicke, 2006b). The indirect effect is that, if tests are given more frequently, students study more. Consider a college class in which there is only a midterm and a final exam compared to a similar class in which weekly quizzes are given every Friday, in addition to the midterm and the final. A large research program is not required to determine that students study more in the class with weekly quizzes than in the class without them. Yet tests also have a direct effect on learning; many studies have shown that students' retrieval of information on tests greatly improves their later retention of the tested material, either compared to a no-intervention control or even compared to a control condition in which students study the material for an equivalent amount of time to that given to students taking the test. That is, taking a test on material often yields greater gains than restudying material, as we document below. These findings have important educational implications, ones that teachers and professors have not exploited.

In this chapter, we first report selectively on findings from our lab on the critical importance of testing (or retrieval) for future remembering. Retrieval is a powerful mnemonic enhancer. However, testing does not lead to improvements under all possible conditions, so the remainder of our chapter will discuss qualifications and boundary conditions of test-enhanced learning, as we call our program (McDaniel, Roediger, & McDermott, 2007b). We consider issues of test format in one section, such as whether multiple-choice or short answer tests produce greater enhancements in performance. Another critical issue, considered in the next section, is the role of feedback: When is it helpful, or is it always helpful? We then discuss how to schedule tests and whether tests should occur frequently with short spacings between them – should we strike memory again when the iron is hot, as it were? Or should tests be spaced out in time, and, if so, how? In the next section, we ask if true/false and multiple-choice tests can ever have negative influences on learning. These tests provide students with erroneous information, either in the form of false statements (in true/false tests) or plausible alternatives that are nearly, but not quite, correct (in multiple-choice tests). Might students pick up misinformation from these kinds of tests, just as they do in other situations (e.g., Loftus, Miller, & Burns, 1978)? We then turn to the issue of metacognition, and examine students' beliefs and practices about testing and how they think it compares to other study strategies. Finally, we discuss how the findings on testing reviewed in this chapter might be applied in the classroom, as recent studies show that test-enhanced learning works in actual classrooms from middle school to college. We end with a few reflections on the role of testing in enhancing educational attainment.

TEST-ENHANCED LEARNING

Psychologists have studied the effects of testing on later memory, off and on, for 100 years (Abbott, 1909). In this section we report two experiments from our own lab to illustrate the power of testing to readers who may not be familiar with this literature and to blunt one main criticism of some testing research (see Roediger & Karpicke [2006b] for a thorough review).

Consider first a study by Wheeler and Roediger (1992). As part of a larger experiment, students in one condition studied 60 pictures while listening to a story. The subjects were told that they should remember the pictures, because they would be tested on the names of the pictures (which were given in the story). The test was free recall, meaning that students were given a blank sheet of paper and asked to recall as many of the items as possible. After hearing the story, one group of students was permitted to leave the lab and asked to return 1 week later for the test. A second group was given a single test that lasted about 7 minutes. A third group was given three successive tests. That is, a minute after their first test, they were given a new blank sheet of paper and asked to recall as many of the 60 pictures as they could for a second time. After they were finished, the procedure was repeated a third time. The group that was given a single recall test produced 32 items on the test; the group that took three tests recalled 32, 35 and 36, respectively. The improvement in recall across repeated tests (even though each later test is further delayed from original study) is called hypermnesia. However, the real interest for present purposes is how students performed on a final test a week later. All subjects had studied the same list of pictures while listening to a story, so the only difference was whether they had taken 0, 1 or 3 tests just after the study phase of the experiment.

The results from the 1-week delayed test are shown in Figure 1.1. Subjects who did not take a test during the first session recalled 17 items, those who had taken one test recalled 23 items, whereas those who had taken three tests recalled 32 items. The number of tests given just after learning greatly

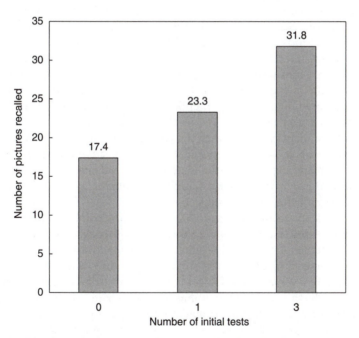

Figure 1.1 Number of pictures recalled on a 1-week delayed test, adapted from Table 1.1 in Wheeler and Roediger (1992). The number of tests given just after learning greatly affected performance a week later; three prior tests raised recall over 80% relative to the no-test condition, and the act of taking three tests virtually eliminated the forgetting process.

affected performance a week later; three prior tests raised recall over 80% relative to the no-test condition (i.e., $(32 - 17)/17 \times 100$). Looked at another way, immediately after study about 32 items could be recalled. If subjects took three tests just after recall, they could still recall 32 items a week later. The act of taking three tests essentially stopped the forgetting process in its tracks, so testing may be a mechanism to permit memories to consolidate or reconsolidate (Dudai, 2006).

Critics, however, could pounce on a potential flaw in the Wheeler and Roediger (1992) experiment just reported. Perhaps, they would carp, repeated testing simply exposes students to information again. That is, all "testing" does is allow for repeated study opportunities, and so the testing effect is no more surprising than the fact that when people study information two (or more) times they remember it better than if they study it once (e.g., Thompson, Wenger, & Bartling, 1978). This objection is plausible, but has been countered in many experiments that compared subjects who were tested to ones who spent the same amount of time restudying the material. The consistent finding is that taking an initial test produces greater recall on a final test than does restudying material (see Roediger & Karpicke, 2006b). Here we report only one experiment that makes the point.

Roediger and Karpicke (2006a, Experiment 1) had students read brief prose passages about a variety of topics, many having to do with science ("The Sun" or "Sea Otters") and other topics. After reading the passage, students either took a 7-minute test on the passage or read it again. Thus, in one condition, students studied the passage twice, whereas in the other they studied it once and took a test. The test consisted of students being given the title of the passage and asked to recall as much of it as possible. The data were scored in terms of the number of idea units recalled. The students taking the test recalled about 70% of the idea units during the test; on the other hand, students who restudied the passage were of course exposed to all the ideas in the passage. Thus, students who reread the passage actually received a greater exposure to the material than did students who took the test. The final test on the passages was either 5 minutes, 2 days or 7 days later, and was manipulated between subjects.

The results are shown in Figure 1.2 and several notable patterns can be seen. First, on the test given after a short (5-minute) delay, students who had repeatedly studied the material recalled it better than those who had studied it once and taken a test. Cramming (repeatedly reading) does work, at least at very short retention intervals. However, on the two delayed tests, the pattern reversed; studying and taking an initial test led to better performance on the delayed test than did studying the material twice. Testing enhanced long-term retention. Many other experiments, some of which are discussed below, have reported this same pattern (see Roediger & Karpicke, 2006b, for a review).

The results reviewed above, along with many others dating back over a century, establish the reality of the testing effect. However, not all experiments reveal testing effects. In the sections below, we consider variables that

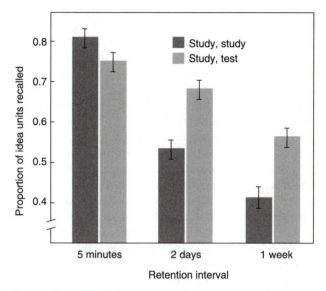

Figure 1.2 Results from Roediger and Karpicke (2006a, Experiment 1). On the 5-minute delayed test, students who had repeatedly studied the material recalled it better than those who had studied it once and taken a test. Cramming (repeatedly reading) does work, at least at very short retention intervals. However, on the two delayed tests, the pattern reversed; studying and taking an initial test led to better performance on the delayed test than did studying the material twice.

modulate the magnitude of the testing effect, beginning with the format of tests.

THE FORMAT OF TESTS

The power of testing to increase learning and retention has been demonstrated in numerous studies using a diverse range of materials; but both study and test materials come in a multitude of formats. Although the use of true/false and multiple-choice exams is now commonplace in high school and college classrooms, there was a time (in the 1920s and 1930s) when these kinds of exams were a novelty and referred to as "new-type," in contrast to the more traditional essay exams (Ruch, 1929). Given the variety of test formats, one question that arises is whether all formats are equally efficacious in improving retention. If we want to provide evidence-based recommendations for educators to utilize testing as a learning tool, it is important to ascertain if particular types of tests are more effective than others.

In a study designed to examine precisely this issue, Kang, McDermott, and Roediger (2007) manipulated the formats of both the initial and final tests – multiple-choice (MC) or short answer (SA) – using a fully-crossed, within-subjects design. Students read four short journal articles, and immediately afterwards they were given an MC quiz, an SA quiz, a list of statements to read, or a filler task. Feedback was given on quiz answers, and the quizzes and the list of statements all targeted the same critical facts. For instance, after reading an article on literacy acquisition, students in the SA condition generated an answer to "What is a phoneme?" (among other questions), students in the MC condition selected one of four possible alternatives to answer the same question, and students in the read-statements condition read "A phoneme is the basic sound unit of a language." This last condition allowed the effects of testing to be compared to the consequences of focused re-exposure to the target information (i.e., similar to receiving the test answers, without having to take the test). This control condition was a very conservative one, given that students in real life generally do not receive the answers to upcoming exams. A more typical baseline condition (i.e., having a filler task after reading the article) was also compared to the testing and focused rereading conditions. Three days later, subjects took a final test consisting of MC and SA questions.

Figure 1.3 shows that final performance was best in the initial SA condition. The initial MC condition led to the next best performance, followed by the read-statements condition and finally the filler-task condition. This pattern of results held for both final MC and final SA questions. Final test scores

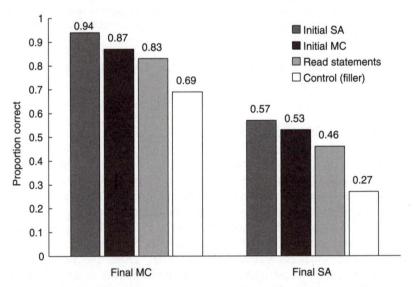

Figure 1.3 Results from Kang, McDermott, and Roediger (2007). Regardless of the format of the final test, the initial test format that required more effortful retrieval (i.e., the SA condition) yielded the best final performance, which was significantly better than being given the test answers without having to take a test. Although taking an initial MC test did benefit final performance relative to the filler-task control condition, the boost was not significantly above the read-statements condition.

were significantly worse in the filler-task condition than the other three conditions, indicating that both testing (with feedback) and focused re-exposure aid retention of the target information. Importantly, only the initial SA condition produced significantly better final performance than the read-statements condition; the initial MC and read-statements conditions did not differ significantly. Retrieval is a potent memory modifier (Bjork, 1975). These results implicate the processes involved in actively producing information from memory as the causal mechanism underlying the testing effect. Regardless of the format of the final test, the initial test format that required more effortful retrieval (i.e., short answer) yielded the best final performance, and this condition was significantly better than having read the test answers in isolation.

Similar results from other studies provide converging evidence that effortful retrieval is crucial for the testing effect (Carpenter & DeLosh, 2006; Glover, 1989). Butler and Roediger (2007), for example, used art history video lectures to simulate classroom learning. After the lectures, students completed short answer or multiple-choice tests, or they read statements as in Kang et al. (2007). On a final SA test given 30 days later, Butler and Roediger found the same pattern of results: (1) retention of target facts was best when students were given an initial SA quiz, and (2) taking an initial MC test produced final performance equivalent to reading the test answers (without taking a test). As discussed in a later section of this chapter, these findings have been replicated in an actual college course (McDaniel, Anderson, Derbish, & Morrisette, 2007b).

Although most evidence suggests that tests that require effortful retrieval yield the most memorial benefits, it should be noted that this depends upon successful retrieval on the initial test (or the delivery of feedback). Kang et al. (2007) had another experiment identical to the one described earlier except that no feedback was provided on the initial tests. Without corrective feedback, final test performance changed: the initial SA condition yielded poorer performance than the initial MC condition. This difference makes sense when performance on the initial tests is considered: accuracy was much lower on the initial SA test ($M = .54$) than on the initial MC test ($M = .86$). The beneficial effect of testing can be attenuated when initial test performance is low (Wenger, Thompson, & Bartling, 1980) and no corrective feedback is provided.

This same conclusion about the role of level of initial performance can be drawn from Spitzer's (1939) early mega-study involving 3605 sixth-graders in Iowa. Students read an article on bamboo, after which they were tested. Spitzer manipulated the frequency of testing (students took between one and three tests) and the delay until the initial test (which ranged from immediately after reading the article to 63 days later). Most important for present purposes is that the benefit of prior testing became smaller the longer one waited after studying for the initial test; i.e., performance on the initial test declined with increasing retention interval, reducing the boost to performance on subsequent tests. In a similar vein, it has been shown that items that elicit errors on a cued recall test have almost no chance of being recalled correctly at a later time unless feedback is given (Pashler, Cepeda, Wixted, & Rohrer, 2005). In other words, learning from the test is handicapped when accuracy is low on the initial test (whereas this problem does not occur with rereading, where there is re-exposure to 100% of the target information). For the testing effect to manifest itself fully, feedback must be provided if initial test performance is low. Recent research showing that retrieval failure on a test (i.e., attempting to recall an answer but failing to) can enhance future encoding of the target information (Kornell, Hays, & Bjork, 2009; Richland, Kornell & Kao, 2009) emphasizes further the utility of providing feedback when initial test performance is poor.

A recent study (Agarwal, Karpicke, Kang, Roediger, & McDermott, 2008) delved more deeply into the issue of whether the kind of test influences the testing effect. In a closed-book test, students take the test without having concurrent access to their study materials, and this is the traditional way in which tests have been administered. In recent years, open-book tests – where students are permitted to consult their notes and textbooks during the test – have grown in popularity, with the belief that such tests promote higher-level thinking skills (e.g., Feller, 1994). The final test only involved short answer questions. We examined the issue of whether administering the initial test open- or closed-book made a difference to later retention of target facts. For the sake of brevity, only the second experiment will be described here (the results replicate the first experiment, which was similar in design). Students studied expository passages in various learning conditions: three study-only conditions (read the passage once, twice, or three times) and four test conditions (a closed-book test, a closed-book test with feedback, or an open-book test after reading the passage once, or a test completed simultaneously while reading the passage).

A final closed-book test was given a week later, and the key results are summarized in Table 1.1. Just taking a closed-book test (without feedback) resulted in final performance that was roughly equivalent to reading the passage three times (.55 vs. .54), and significantly better than reading the passage twice (.55 vs. 50), once again demonstrating the power of testing. The two learning conditions that tied for the best performance, however, were the closed-book test with feedback and the open-book test conditions (Ms = .66), both of which produced significantly more correct responses on the final test than all the other conditions. In our view, these two learning conditions contained two critical components – testing (retrieval) and feedback – that the other learning conditions lacked (or had only one or the other), and this combination contributed to best performance on the delayed test.

Although the current data suggest the equivalence of closed-book tests with feedback and open-book tests in enhancing later retention, further investigation into this issue is warranted, because on theoretical grounds one might expect a closed-book test to involve more retrieval effort than an

Table 1.1 Mean proportion recalled in Agarwal et al.'s (2008) Experiment 2 on test formats. Proportion correct was greater for test conditions than study conditions; however, subjects predicted learning would be greater for study conditions relative to test conditions. Learning conditions that contained both testing and feedback, namely the closed-book test with feedback and the open-book test conditions, contributed to best performance on the delayed test.

Condition	Proportion correct	
	Initial test	*One-week delayed test*
Study 1×		.40
Study 2×		.50
Study 3×		.54
Closed-book test	.67	.55
Closed-book test with feedback	.65	.66
Open-book test	.81	.66
Simultaneous answering	.83	.59
Non-studied control		.16

open-book test. Perhaps a difference between these two conditions will emerge with a longer delay for the final test, an outcome that has occurred in other experiments (e.g., Roediger & Karpicke, 2006a). Such a finding would probably further depend on how students approach the open-book tests (e.g., whether they attempt retrieval of an answer before consulting the study material for feedback, or whether they immediately search the study material in order to identify the target information). Future research in our lab will tackle this topic.

In summary, one reason why testing benefits memory is that it promotes active retrieval of information. Not all formats of tests are equal. Test formats that require more effortful retrieval (e.g., short answer) tend to produce a greater boost to learning and retention, compared to test formats that engage less effortful retrieval (e.g., multiple-choice). However, tests that are more effortful or challenging also increase the likelihood of retrieval failure, which has been shown to reduce the beneficial effect of testing. Therefore, to ameliorate low performance on the initial test, corrective feedback should be provided. The practical implications of these findings for improving learning in the classroom are straightforward: instead of giving students summary notes to read, teachers should implement more frequent testing (of important facts and concepts) – using test formats that entail effortful retrieval – and provide feedback to correct errors. We turn now to a greater consideration of the issue of how and when feedback should be given after tests.

TESTING AND FEEDBACK

Broadly defined, feedback is information provided following a response or recollection, which informs the learner about the status of current performance, often leading to improvement in future performance (Roediger, Zaromb, & Butler, 2008). A great deal of laboratory and applied research has examined the conditions under which feedback is, and is not, effective in improving learning and performance. We have already mentioned the critical importance of feedback when initial performance is low, as well as the benefit of feedback regardless of test format. In a later section, we discuss the benefits of feedback in reducing the negative effects of multiple-choice tests. For now, we focus on the effect of feedback type (e.g., corrective or right/wrong) and delay (e.g., immediate vs. delayed) on a learner's future responses and confidence regarding their own performance.

To begin, feedback can encompass a range of information: re-presentation of the original material, information regarding whether the learner is simply correct or incorrect, or specific information regarding the correct response, just to name a few. In a study by Pashler et al. (2005), subjects studied Luganda–English word pairs (e.g., *leero – today*) and received no feedback, right/wrong feedback, or correct answer feedback following each response on an initial test. After one week, performance following the correct answer feedback condition was significantly greater than performance in either of the other conditions. In addition, right/wrong feedback did not benefit retention over and above the absence of feedback, a finding replicated in other studies (e.g., see Bangert-Drowns, Kulik, Kulik, & Morgan, 1991, for a review). Furthermore, Moreno (2004) demonstrated that explanatory feedback (e.g., providing students with the correct answer and an explanation) increased final retention and transfer relative to corrective feedback (e.g., only providing students with the correct answer). In general, in order to improve performance, feedback must include corrective information, and the learner may further benefit when an explanation follows the corrective feedback.

Although Pashler et al. (2005) found the benefits of corrective feedback to be limited to revising errors, Butler, Karpicke, and Roediger (2007) found that feedback benefits initially correct answers as well as incorrect responses. This recent finding is consistent with earlier research, which demonstrated that subjects who receive feedback are more likely to fix initial errors and remember initially correct responses on a final criterial test (Kulhavy, Yekovich, & Dyer, 1976, 1979). More specifically, subjects spend more time processing feedback following errors made with high confidence and correct answers made with low confidence. Butterfield and Metcalfe (2006) held feedback time constant, and still found subjects were more likely to later correct errors made with high confidence than those made with low confidence. They named this the hypercorrection effect, and argued that subjects attend more to feedback that is at odds with their expectations (see also Fazio

& Marsh, 2009). Similarly, Butler, Karpicke, and Roediger (2008) suggested that feedback reinforces the association between a cue and its target response, increasing the likelihood that an initially low-confidence correct response will be produced on a final criterial test.

Regarding the best time to deliver feedback, there exists a great deal of debate and confusion, as immediate and delayed feedback are operationalized differently across studies. For instance, the term "immediate feedback" has been used to imply feedback given just after each test item or feedback provided immediately after a test. On the other hand, "delayed feedback" can take place anywhere from 8 seconds after an item to 2 days after the test (Kulik & Kulik, 1988), although in many educational settings the feedback may actually occur a week or more later.

Butler et al. (2007) investigated the effects of type and timing of feedback on long-term retention. Subjects read prose passages and completed an initial multiple-choice test. For some responses, they received standard feedback (i.e., the correct answer); for others they received feedback by answering until correct (labeled AUC: i.e., each response was labeled as correct or incorrect, and if incorrect they chose additional options until they answered the question correctly). Half of the subjects received the feedback immediately after each question, while the rest received the feedback after a 1-day delay. One week later, subjects completed a final cued recall test, and these data are shown in Figure 1.4. On the final test, delayed feedback led to substantially better performance than immediate feedback, while the standard feedback condition and the answer-until-correct feedback condition resulted in similar performance. Butler et al. discussed why some studies find immediate feedback to be more beneficial than delayed feedback (e.g., see Kulik & Kulik, 1988, for a review). Namely, this inconsistency might occur if learners do not fully process delayed feedback, which would be particularly likely in applied studies where less experimental control is present. That is, even if students receive delayed feedback they may not look at it or look only at feedback on questions that they missed. When feedback processing is controlled, as in the Butler et al. study, a benefit for delayed feedback on long-term retention emerges.

In sum, the provision of feedback leads to substantial increases in long-term learning. Delayed feedback virtually always boosts final performance if the feedback includes both the correct answer as well as an explanation of that answer. Feedback also serves a variety of purposes: correcting errors, improving retention of correct responses, and enhancing metacognition. Feedback should be incorporated into all educational testing.

SCHEDULES FOR TESTING

The great bulk of the literature on testing effects shows the benefit of a single initial test relative to either no test or to a reading control condition. The fact

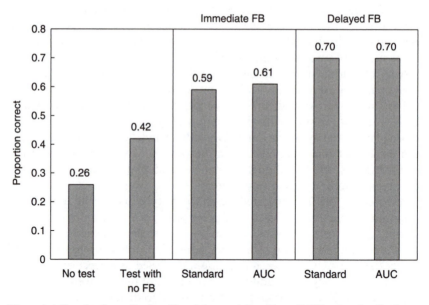

Figure 1.4 Results from Butler, Karpicke, and Roediger (2007). On the final test, delayed feedback (FB) led to substantially better performance than immediate feedback, while the standard feedback condition and the answer-until-correct (AUC) feedback condition resulted in similar performance. When feedback processing is controlled, a benefit for delayed feedback on long-term retention emerges.

that the testing effect occurs robustly in such situations indicates the power of testing, but one can ask whether students would learn better if they received multiple tests on the same material. For example, the Wheeler and Roediger (1992) data shown in Figure 1.1 indicate that three tests shortly after study led to better recall a week later relative to one test. Is this effect general?

Anecdotally, one might expect that it is. For example, when children in the early primary grades are taught their multiplication tables, they often use or construct flashcards. All problems up to 9 × 9 (or even higher) are created so that one side of the card might say 6 × 8 = ?? and the other side has 48. Students are instructed to test themselves repeatedly on the cards, flipping over to the other side when they need feedback. Students are usually instructed to do this until answering the item becomes quick and effortless, but it takes repeated practice to reach this state.

Flashcards are used in many other situations to learn large bodies of factual information, and educational companies make flashcards for a huge number of purposes, including learning foreign language vocabulary, the parts of the skeletal system, birds and their names, and so on. Research on how to effectively use flashcards is relatively new, however. One instruction often given in mastering a set of flashcards is to learn to give the correct answer, then practice it once, and then to drop that card from the pile to concentrate on others that have not yet been learned. The assumption is that learning to a criterion of one correct recitation means that the item is learned and that further practice on it will be for naught.

Karpicke and Roediger (2008) published a study that questions this common wisdom. In their study, students learned foreign language vocabulary in the form of Swahili–English words pairs. (Swahili was used because students were unfamiliar with the language, and yet the word forms were easily pronounceable for English speakers, such as *mashua–boat*). Students learned 40 pairs under one of four conditions. In one condition, students studied and were tested on the 40 pairs in the usual multitrial learning situation favored by psychologists (study–test, study–test, study–test, study–test, labeled the ST condition). In a second condition, students received a similar first study–test cycle, but if they correctly recalled pairs on the test, these pairs were dropped from the next study trial. Thus, across the four trials, the study list got smaller and smaller as students recalled more items. However, in this condition, labeled S_NT, students were tested on all 40 pairs during each test period. Thus, relative to the ST condition, the S_NT condition involved fewer study opportunities but the same number of tests. In a third condition, labeled ST_N, students studied and were tested the same way as in the other conditions on the first trial, but after the first trial they repeatedly studied the pairs three more times, but once they had recalled a pair, it was dropped from the test. In this condition, the study sequence stayed the same on four occasions, but the number of items tested became smaller and smaller. Finally, in a fourth condition denoted S_NT_N, after the first study–test trial, items that were recalled were dropped both from the study and test phase of the experiment for the additional trials. In this case, then, the study list and the test sequence became shorter over trials. This last condition is most like standard advice for using flashcards – students studied and were tested on the pairs until they were recalled, and then they were dropped so that attention could be devoted to unlearned pairs.

Initial learning on the 40 pairs in the four conditions is shown in Figure 1.5, where it can be seen that all four conditions produced equivalent learning. The data in Figure 1.5 show cumulative performance, such that students were given credit the first time they recalled a pair and not again (for those conditions in which multiple recalls of a pair were required, ST and S_NT). At the end of the learning phase, students were told that they would come back a week later to be tested again and were asked to predict how many pairs they would recall. Students in all four groups estimated that they would recall about 20 pairs, or 50% of the pairs, a week later. After all, the learning curves were equal, so why would we expect students' judgments to differ?

Figure 1.6 shows the proportion of items recalled 1 week later, in each of the four conditions. Students in two conditions did very well (ST and S_NT, around 80%) and in the other two conditions students did much more poorly (ST_N and S_NT_N, around 35%). What do the former two conditions have in common that the latter two conditions lack? The answer is retrieval practice.

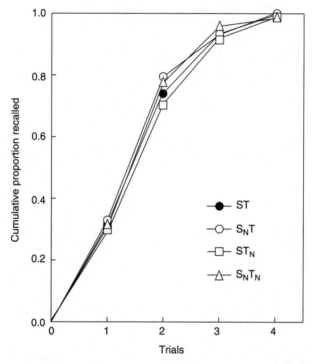

Figure 1.5 Initial cumulative learning performance from Karpicke and Roediger (2008). All four conditions produced equivalent learning.

In both the ST and S_NT conditions, students were tested on all 40 pairs for all four trials. Note that in the ST condition students studied all 40 items four times, whereas in the S_NT condition, the items were dropped from study. However, this reduced amount of study did not matter a bit for retention a week later. Students in the ST_N and S_NT_N conditions had only enough testing for each item to be recalled once and, without repeated retrieval, final recall was relatively poor. Once again, the condition with many more study opportunities (ST_N) did not lead to any appreciably better recall a week later than the condition that had minimal study opportunities (S_NT_N).

The bottom line from the Karpicke and Roediger (2008) experiment is that after students have retrieved a pair correctly once, repeated retrieval is the key to improved long-term retention. Repeated studying after this point does not much matter.

Recall that the students in the four conditions predicted that they would do equally well, and recall about 50% after a week. As can be seen in Figure 1.6, the students who were repeatedly tested actually outperformed their predictions, so they underestimated the power of testing. On the other hand, the students who did not have repeated testing overestimated how well they would do. In a later section, we return to the issue of what students know

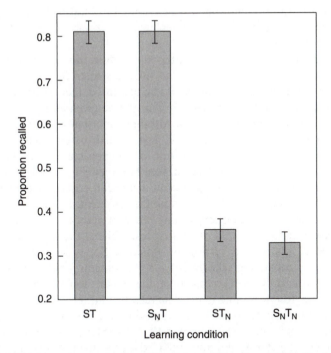

Figure 1.6 Final learning results from Karpicke and Roediger (2008). Students in the ST and S_NT conditions performed very well, and students in the ST_N and S_NT_N conditions did much more poorly. In both the ST and S_NT conditions, students were tested on all 40 pairs for all four trials. Students in the ST_N and S_NT_N conditions had only enough testing for each item to be recalled once and, without repeated retrieval, recall was relatively poor. The condition with many more study opportunities (ST_N) did not lead to any appreciably better recall a week later than the condition that had minimal study opportunities (S_NT_N).

about the effects of testing and whether they use testing as a study strategy when left to their own devices.

Repeated testing seems to be great for consolidating information into long-term memory, but is there an optimal schedule for repeated testing? Landauer and Bjork (1978) argued that a condition they called expanding retrieval was optimal, or at least was better than two other schedules called massed practice and equal interval practice. To explain, let us stick with our foreign-language vocabulary learning example above, *mashua–boat*, and consider patterns in which three retrievals of the target might be carried out. In the immediate test condition, after the item has been presented, *mashua* would be presented three times in a row for boat to be recalled each time. This condition might provide good practice because, of course, performance on each test would be nearly perfect. (In fact, in most experiments, this massed testing condition leads to 98% or higher correct recall with paired-associates.)

The massed retrieval condition will be denoted a 0-0-0 to indicate that the three retrievals occurred back to back, with no other study or test items between retrievals of the target.

A second condition is the equal interval schedule, in which tests are given after a delay from study and at equal intervals after that. So, in a 5-5-5 schedule, a pair like *mashua–boat* would be presented, then five other pairs or tests would occur, and then *mashua – ??* would be given as a cue. This same process would occur two more times. Although distributed retrieval could be beneficial relative to massed retrieval, just as distributed study practice is beneficial relative to massed practice, one looming problem occurs in the case of retrieval – if the first test is delayed, recall on the first test may be low and, as discussed above, low performance on a test can reduce or eliminate the power of the testing effect. To overcome this problem, Landauer and Bjork (1978) introduced the idea of expanding retrieval practice, to insure a nearly errorless early retrieval with a quick first test while at the same time gaining advantages of distributed testing or practice. So, to continue with our example, in an expanding schedule of 1-4-10, students would be tested with *mashua – ??* after only 1 intervening item, then again after 4 intervening items, and then after 10 intervening items. The idea behind the expanding schedule is familiar to psychologists because it resembles the idea of shaping behavior by successive approximations (Skinner, 1953, Chapter 6); just as schedules of reinforcement (Ferster & Skinner, 1957) exist to shape behavioral responses, so schedules of retrieval may shape the ability to remember. If a student wants to be able to retrieve a vocabulary word long after study, the expanding retrieval schedule may help to shape its retrieval.

Landauer and Bjork (1978) conducted two experiments pitting massed, equal interval, and expanding interval schedules of retrieval against one another. For the latter conditions, they used 5-5-5 spacing and 1-4-10 spacing. Note that this comparison equates the average interval of spacing at 5. The materials in one experiment were fictitious first and last names, such that students were required to produce a last name when given the first name. Landauer and Bjork measured performance on the three initial tests and then on a final test given at the end of the experimental session. The results for the expanding and equal interval retrieval sequences are shown in Table 1.2 for

Table 1.2 Mean proportion recalled in Landauer and Bjork's (1978) experiment on schedules of testing; data are estimated from Figures 1.1 and 1.2. Expanding retrieval schedules were better than equal interval schedules on both the initial three tests and the final criterial test.

| | *Initial tests* | | | *Final test* |
	1	2	3	
Expanding	.61	.55	.50	.47
Equal	.42	.42	.43	.40

the three initial tests and then the final, criterial, test. Expanding retrieval schedules were better than equal interval schedules, as Landauer and Bjork predicted, on both the initial three tests and then the final criterial test. The 7% advantage of expanding interval retrieval to equally spaced retrieval on the final test was small but statistically significant, and this is the comparison that the authors emphasized in the paper. They replicated the effect in a separate experiment with face–name pairs. However, note a curious fact about the data in Table 1.2: Over the four tests shown, performance drops steadily in the expanding interval condition (from .61 to .47) whereas in the equal interval condition performance is essentially flat (.42 to .40). This pattern suggests that on a more delayed final test, the curves might cross over and equal interval retrieval might prove superior to expanding retrieval.

Strangely, for some years researchers did not investigate Landauer and Bjork's (1978) intriguing findings, perhaps because they made such good sense. Most of the studies on retrieval schedules compared expanding and massed retrieval, but did not include the critical equal interval condition needed to compare expanding retrieval to another distributed schedule (e.g., Rea & Modigliani, 1985). All studies making the massed versus expanding retrieval comparison showed expanding retrieval to be more effective, and Balota, Duchek, and Logan (2007) have provided an excellent review of this literature. They show conclusively that massed testing is a poor strategy relative to distributed testing, despite the fact that massed testing produces very high performance on the initial tests (much higher than equal interval testing). Although this might seem commonplace to cognitive psychologists steeped in the literature of massed versus spaced presentation (the spacing effect), from a different perspective the outcome is surprising. Skinner (1958) promoted the notion of errorless retrieval as being the key to learning, and he implemented this approach into his teaching machines and programmed learning. However, current research shows that distributed retrieval is much more effective in promoting later performance than is massed retrieval, even though massed retrieval produces errorless performance.

On the other hand, when comparisons are made between expanding and equal interval schedules, the data are much less conclusive. The other main point established in the Balota et al. (2007) review is that no consistent evidence exists for the advantage of expanding retrieval schedules over equal interval testing sequences. A few studies after Landauer and Bjork's (1978) seminal study obtained the effect, but the great majority did not. For example, Cull (2000) reported four experiments in which students learned difficult word pairs. Across experiments, he manipulated variables such as intertest interval, feedback or no feedback after the tests, and testing versus restudying the material. The general conclusion drawn from the four experiments was that distributed retrieval produced much better retention on a final test than did massed retrieval, but that it did not matter whether the schedule had uniform or expanded spacing of tests.

Recent research by Karpicke and Roediger (2007) and Logan and Balota

(2008) actually shows a more interesting pattern. On tests that occur a day or more after original learning, equal interval schedules of initial testing actually produce greater long-term retention than do expanding schedules (just the opposite of Landauer and Bjork's findings). Recall the data in Table 1.2 and how the expanding retrieval testing condition showed a steady decline with repeated tests whereas the equal interval schedule showed essentially no decline. Because the final test in these studies occurred during the same session as initial learning, the retention interval for the final test was fairly short, leaving open the possibility that on a long-delayed test the functions would actually cross. This is just what both Karpicke and Roediger and Logan and Balota found.

Karpicke and Roediger (2007) had students learn word pairs taken from practice tests for the Graduate Record Exam (e.g., *sobriquet–nickname, benison–blessing*) and tests consisted of giving the first member of the pair and asking for the second. Their initial testing conditions were massed (0-0-0), expanding (1-5-9) and equal interval (5-5-5). In addition, they included two conditions in which students received only a single test after either 1 intervening pair or 5. The design and initial test results are shown on the left side of Table 1.3. Initial test performance was best in the massed condition, next in the expanding condition, and worst in the equally spaced condition, the usual pattern, and students in the single test condition recalled less after a delay of 5 intervening items than after 1. There are no surprises in the initial recall data. Half the students took a final test 10 minutes after the initial learning phase, whereas the rest received the final test 2 days later. These results are shown in the right side of Table 1.3. First consider data at the 10-minute delay. The top three rows show a very nice replication of the pattern reported by Landauer and Bjork (1978): Expanding retrieval in the initial phase produced better recall on the final test than the equal interval schedule, and both of these schedules were better than the massed retrieval

Table 1.3 Mean proportion recalled in Karpicke and Roediger's (2007) experiment on schedules of testing. Expanding retrieval in the initial phase produced better recall than the equal interval schedule on the 10-minute delayed test, and both of these schedules were better than the massed retrieval schedule. However, after a 2-day delay, recall was best in the equal interval condition relative to the expanding condition, although both conditions still produced better performance than in the massed condition.

	Initial tests			Final tests	
	1	*2*	*3*	*10 min*	*48 h*
Massed (0-0-0)	.98	.98	.98	.47	.20
Expanding (1-5-9)	.78	.76	.77	.71	.33
Equal (5-5-5)	.73	.73	.73	.62	.45
Single-immediate (1)	.81			.65	.22
Single-delayed (5)	.73			.57	.30

schedule. Also, the single-immediate test produced better delayed recall than the single-delayed test. However, the startling result in this experiment appeared for those subjects who took the test after a 2-day delay. Recall was now best in the equal interval condition (M = .45) relative to the expanding condition (M = .33), although both conditions still produced better performance than in the massed condition (M = .20). Interestingly, performance also reversed across the delay for the two single test conditions: recall was better in the single-immediate condition after 10 minutes, but was reliably better in the single-delayed condition after 2 days.

Karpicke and Roediger (2007) argued that, congenial as the idea is, expanding retrieval is not conducive to good long-term retention. Instead, what seems to be important for long-term retention is the difficulty of the first retrieval attempt. When subjects try to retrieve an item after 5 intervening items, they exert more effort during retrieval than after 1 intervening item, which in turn is more difficult than after no intervening items (the massed condition). Notice that the same pattern occurs for items that were tested only once, after either 1 or 5 intervening items. Karpicke and Roediger (2007) replicated these results in a second experiment in which feedback was given after the initial tests. A third experiment confirmed that delaying the first test is the critical ingredient in enhancing long-term retention and that the method of distributing retrieval (expanding or equal interval) does not matter. Logan and Balota (2008) reported similar data and reached the same general conclusion.

The conclusion that retrieval difficulty is the key element promoting better long-term retention for equal interval (relative to expanding or massed) schedules fits well with data reviewed in previous parts of the chapter, such as recall tests producing a greater testing effect than recognition tests. However, as Balota et al. (2007) have noted, the literature on expanding retrieval sequences has used a relatively small array of conditions (three tests, paired associate learning of one sort or another, relatively immediate tests). One can imagine that an expanding retrieval schedule could be better than equal intervals if there were more presentations and these occurred over longer periods of time. However, this conjecture awaits future testing.

DANGERS OF MULTIPLE-CHOICE AND TRUE/FALSE TESTS

We have established that students learn from tests, and that this learning seems to be especially durable. However, the fact that we learn from tests can also pose a danger in some situations. Although professors would never knowingly present wrong information during lectures or in assigned readings, they do it routinely when they give certain types of tests, viz., true/false and multiple-choice tests. If students learn from tests, might they learn wrong information if it is presented on the tests? On true/false tests it is common for half the statements to be right and half to be wrong, and normally false items are plausible in order to require rather fine discriminations. Similarly, for multiple-choice tests, students receive a question stem and then four possible completions, one of which is correct and three others that are erroneous (but again, statements that might be close to correct). Because erroneous information is presented on the tests, students might learn that incorrect information, especially if no feedback is given (as is often the case in college courses). If the test is especially difficult (meaning a large number of wrong answers are selected), the students may actually leave a test more confused about the material than when they walked in. However, even if conditions are such that students rarely commit errors, it might be that simply reading and carefully considering false statements on true/false tests and distractors on multiple-choice tests can lead later to erroneous knowledge. Several studies have shown that having people simply read statements (whether true or false) increases later judgments that the statements are true (Bacon, 1979; Begg, Armour, & Kerr, 1985; Hasher, Goldstein, & Toppino, 1977). This effect underlies the tactics of propagandists using "the big lie" technique by repeating a statement over and over until the populace believes it, and is also a favored tactic in most US presidential elections. If you repeat an untruth about an opponent repeatedly, the statement comes to be believed.

Remmers and Remmers (1926) first discussed the idea that incorrect information on tests might mislead students, when the "new" techniques of true/false and multiple-choice testing were introduced into education (Ruch, 1929). They called this outcome the negative suggestibility effect, although not much research was done on it for many years. Much later Toppino and his colleagues showed that statements presented as distractors on true/false and multiple-choice tests did indeed accrue truth value from their mere presentation, because these statements were judged as more true when mixed with novel statements in appropriately designed experiments (Toppino & Brochin, 1989; Toppino & Luipersbeck, 1993). In a similar vein, Brown (1988) and Jacoby and Hollingshead (1990) showed that exposing students to misspelled words increased misspelling of those words on a later oral test.

Roediger and Marsh (2005) asked whether giving a multiple-choice test (without feedback) would lead to a kind of misinformation effect (Loftus et al., 1978). That is, if students take a multiple-choice test on a subset of facts, and then take a short answer test on all facts, will prior testing increase intrusions of multiple-choice lures on the final test? Roediger and Marsh conducted a series of experiments to address this question, manipulating the difficulty of the material (and hence level of performance on the multiple-choice test) and the number of distractors given on the multiple-choice test. Three experiments were submitted using these tactics, but the editor asked us to drop our first two experiments (which established the phenomenon) and report only a third, control, experiment that showed that the negative suggestibility effect occurred under tightly controlled but not necessarily realistic conditions. We complied and published the third experiment, but the two most interesting experiments (in our opinion) were not reported. We present them here to show that negative effects of testing do accrue from taking multiple-choice tests and to have the experiments published, albeit in terse form.

Our first experiment was exploratory, just to make sure we could get the effects we sought. We predicted that we would see a positive testing effect to the extent students were able to answer the multiple-choice questions. Of interest was whether selecting distractors on the multiple-choice test would lead to their intrusion on a later test. We selected 80 easy and 80 hard general knowledge questions from the Nelson and Narens (1980) norms. Subjects in the norming study correctly answered an average of 72% of easy questions ("What sport uses the terms 'gutter' and 'alley'? [bowling]") and 13% of the difficult items ("Which union general defeated the Confederate Army at the Civil War battle of Gettysburg?" [Meade]). Because the norms are for short answer questions, we generated three plausible distractors for each item. Four sets of 40 items (20 easy and 20 hard) were created and rotated through four multiple-choice test conditions: 40 items were not tested, 40 were tested with one distractor, 40 with two distractors, and 40 with 3 distractors. Thus the multiple-choice test consisted of 120 questions, and no feedback was given as to the correctness of the answers. Following this test, the 40 subjects in the experiment spent 5 minutes doing a visuospatial filler task before they took a final short answer (cued recall) test. They were given the 160 general knowledge questions (120 items previously tested with multiple-choice and the 40 nontested items).

Performance on the multiple-choice test is shown in the top panel of Table 1.4, in the section devoted to Experiment 1 data. Not surprisingly, performance was better on easy than difficult items and declined with the number of alternatives. However, we did succeed in manipulating the level of

Table 1.4 Proportion correct on a multiple-choice test as a function of question difficulty and number of alternatives (including correct) for each question in Experiments 1 and 2 of Roediger and Marsh (reported in this chapter). Performance was better on easy than difficult items and declined with the number of alternatives. Similarly, performance on unread passages was lower than for read passages, and performance generally declined with the number of distractors (albeit more for unread than read passages).

	Number of alternatives		
	Two	*Three*	*Four*
Experiment 1			
Easy questions	.91	.85	.85
Hard questions	.66	.55	.48
Experiment 2			
Passages read	.86	.86	.84
Passages not read	.68	.62	.51

multiple-choice performance, and this allowed us to see if any negative effects of testing were limited to conditions in which subjects made more errors on the multiple-choice test (i.e., difficult items and relatively many distractors).

The interesting data are contained in Tables 1.5 and 1.6 (again, the top panels devoted to Experiment 1). Table 1.5 shows the proportion of short answer questions answered correctly ("bowling" in response to "What sport uses the terms 'gutter' and 'alleys'?"). A strong positive testing effect appeared: Relative to the nontested questions, subjects correctly answered more previously-tested questions, for both easy and hard items. When previously tested with more multiple-choice distractors, the size of the positive effect dropped a bit for the hard items. However, the positive testing effect was robust in all conditions. Subjects had been required to guess on the short answer test (and they provided confidence ratings), but when we removed the "not sure" responses from the data, the same pattern held (for both high confidence and medium confidence answers). These data with "not sure responses removed" are shown in parentheses in Table 1.5.

Table 1.6 shows errors committed on the short answer test, and we found that prior multiple-choice testing also led to a negative effect (in addition to the positive testing effect just documented). The prior multiple-choice test led to more multiple-choice lure answers on the final test and this effect grew larger when more distractors had been presented on the multiple-choice test. Again, removing the "not sure" responses reduced the size of the negative suggestibility effect, but left the basic pattern intact. Those data are again in parentheses.

Table 1.5 Proportion correct on the cued recall test as a function of question difficulty and number of alternatives (including the correct answer) on the prior multiple-choice test. Non-guess responses are in parentheses (proportion correct not including those that received a "not sure" rating). A positive testing effect is evident for both easy and hard questions, and read and unread passages, although the effect declined with the number of distractors on the prior multiple-choice test for the unread items. In both experiments, a positive testing effect was observed under all conditions, and the effect was maintained even when "not sure" responses were removed.

	Number of previous alternatives			
	Zero (not-tested)	*Two*	*Three*	*Four*
Experiment 1				
Easy questions	.69	.86	.84	.84
	(.65)	(.83)	(.81)	(.80)
Hard questions	.18	.44	.41	.38
	(.16)	(.40)	(.36)	(.33)
Experiment 2				
Read passages	.56	.79	.79	.75
	(.52)	(.73)	(.72)	(.70)
Non-read passages	.23	.56	.53	.44
	(.14)	(.43)	(.40)	(.31)

Table 1.6 Proportion target incorrect answers on the cued recall test as a function of question difficulty and number of alternatives (including the correct answer) on the prior multiple-choice test. Non-guess responses are in parentheses (proportion correct not including those that received a "not sure" rating). The prior multiple-choice test led to more errors on the final test and this effect grew larger when more distractors had been presented on the multiple-choice test. Removing the "not sure" responses reduced the size of the negative suggestibility effect, but left the basic pattern intact.

	Number of previous alternatives			
	Zero (not-tested)	*Two*	*Three*	*Four*
Experiment 1				
Easy questions	.08	.09	.11	.11
	(.05)	(.06)	(.09)	(.08)
Hard questions	.17	.26	.34	.36
	(.10)	(.20)	(.21)	(.24)
Experiment 2				
Read passages	.05	.09	.10	.11
	(.01)	(.06)	(.05)	(.07)
Non-read passages	.11	.24	.25	.37
	(.03)	(.13)	(.12)	(.15)

The data show clearly that taking a multiple-choice test can simultaneously enhance performance on a later cued recall test (a positive testing effect) and harm performance (a negative suggestibility effect). The former effect comes from questions answered correctly on the multiple-choice test, whereas the latter effect arises from errors committed on the multiple-choice test. In fact, 78% of the multiple-choice lure answers on the final test had been selected erroneously on the prior multiple-choice test. This result is noteworthy because it suggests that any negative effects of multiple-choice testing require selection of an incorrect answer, and that simply reading the lures (and then selecting the correct answer) is not problematic.

In Experiment 2 we examined whether students would show the same effects when learning from prose materials. We used 20 nonfiction passages on a wide variety of topics (the sun, Mt. Rainier, Louis Armstrong). For each passage we constructed four questions, each of which could be tested in both multiple-choice and short answer formats. Students read half the passages and not the other half, and then took a multiple-choice test where the number of multiple-choice lures was manipulated from zero (the item was not tested) through three alternatives. Thus, the design conformed to a 2 (studied, non-studied passages) × 4 (number of distractors on the test, 0–3) design. Five minutes after completing the multiple-choice test, the students took the final short answer test that contained 80 critical items (60 from the previous multiple-choice test and 20 previously nontested items). As in the first experiment, they were required to answer all questions and to rate their confidence in each answer.

The multiple-choice data are displayed in the bottom part of Table 1.4. Again, the results are straightforward: Not surprisingly, performance on unread passages was lower than for read passages, and performance generally declined with the number of distractors (albeit more for unread than read passages). Once again, the manipulations succeeded in varying multiple-choice performance across a fairly wide range.

The consequences of multiple-choice testing can be seen in the bottom of Table 1.5, which shows the proportion of final short answer questions answered correctly. A positive testing effect occurred for both read and unread passages, although for unread passages the effect declined with the number of distractors on the prior multiple-choice test. Still, as in the first experiment, a positive testing effect was observed in all conditions, even when "not sure" responses were removed (the data in parentheses).

As can be seen in Table 1.6, the negative suggestibility effect also appeared in full force in Experiment 2, although it was greater for the nonread passages, with their corresponding higher rate of errors on the multiple-choice test than for the read passages. For the read passages, the error rate nearly doubled after the multiple-choice test, from 5% to 9%. When the "not sure" responses were removed, the difference grew from 1% (not tested) to 6% (tested). This is not large, but is statistically significant. Also, note that students in this experiment were tested under conditions that usually do not hold in actual educational settings – they had carefully read the relevant passages only moments before the multiple-choice test and only 20 or so minutes before taking the final criterial test. The data from the nonread passages with their higher error rates may in some ways be more educationally informative, as unfortunately students are often unprepared for exams. The negative suggestibility effect was much larger in the nonread condition whether or not the "not sure" responses were included.

The generalization that may be taken from these two experiments is that when multiple-choice performance is relatively high, a large positive testing effect and a relatively small negative suggestibility effect will be found. Correspondingly, under conditions of relatively poor multiple-choice performance, the positive testing effect will be diminished and the negative effect will be increased. These conclusions hold over more recent experiments, and also agree with the third experiment conducted, the one that did appear in the Roediger and Marsh (2005) paper. In this study, we replicated Experiment 2 but changed the instruction on the final short answer test from forced recall with confidence ratings to recall with a strong warning against guessing. That is, subjects were told to give an answer on the final test only if they were reasonably sure they were right. Under these stricter conditions, we still obtained the negative suggestibility effect (and, of course, the positive testing effect). These strict conditions are unlike those used in educational settings, though, where students are typically free to respond without fear of penalty for wrong answers.

The subjects in the three experiments just described were all from

Washington University, a highly selective university, and therefore these expert test takers are unrepresentative of test takers in general. To take a step towards a more typical sample, we (Marsh, Agarwal, & Roediger, 2009) recently tested high school juniors at a suburban high school in Illinois, on practice SAT II questions on chemistry, biology, and history. SAT II tests (now renamed SAT subject tests) are often taken by high school juniors and used for college admissions and class placement decisions. We examined the effects of answering SAT II questions on a later short answer test, in both the high school students and a Duke University sample tested with similar procedures. Duke University students are expert test takers, who took tests similar to the SAT II for admission. Not surprisingly, the undergraduates did much better on the initial multiple-choice questions than did the high school students; undergraduates answered 55% correctly whereas high schoolers only answered 34% correctly. High schoolers also endorsed far more multiple-choice lures than did the university students; SAT II questions always offer a "don't know" option as the test penalizes wrong answers. So even if high school students didn't know the answers, they still could have responded "don't know" rather than endorsing a distractor – but they endorsed distractors for 56% of the multiple-choice questions! The results on the final short answer test were consistent with what we predicted – the negative testing effect was much larger in the group (high school students) who endorsed more multiple-choice lures. Testing led to a smaller positive testing effect in high school students, and a larger negative testing effect, emphasizing the need for future research to include populations other than undergraduates.

None of the experiments described thus far in this section provided any corrective feedback to students. Importantly, Butler and Roediger (2008) showed that feedback given shortly after a multiple-choice test enhanced the positive testing effect and neutralized the negative suggestibility effect. However, it is critical that feedback be provided under conditions in which it is carefully processed to have this positive impact (see too Butler et al., 2007). Giving feedback is thus one obvious method of preventing the negative suggestibility effect. However, in our experience feedback is rarely given in university and college settings and when provided it occurs under suboptimal conditions. In large introductory courses using multiple-choice and short answer tests, professors often want to protect items in their test banks (so they do not have to create new tests and can refine their old tests with the data students provide). Even when professors do give feedback on tests, it is often given relatively long after taking the test (due to time for grading) and/or the feedback is provided under conditions in which students may not attend to it (e.g., just giving back the marked tests or requiring students to stop by the professor's office to see the corrected tests).

Most professors we know give credit (and partial credit) as deserved, but do not deduct points for bad answers – the worst possible score on an item is a zero, not some negative number. However, giving a penalty for wrong answers sounds more interesting when one thinks about the importance of endorsing multiple-choice lures for the negative suggestibility effect. We examined this more directly in another experiment using SAT II practice questions and Duke undergraduates (Marsh et al., 2009). One group of undergraduates was warned they would receive a penalty for wrong answers and that they should choose a "don't know" option if they were not reasonably sure of their answer. Another group was required to answer all of the multiple-choice questions. Both groups showed large positive testing effects, and smaller negative testing effects. Critically, the penalty instruction significantly reduced the negative testing effect, although it was still significant.

Research on negative suggestibility is just beginning, and only a few variables have been systematically investigated. Three classes of variables are likely to be interesting: ones that affect how likely subjects are to select multiple-choice lures (e.g., reading related material, a penalty for wrong answers on the MC test), ones that affect the likelihood that selected multiple-choice lures are integrated with related world knowledge (e.g., corrective feedback), and ones that affect monitoring at test (e.g., the warning against guessing on the final test used in Roediger & Marsh, 2005). The negative testing effect could change in size for any of these reasons. For example, consider one recent investigation involving the effects of adding a "none of the above" option to the MC test (Odegard & Koen, 2007). When "none of the above" was the correct answer on the MC test, the negative testing effect increased. It turned out that subjects were less willing to endorse "none of the above" than a specific alternative, meaning that MC performance was worst for items containing a "none of the above" option (and MC lure endorsements increased), with consequences for later performance.

In summary, most experiments show that the positive testing effect is larger than any negative testing effect; even if subjects learn some false facts from the test, the net effect of testing is positive (see Marsh, Roediger, Bjork, & Bjork, 2007, for a review). The exception may be when students are totally unprepared for the test and endorse many multiple-choice lures – this is a scenario that needs further research. The best advice we can give is to make sure the students receive corrective feedback, and to consider penalizing students for wrong answers.

METACOGNITION AND SELF-REGULATED LEARNING

While we have focused on testing as a pedagogical tool to enhance learning in the classroom, we are mindful that the bulk of learning in real life takes place outside the classroom. More often than not learning is self-regulated – the learner has to decide what information to study, how long to study, the kind of strategies or processing to use when studying, and so on. All these decisions depend on the learner's goals (e.g., the desired level of mastery), beliefs (e.g., that a particular type of study strategy is more effective), external constraints (e.g., time pressure), and online monitoring during the learning experience (i.e., subjective assessments of how well the material has been learned; Benjamin, 2007). In other words, a student's beliefs about learning and memory and his or her subjective evaluations during the learning experience are vital to effective learning (Dunlosky, Hertzog, Kennedy, & Thiede, 2005). In this section we shall discuss the metacognitive factors concomitant with testing, how testing can improve monitoring accuracy, as well as the use of self-testing as a study strategy by students.

Research on metacognition provides a framework for examining how students strategically monitor and regulate their learning. *Monitoring* refers to a person's subjective assessment of their cognitive processes, and *control* refers to the processes that regulate behavior as a consequence of monitoring (Nelson & Narens, 1990). One indirect way in which testing can enhance future learning is by allowing students to better monitor their learning (i.e., discriminate information that has been learned well from that which has not been learned). Enhanced monitoring in turn influences subsequent study behavior, such as having students channel their efforts towards less well-learned materials. A survey of college students' study habits revealed that students are generally aware of this function of testing (Kornell & Bjork, 2007). In response to the question "If you quiz yourself while you study, why do you do so?" 68% of respondents chose "To figure out how well I have learned the information I'm studying," while only 18% selected "I learn more that way than through rereading," suggesting that relatively few students view testing as a learning event (see too Karpicke, Butler, & Roediger, 2009).

To gain insight into subjects' monitoring abilities, researchers ask them to make judgments of learning (JOLs). Normally done during study, students predict their ability to remember the to-be-learned information at a later point in time (usually on a scale of 0–100%), and then these predictions are compared to their actual performance. Usually people are moderately accurate when making these predictions in laboratory paradigms (e.g., Arbuckle & Cuddy, 1969), but JOLs are inferential in nature and can be based on a variety of beliefs and cues (Koriat, 1997). The accuracy of one's metacognitive monitoring depends on the extent to which the beliefs and cues that one uses are diagnostic of future memory performance – and some of students' beliefs about learning are wrong. For example, subjects believe that items that are easily processed will be easy to retrieve later (e.g., Begg, Duft, Lalonde, Melnick, & Sanvito, 1989), whereas we have already discussed that more effortful retrieval is more likely to promote retention. Similarly, students tend to give higher JOLs after repeated study than after receiving initial tests on the to-be-remembered material, but actual final memory performance exhibits the opposite pattern (i.e., the testing effect; Agarwal et al., 2008; Kang, 2009a; Roediger & Karpicke, 2006a). Repeated studying of the material probably engenders greater processing fluency, which leads to an overestimation of one's future memory performance.

Students' incorrect beliefs about memory mean that they often engage in

suboptimal learning strategies. For example, JOLs are often negatively correlated with study times during learning, meaning that students spend more
time studying items that they feel are difficult and that they still need to
master (Son & Metcalfe, 2000; although see Metcalfe & Kornell [2003]
for conditions that produce an exception to this generalization). Not only is
testing a better strategy, but sometimes substantial increases in study time are
not accompanied by equivalent increases in performance, an outcome termed
the "labor-in-vain" effect (Nelson & Leonesio, 1988).

Consider a study by Karpicke (in press) that examined subjects' strategies
for learning Swahili–English word pairs. Critically, the experiment had
repeated study–test cycles (multi-trial learning) and once subjects were able to
correctly recall the English word (when cued with the Swahili word) they were
given the choice of whether to restudy, test, or drop an item for the upcoming
trial, with the goal of maximizing performance on a final test 1 week later.
Subjects chose to drop the majority of items (60%), while about 25% and 15%
of the items were selected for repeated testing and restudy, respectively.
Subjects also made JOLs before making each choice, and items selected for
restudy were subjectively the most difficult (i.e., lowest JOLs), dropped items
were perceived to be the easiest, and items selected for testing were in
between. As expected, final performance increased as a function of the proportion of items chosen to be tested, whereas there was no relationship
between the proportion of items chosen for restudy and final recall. Finally,
there was a negative correlation between the proportion of items dropped
and final recall, indicating that subjects dropped items before they had firmly
registered the pair.

These results suggest that learners often make suboptimal choices during
learning, opting for strategies that do not maximize subsequent retention.
Also, the tendency to drop items once they were recalled the first time reflects
overconfidence and under-appreciation of the value of practicing retrieval.
Follow-up research in our lab (Kang, 2009b) is investigating whether
experiencing the testing effect (i.e., performing well on a final test for items
previously tested, relative to items that were previously dropped or restudied)
can induce learners to select preferentially self-testing study strategies that
enhance future recall. We suspect this may be possible, given that testing can
help improve metacognitive monitoring and sensitize learners to retrieval
conditions, as described in the next two experiments.

Comparisons between immediate and delayed JOLs suggest an important
role for testing in improving monitoring accuracy. Delayed JOLs refer to ones
solicited at some delay after the items have been studied, whereas immediate
JOLs are solicited immediately after each item has been studied. Delayed
JOLs are typically more accurate than immediate JOLs (e.g., Nelson &
Dunlosky, 1991). This delayed JOL effect is obtained only under certain
conditions, specifically when the JOLs are "cue-only" JOLs. This term refers
to the situation in which studied items are A–B pairs and subjects are provided only with A when asked to make their prediction for later recall of the

target B; the effect does not occur when JOLs are sought with intact cue-target pairs presented (Dunlosky & Nelson, 1992). One explanation for this finding is that subjects attempt retrieval of the target for cue-only delayed JOLs, and success or failure at retrieval then guides subjects' predictions (i.e., a high JOL is given if the target is successfully retrieved; if not then a low JOL is given). This enhanced ability to distinguish well-learned from less well-learned items, coupled with the testing effect on items retrieved successfully during the delayed JOL, has been proposed to account for the increased accuracy of delayed JOLs (Spellman & Bjork, 1992; Kelemen & Weaver, 1997).

Testing can also augment monitoring accuracy by sensitizing learners to the actual conditions that prevail at retrieval. Consider one study where JOLs were not always accurate: Koriat and Bjork (2005) had subjects learn paired associates, including forward-associated pairs (e.g., *cheddar–cheese*), backwards-associated pairs (e.g., *cheese–cheddar*), and unrelated pairs. During learning, subjects were asked to judge how likely it was that they would remember the 2nd word in the pair. Subjects over-predicted their ability to remember the target in the backwards-associated pairs, and the authors dubbed this an "illusion of competence." When subjects see "*cheese–cheddar*" they think they will easily remember *cheddar* when they later see *cheese* because the two words are related. However, when *cheese* occurs on the later test, it does not cue *cheddar* because the association between them is asymmetric and occurs in the opposite direction (*cheddar* reminds people of *cheese*, but *cheese* is much less likely to remind people of *cheddar*). Castel, McCabe, and Roediger (2007) reported the same overconfidence in students believing they would remember identical pairs of words (*cheese–cheese*). Critically, Koriat and Bjork (2006) found that study–test experience could alleviate this metacognitive illusion. On the first study–test cycle, subjects showed the same overconfidence for the backward-associated pairs, but JOLs and recall performance became better calibrated with further study–test opportunities. This finding suggests that prior test experience can enhance learners' sensitivity to retrieval conditions on a subsequent test, and can be a way to improve metacognitive monitoring.

The studies discussed in this section converge on the general conclusion that the majority of college students are unaware of the mnemonic benefit of testing: When students monitor their learning they feel more confident after repeated reading than after repeated testing, and when allowed to choose their study strategies self-testing is not the dominant choice. Students' self-reported study strategies mirror these laboratory findings (Karpicke et al., 2009). When preparing for tests, rereading notes or textbooks was by far the most preferred strategy (endorsed by almost 55% of students completing the survey), whereas strategies that involve retrieval practice (e.g., doing practice problems, using flashcards, self-testing) were preferred by fewer than 20% of students. It is clear that, when left to their own devices, many students engage in suboptimal study behavior. Even though college students might be expected to be expert learners (given their many years of schooling and experience preparing for exams), they often labor in vain (e.g., rereading the text) instead of employing strategies that contribute to robust learning and retention. Self-testing may be unappealing to many students because of the greater effort required compared to rereading, but this difficulty during learning turns out to be beneficial for long-term performance (Bjork, 1994). Therefore, the challenge for future research is to uncover conditions that encourage learners to set aside their naïve intuitions when studying and opt for retrieval-based strategies that yield lasting results.

APPLICATIONS OF TESTING IN CLASSROOMS

Recently, several journal articles have highlighted the importance of using tests and quizzes to improve learning in real educational situations. The notion of using testing to enhance student learning is not novel, however, as Gates employed this practice with elementary school students in 1917 (see too Jones [1923] and Spitzer [1939]). One cannot, however, assume that laboratory findings necessarily generalize to classroom situations, given that some laboratory parameters (e.g., relatively short retention intervals, tight experimental control) do not correspond well to naturalistic contexts. This distinction has garnered interest recently and we will outline a few studies that have evaluated the efficacy of test-enhanced learning within a classroom context.

Leeming (2002) adopted an "exam-a-day" procedure in two sections of Introductory Psychology and two sections of his summer Learning and Memory course, for a total of 22 to 24 exams over the duration of the courses. In comparable classes taught in prior semesters, students had received only four exams. Final retention was measured after 6 weeks. Leeming found significant increases in performance between the exam-a-day procedure and the four exam procedure in both the Introductory Psychology sections (80% vs. 74%) and Learning and Memory sections (89% vs. 81%). In addition, the percentage of students who failed the course decreased following the exam-a-day procedure. Leeming's students also participated in a survey, and students in the exam-a-day sections reported increased interest and studying for class.

McDaniel et al. (2007a) described a study in an online Brain and Behavior course that used two kinds of initial test questions, short answer and multiple-choice, as well as a read-only condition. Weekly initial quizzes were administered via the Web; questions were followed by immediate feedback and in the read-only condition, the facts were re-presented. Two unit examinations in multiple-choice format were given after 3 weeks of quizzes, and a final cumulative multiple-choice assessment at the end of the semester covered material from both units. Although facts targeted on the initial quizzes were repeated on the unit/final exams, the question stems were phrased differently so that the learning of concepts was assessed rather than memory for a prior test response. On the two unit exams, retention for quizzed material was significantly greater than that for non-quizzed material, regardless of the initial quiz format. On the final exam, however, only short answer (but not multiple-choice) initial quizzes produced a significant benefit above non-quizzed and read-only material. The results from this study provide further evidence of the strength of the testing effect in classroom settings, as well as replicating prior findings showing that short answer tests produce a greater testing effect than do multiple-choice tests (e.g., Butler & Roediger, 2007; Kang et al., 2007).

McDaniel and Sun (2009) replicated these findings in a more traditional college classroom setting, in which students took two short-answer quizzes per week. The quizzes were emailed to the students, who had to complete them by noon the next day. After emailing their quiz back to the professor, students received an email with the quiz questions and correct answers. Retention was measured on unit exams, composed of quizzed and non-quizzed material, and administered at the end of every week. Performance for quizzed material was significantly greater than performance on non-quizzed material.

Finally, Roediger, McDaniel, McDermott, and Agarwal (2010) conducted various test-enhanced learning experiments at a middle school in Illinois. The experiments were fully integrated into the classroom schedules and used material drawn directly from the school and classroom curriculum. In the first study, 6th grade social studies, 7th grade English, and 8th grade science students completed initial multiple-choice quizzes over half of the classroom material. The other half of the material served as the control material. The teacher in the class left the classroom during administration of quizzes, so she did not know the content of the quizzes and could not bias her instruction toward (or against) the tested material. The initial quizzes included a pre-test before the teacher reviewed the material in class, a post-test immediately following the teacher's lecture, and a review test a few days after the teacher's lecture. Upon completion of a 3- to 6-week unit, retention was measured on chapter exams composed of both quizzed and non-quizzed material. At all three grade levels, and in all three content areas, significant testing effects were revealed such that retention for quizzed material was greater than for non-quizzed material, even up to 9 months later (at the end of the school year). The results from 8th grade science, for example, can be seen in Figure 1.7.

This experiment was replicated with 6th grade social studies students who, instead of completing in-class multiple-choice quizzes, participated in games online using an interactive website at their leisure. This design was implemented in order to minimize the amount of class time required for a test-enhanced learning program. Despite being left to their own devices, students still performed better on quizzed material available online than non-quizzed material on their final chapter exams. Furthermore, in a subsequent

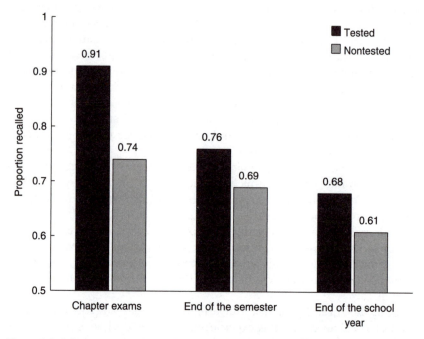

Figure 1.7 Science results from Roediger, McDaniel, McDermott, and Agarwal (2009). Significant testing effects in a middle school setting were revealed such that retention for quizzed material was greater than for non-quizzed material, even up to 9 months later (at the end of the school year).

experiment with 6th grade social studies students, a read-only condition was included, and performance for quizzed material was still significantly greater than read-only and non-quizzed material, even when the number of exposures were equated between the quizzed and read-only condition.

In sum, recent research is beginning to demonstrate the robust effects of testing in applied settings, including middle school and college classrooms. Future research extending to more content areas (e.g., math), age groups (e.g., elementary school students), methods of quizzing (e.g., computer-based and online), and types of material (e.g., application and transfer questions), we expect, will only provide further support for test-enhanced learning programs.

CONCLUSION

In this chapter, we have reviewed evidence supporting test-enhanced learning in the classroom and as a study strategy (i.e., self-testing) for improving student performance. Frequent classroom testing has both indirect and direct benefits. The indirect benefits are that students study for more time and with greater regularity when tests are frequent, because the specter of a looming test encourages studying. The direct benefit is that testing on material serves as a potent enhancer of retention for this material on future tests, either relative to no activity or even relative to restudying material. Providing correct answer feedback on tests and insuring that students carefully process this feedback greatly enhances this testing effect. Feedback is especially important when initial test performance is low. Multiple tests produce a larger testing effect than does a single test. In addition, tests requiring production of answers (short answer or essay tests) produce a greater testing effect than do recognition tests (multiple-choice or true/false). The latter tests also have the disadvantage of exposing students to erroneous information, but giving feedback eliminates this problem. Test-enhanced learning is not limited to laboratory materials; it improves performance with educational materials (foreign language vocabulary, science passages) and in actual classroom settings (ranging from middle school classes in social studies, English, and science, to university classes in introductory psychology and biological bases of behavior). We believe that the application of frequent testing in classrooms can greatly improve academic performance across the curriculum.

References

Abbott, E. E. (1909). On the analysis of the factors of recall in the learning process. *Psychological Monographs, 11*, 159–177.

Agarwal, P. K., Karpicke, J. D., Kang, S. H. K., Roediger, H. L., & McDermott, K. B. (2008). Examining the testing effect with open- and closed-book tests. *Applied Cognitive Psychology, 22*, 861–876.

Arbuckle, T. Y., & Cuddy, L. L. (1969). Discrimination of item strength at time of presentation. *Journal of Experimental Psychology, 81*, 126–131.

Bacon, F. T. (1979). Credibility of repeated statements: Memory for trivia. *Journal of Experimental Psychology: Human Learning and Memory, 5*, 241–252.

Balota, D. A., Duchek, J. M., & Logan, J. M. (2007). Is expanded retrieval practice a superior form of spaced retrieval? A critical review of the extant literature. In J. S. Nairne (Ed.), *The foundations of remembering: Essays in honor of Henry L. Roediger, III* (pp. 83–105). New York: Psychology Press.

Bangert-Drowns, R. L., Kulik, C. C., Kulik, J. A., & Morgan, M. (1991). The instructional feedback in test-like events. *Review of Educational Research, 61*, 213–238.

Begg, I., Armour, V., & Kerr, T. (1985). On believing what we remember. *Canadian Journal of Behavioral Science, 17*, 199–214.

Begg, I., Duft, S., Lalonde, P., Melnick, R., & Sanvito, J. (1989). Memory predictions are based on ease of processing. *Journal of Memory and Language, 28*, 610–632.

Benjamin, A. S. (2007). Memory is more than just remembering: Strategic control of encoding, accessing memory, and making decisions. In A. S. Benjamin & B. H. Ross (Eds.), *The psychology of learning and motivation: Skill and strategy in memory use* (Vol. 48, pp. 175–223). London: Academic Press.

Bjork, R. A. (1975). Retrieval as a memory modifier: An interpretation of negative recency and related phenomena. In R. L. Solso (Ed.), *Information processing and cognition: The Loyola Symposium* (pp. 123–144). New York: Wiley.

Bjork, R. A. (1994). Memory and metamemory considerations in the training of human beings. In J. Metcalfe and A. Shimamura (Eds.), *Metacognition: Knowing about knowing* (pp. 185–205). Cambridge, MA: MIT Press.

Brown, A. S. (1988). Encountering misspellings and spelling performance: Why wrong isn't right. *Journal of Educational Psychology, 4,* 488–494.

Butler, A. C., Karpicke, J. D., & Roediger, H. L. (2007). The effect of type and timing of feedback on learning from multiple-choice tests. *Journal of Experimental Psychology: Applied, 13,* 273–281.

Butler, A. C., Karpicke, J. D., & Roediger, H. L. (2008). Correcting a metacognitive error: Feedback increases retention of low-confidence correct responses. *Journal of Experimental Psychology: Learning, Memory, and Cognition, 34,* 918–928.

Butler, A. C., & Roediger, H. L. (2007). Testing improves long-term retention in a simulated classroom setting. *European Journal of Cognitive Psychology, 19,* 514–527.

Butler, A. C., & Roediger, H. L. (2008). Feedback enhances the positive effects and reduces the negative effects of multiple-choice testing. *Memory and Cognition, 36,* 604–616.

Butterfield, B., & Metcalfe, J. (2006). The correction of errors committed with high confidence. *Metacognition and Learning, 1,* 69–84.

Carpenter, S. K., & DeLosh, E. L. (2006). Impoverished cue support enhances subsequent retention: Support for the elaborative retrieval explanation of the testing effect. *Memory and Cognition, 34,* 268–276.

Castel, A. D., McCabe, D. P., & Roediger, H. L. (2007). Illusions of competence and overestimation of associative memory for identical items: Evidence from judgments of learning. *Psychonomic Bulletin and Review, 14,* 107–111.

Cull, W. L. (2000). Untangling the benefits of multiple study opportunities and repeated testing for cued recall. *Applied Cognitive Psychology, 14,* 215–235.

Dudai, Y. (2006). Reconsolidation: The advantage of being refocused. *Current Opinion in Neurobiology, 16,* 174–178.

Dunlosky, J., Hertzog, C., Kennedy, M. R. T., & Thiede, K. W. (2005). The self-monitoring approach for effective learning. *Cognitive Technology, 10,* 4–11.

Dunlosky, J., & Nelson, T. O. (1992). Importance of the kind of cue for judgments of learning (JOL) and the delayed-JOL effect. *Memory and Cognition, 20,* 374–380.

Fazio, L. K., & Marsh, E. J. (2009). Surprising feedback improves later memory. *Psychonomic Bulletin and Review, 16,* 88–92.

Feller, M. (1994). Open-book testing and education for the future. *Studies in Educational Evaluation, 20,* 235–238.

Ferster, C. B., & Skinner, B. F. (1957). *Schedules of reinforcement.* New York: Appleton-Century-Crofts.

Gates, A. I. (1917). Recitation as a factor in memorizing. *Archives of Psychology, 6*(40).

Glover, J. A. (1989). The "testing" phenomenon: Not gone but nearly forgotten. *Journal of Educational Psychology, 81,* 392–399.

Hasher, L., Goldstein, D., & Toppino, T. (1977). Frequency and the conference of referential validity. *Journal of Verbal Learning and Verbal Behavior, 16,* 107–112.

Jacoby, L. L., & Hollingshead, A. (1990). Reading student essays may be hazardous to your spelling: Effects of reading incorrectly and correctly spelled words. *Canadian Journal of Psychology, 44*, 345–358.

Jones, H. E. (1923). The effects of examination on the performance of learning. *Archives of Psychology, 10*, 1–70.

Kang, S. H. K. (2009a). Enhancing visuo-spatial learning: The benefit of retrieval practice. Manuscript under revision.

Kang, S. H. K. (2009b). The influence of text expectancy, test format and test experience on study strategy selection and long-term retention. Unpublished doctoral dissertation, Washington University, St Louis, MO, USA.

Kang, S. H. K., McDermott, K. B., & Roediger, H. L. (2007). Test format and corrective feedback modify the effect of testing on long-term retention. *European Journal of Cognitive Psychology, 19*, 528–558.

Karpicke, J. D. (in press). Metacognitive control and strategy selection: Deciding to practice retrieval during learning. *Journal of Experimental Psychology: General.*

Karpicke, J. D., Butler, A. C., & Roediger, H. L. (2009). Metacognitive strategies in student learning: Do students practise retrieval when they study on their own? *Memory, 17*, 471–479.

Karpicke, J. D., & Roediger, H. L. (2007). Expanding retrieval practice promotes short-term retention, but equally spaced retrieval enhances long-term retention. *Journal of Experimental Psychology: Learning, Memory, and Cognition, 33*, 704–719.

Karpicke, J. D., & Roediger, H. L. (2008). The critical importance of retrieval for learning. *Science, 319*, 966–968.

Kelemen, W. L., & Weaver, C. A. (1997). Enhanced memory at delays: Why do judgments of learning improve over time? *Journal of Experimental Psychology: Learning, Memory, and Cognition, 23*, 1394–1409.

Koriat, A. (1997). Monitoring one's own knowledge during study: A cue-utilization approach to judgments of learning. *Journal of Experimental Psychology: General, 126*, 349–370.

Koriat, A., & Bjork, R. A. (2005). Illusions of competence in monitoring one's knowledge during study. *Journal of Experimental Psychology: Learning, Memory, and Cognition, 31*, 187–194.

Koriat, A., & Bjork, R. A. (2006). Illusions of competence during study can be remedied by manipulations that enhance learners' sensitivity to retrieval conditions at test. *Memory and Cognition, 34*, 959–972.

Kornell, N., & Bjork, R. A. (2007). The promise and perils of self-regulated study. *Psychonomic Bulletin and Review, 14*, 219–224.

Kornell, N., Hays, M. J., & Bjork, R. A. (2009). Unsuccessful retrieval attempts enhance subsequent learning. *Journal of Experimental Psychology: Learninig, Memory, and Cognition, 35*, 989–998.

Kulhavy, R. W., Yekovich, F. R., & Dyer, J. W. (1976). Feedback and response confidence. *Journal of Educational Psychology, 68*, 522–528.

Kulhavy, R. W., Yekovich, F. R., & Dyer, J. W. (1979). Feedback and content review in programmed instruction. *Contemporary Educational Psychology, 4*, 91–98.

Kulik, J. A., & Kulik, C. C. (1988). Timing of feedback and verbal learning. *Review of Educational Research, 58*, 79–97.

Landauer, T. K., & Bjork, R. A. (1978). Optimal rehearsal patterns and name learning. In M. M. Gruneberg, P. E. Harris, & R. N. Sykes (Eds.), *Practical aspects of memory* (pp. 625–632). New York: Academic Press.

Leeming, F. C. (2002). The exam-a-day procedure improves performance in Psychology classes. *Teaching of Psychology, 29*, 210–212.

Loftus, E. F., Miller, D. G., & Burns, H. J. (1978). Semantic integration of verbal information into a visual memory. *Journal of Experimental Psychology: Human Learning and Memory, 4*, 19–31.

Logan, J. M., & Balota, D. A. (2008). Expanded vs. equal interval spaced retrieval practice: Exploring different schedules of spacing and retention interval in younger and older adults. *Aging, Neuropsychology, and Cognition, 15*, 257–280.

McDaniel, M. A., Anderson, J. L., Derbish, M. H., & Morrisette, N. (2007a). Testing the testing effect in the classroom. *European Journal of Cognitive Psychology, 19*, 494–513.

McDaniel, M. A., Roediger, H. L., III, & McDermott, K. B. (2007b). Generalizing test-enhanced learning from the laboratory to the classroom. *Psychonomic Bulletin and Review, 14*, 200–206.

McDaniel, M. A., & Sun, J. (2009). The testing effect: Experimental evidence in a college course. Manuscript under revision.

Marsh, E. J., Agarwal, P. K., & Roediger, H. L., III (2009). Memorial consequences of answering SAT II questions. *Journal of Experimental Psychology: Applied, 15*, 1–11.

Marsh, E. J., Roediger, H. L., III, Bjork, R. A., & Bjork, E. L. (2007). The memorial consequences of multiple-choice testing. *Psychonomic Bulletin and Review, 14*, 194–199.

Metcalfe, J., & Kornell, N. (2003). The dynamics of learning and allocation of study time to a region of proximal learning. *Journal of Experimental Psychology: General, 132*, 530–542.

Moreno, R. (2004). Decreasing cognitive load for novice students: Effects of explanatory versus corrective feedback in discovery-based multimedia. *Instructional Science, 32*, 99–113.

Nelson, T. O., & Dunlosky, J. (1991). When people's judgments of learning (JOLs) are extremely accurate at predicting subsequent recall: The "delayed-JOL effect." *Psychological Science, 2*, 267–270.

Nelson, T. O., & Leonesio, R. J. (1988). Allocation of self-paced study time and the "labor-in-vain effect." *Journal of Experimental Psychology: Learning, Memory, and Cognition, 14*, 676–686.

Nelson, T. O., & Narens, L. (1980). Norms of 300 general-information questions: Accuracy of recall, latency of recall, and feeling-of-knowing ratings. *Journal of Verbal Learning and Verbal Behavior, 19*, 338–368.

Nelson, T. O., & Narens, L. (1990). Metamemory: A theoretical framework and new findings. In G. H. Bower (Ed.), *The psychology of learning and motivation* (Vol. 26, pp. 125–173). New York: Academic Press.

Odegard, T. N., & Koen, J. D. (2007). "None of the above" as a correct and incorrect alternative on a multiple-choice test: Implications for the testing effect. *Memory, 15*, 873–885.

Pashler, H., Cepeda, N. J., Wixted, J. T., & Rohrer, D. (2005). When does feedback facilitate learning of words? *Journal of Experimental Psychology: Learning, Memory, and Cognition, 31*, 3–8.

Rea, C. P., & Modigliani, V. (1985). The effect of expanded versus massed practice on the retention of multiplication facts and spelling lists. *Human Learning: Journal of Practical Research and Applications, 4*, 11–18.

Remmers, H. H., & Remmers, E. M. (1926). The negative suggestion effect on true-false examination questions. *Journal of Educational Psychology, 17*, 52–56.

Richland, L. E., Kornell, N. & Kao, L. S. (2009). The pretesting effect: Do unsuccessful retrieval attempts enhance learning? *Journal of Experimental Psychology: Applied, 15*, 243–257.

Roediger, H. L., & Karpicke, J. D. (2006a). Test enhanced learning: Taking memory tests improves long-term retention. *Psychological Science, 17*, 249–255.

Roediger, H. L., & Karpicke, J. D. (2006b). The power of testing memory: Basic research and implications for educational practice. *Perspectives on Psychological Science, 1*, 181–210.

Roediger, H. L., McDaniel, M. A., McDermott, K. B., & Agarwal, P. K. (2010). Test-enhanced learning in the classroom: The Columbia Middle School project. Manuscript in preparation.

Roediger, H. L., & Marsh, E. J. (2005). The positive and negative consequences of multiple-choice testing. *Journal of Experimental Psychology: Learning, Memory, and Cognition, 31*, 1155–1159.

Roediger, H. L., Zaromb, F. M., & Butler, A. C. (2008). The role of repeated retrieval in shaping collective memory. In P. Boyer and J. V. Wertsch (Eds.), *Memory in Mind and Culture* (pp. 29–58). Cambridge: Cambridge University Press.

Ruch, G. M. (1929). *The objective or new-type examination: An introduction to educational measurement.* Chicago: Scott, Foresman, and Co.

Skinner, B. F. (1953). *Science and human behavior.* New York: Macmillan.

Skinner, B. F. (1958). Teaching machines. *Science, 128*, 969–977.

Son, L. K., & Metcalfe, J. (2000). Metacognitive and control strategies in study-time allocation. *Journal of Experimental Psychology: Learning, Memory, and Cognition, 26*, 204–221.

Spellman, B. A., & Bjork, R. A. (1992). When predictions create reality: Judgments of learning may alter what they are intended to assess. *Psychological Science, 3*, 315–316.

Spitzer, H. F. (1939). Studies in retention. *Journal of Educational Psychology, 30*, 641–656.

Thompson, C. P., Wenger, S. K., & Bartling, C. A. (1978). How recall facilitates subsequent recall: A reappraisal. *Journal of Experimental Psychology: Human Learning and Memory, 4*, 210–221.

Toppino, T. C., & Brochin, H. A. (1989). Learning from tests: The case of true–false examinations. *Journal of Educational Research, 83*, 119–124.

Toppino, T. C., & Luipersbeck, S. M. (1993). Generality of the negative suggestion effect in objective tests. *Journal of Educational Research, 86*, 357–362.

Wenger, S. K., Thompson, C. P., & Bartling, C. A. (1980). Recall facilitates subsequent recognition. *Journal of Experimental Psychology: Human Learning and Memory, 6*, 135–144.

Wheeler, M. A., & Roediger, H. L. (1992). Disparate effects of repeated testing: Reconciling Ballard's (1913) and Bartlett's (1932) results. *Psychological Science, 3*, 240–245.

2 Retrieval-induced forgetting

The unintended consequences of unintended forgetting

Malcolm D. MacLeod, Jo Saunders
and Laura Chalmers

When we are asked to think about memory and how it works we often tend to conceptualize it in terms of what we can remember, how much we can remember, and for how long we can remember it. Even for memory theorists, memory tends to be characterized in terms of its storage capacity, retention capabilities, and the processes underlying these properties (i.e., encoding, storage, and retrieval). Forgetting, in contrast, hardly gets a mention. To some extent, the reason for this is that forgetting is a largely 'invisible' phenomenon. Unless we know what we have forgotten, it is difficult to know that we have forgotten it! When we do become aware of weaknesses in our memorial armature, forgetting is typically seen as a nuisance or hindrance – something that should, wherever possible, be avoided. At its most benign, forgetting can be regarded as a 'blip' or error in an otherwise smooth-running system; something that happens from time to time when insufficient attention is being paid to what we are doing. At its most insidious, forgetting may irreconcilably alter our awareness of what is current and what is real, and even undermine our concept of self (e.g., in the advanced stages of dementia).

Implicit in these conceptions of memory is the notion that forgetting is maladaptive or, at the very least, something that happens when memory is not working properly. Yet, there are indications that some forms of forgetting may be just as important as remembering in order for our memories to work effectively. Théodule Ribot (1887), over a century ago, recognized the potential importance of forgetting when he noted that 'Forgetfulness, except in certain cases, is not a disease of memory, but a condition of health and life' (p. 61). Similarly, William James (1890) drew our attention to the possibility that our memories would be much poorer if it were not for the fact that we forget. In other words, rather than considering forgetting as the inevitable product of a system that is operating less than optimally, we need to consider the possibility of forgetting as an integral part of memory – something that is intrinsically linked to our ability to remember. Arguably, without the capacity to forget, we would find it impossible to remember, at least in any purposive goal-directed manner (Macrae & MacLeod, 1999).

In the current chapter we explore this possibility by considering the nature of the relationship between remembering and forgetting and, in doing so, consider some of the costs and benefits associated with a particular form of unintended forgetting called *retrieval-induced forgetting*. This form of forgetting refers to a selective loss in memory performance caused by the retrieval of other related material; an instance of when 'remembering can cause forgetting'. As we will see from our discussion of the most recent work in this field, this phenomenon can also be characterized as a case of when 'forgetting can cause remembering'. Specifically, we and others have argued that retrieval-induced forgetting plays a pivotal role in moderating the availability of memories; that is, it provides a targeted means of controlling which particular memories come into conscious awareness (M. C. Anderson, Bjork, & Bjork, 1994; M. C. Anderson & Spellman, 1995; Macrae & MacLeod, 1999; M. D. MacLeod & Macrae, 2001). Thus, strange though it might first seem, some forms of forgetting may actually help us to achieve a range of everyday tasks that depend heavily upon our ability to draw upon information from memory on demand. In doing so, our chapter also explores the possibility that, despite the many benefits that can accrue from this kind of forgetting, there may also be a number of unforeseen associated consequences. In particular, we consider that the act of retrieval can, under certain circumstances, prompt the forgetting of the very material we wish to remember and explore how such cases of unintended forgetting might be obviated.

FORGETTING AS AN ADAPTIVE MECHANISM

Despite the prescient observations of Ribot and James, the potential advantages associated with forgetting have only recently begun to receive serious attention from memory researchers. Some have explored the role of forgetting in terms of behavioural plasticity and, in particular, our ability to adapt to changes in our physical environment (J. R. Anderson & Schooler, 2000; R. A. Bjork & Bjork, 1992). Others have considered the possibility that certain forms of forgetting may play a critical role in helping us to adjust to the aftermath sometimes associated with combat, illness, crime, or ethnic conflict (E. L. Bjork, Bjork, & Anderson, 1998; M. D. MacLeod, 1999; M. D. MacLeod, Bjork, & Bjork, 2003). Some have explored the pivotal role played by forgetting in the updating of memory. The basic argument here is that, by being able to set aside or discriminate out-of-date information, we are better able to remember current information (R. A. Bjork, 1989; M. D. MacLeod & Saunders, 2008). Others have considered the role of forgetting in moderating the accessibility of memories and how such forgetting can help us to retrieve the information we wish to remember (see M. C. Anderson, 2003, for a review).

Common to all these theoretical perspectives is the notion that, rather than something to be avoided at any cost, forgetting may be exactly what is required in order for us to keep our memories functioning optimally in a world that is constantly changing (E. L. Bjork, Bjork, & MacLeod, 2006;

M. D. MacLeod, Bjork, & Bjork, 2003; M. D. MacLeod & Macrae, 2001). Consider the problem posed by trying to remember the telephone number of a recently acquired girlfriend or boyfriend. Typically, the cues employed during memory retrieval are underspecified; that is, there is a tendency to access not only the target material we wish to remember but also related memories for irrelevant telephone numbers (e.g., in this case, the telephone numbers of previous girlfriends or boyfriends). These related memories, in turn, end up competing for activation with target memories we wish to retrieve. Clearly, these related but unwanted memories represent a source of unwelcome competition. Imagine the potential embarrassment of calling up an old flame because older memories are activated at retrieval in preference to memory for the telephone number of one's current partner. Retrieval inhibition – an active form of forgetting – is thought to promote the likelihood of retrieving target material by moderating the retrieval accessibility of competing memories via a process of dampening down or inhibiting competing unwanted memories. As a result, related unwanted material no longer poses a threat to the retrieval of the material we wish to recall; that is, it is effectively forgotten. Thus, by forgetting the telephone numbers associated with old flames, one is more likely to be able to remember the telephone number of one's current partner – something, no doubt, one's current partner would be more than happy to learn! But one's partner should not become too complacent about this state of affairs as these older telephone numbers may only be temporarily forgotten.

Forgetting and flexible memory updating

Consider the fact that human memory operates within a dynamic social context – a context in which the goals we need to achieve are continually subject to change (M. D. MacLeod & Macrae, 2001). One of the major problems we face in our daily lives is that we have little or no idea as to what these goals might be from one minute to the next. Thus, we have no way of knowing in advance what information may be required to complete such tasks later today, let alone next week or next month. Information deemed irrelevant for the completion of a current task may prove critical to the successful execution of some future task. Following this line of logic, it rapidly becomes apparent that the notion that memory updating comprises the replacement of old memories with new is far too simplistic. By erasing older memories one would immediately lose the kind of retrieval flexibility that is arguably needed to accomplish such tasks. If we continually failed to retrieve target material from memory when it was most needed, memory would no longer prove adaptive in any purposive sense.

Thus, the notion of destructive updating where memory is kept up to date by overwriting older or out-of-date information with new (cf. Loftus, Miller, & Burns, 1978) seems a potentially costly enterprise – not only in terms of the social gaffes we are likely to make (e.g., phoning up our old flames by mistake) but also in terms of the cognitive effort and time that would be needed to relearn material (e.g., the telephone number of one's current partner). Rather, it would seem that there is a need for memory updating to be achieved in a much more subtle and flexible manner – one in which memories that are deemed irrelevant for a current task can be excised from conscious inspection but not irrevocably lost (E. L. Bjork, Bjork, & MacLeod, 2006; M. D. MacLeod & Macrae, 2001). Thus, related but unwanted memories can be temporarily forgotten for as long as it takes to complete the current task but subsequently become available for some future task should they be required. We believe that the mechanism underlying retrieval-induced forgetting (i.e., inhibition) may offer just this kind of flexibility in memory updating.

Retrieval practice and memory performance

Retrieval-induced forgetting refers to a particular pattern of forgetting that occurs as a result of the selective retrieval practice of other related material. Unlike directed forgetting (e.g., Johnson, 1994; C. MacLeod, 1989), this specific form of forgetting occurs *implicitly* as a result of the retrieval process itself (i.e., there are no explicit instructions to forget material). Rather, forgetting occurs as a function of the retrieval competition emanating from related memories. In order to deal with unwanted competition at retrieval, related memories are actively inhibited or suppressed, thereby promoting the retrieval of the material we wish to remember.

The standard procedure used to explore retrieval-induced forgetting typically comprises a four-phase retrieval practice paradigm (M. C. Anderson et al., 1994). Although there are a number of variations, the basic paradigm generally involves the presentation of a series of category–exemplar pairs (e.g., sport–football, sport–tennis, sport–rugby, sport–cricket ... tree–sycamore, tree–oak, tree–spruce, tree–poplar ... bird–sparrow, bird–eagle, bird–robin, bird–mallard ... vegetable–carrot, vegetable–onion, vegetable–celery, vegetable–broccoli ...). On completion, participants are cued to retrieve half of the exemplars from half of the categories. For example, participants might be required to complete the following cued stem tests (e.g., sport–fo____, sport–te____; bird–sp____, bird–ea____) but are not prompted to retrieve exemplars from the remaining categories (i.e., exemplars from tree or vegetable categories). Following a distractor task (between 5 and 20 minutes), participants are asked to recall all the exemplars that had originally been presented.

As one would expect, a facilitation effect emerges for those exemplars that received retrieval practice (i.e., Rp+ items). Specifically, Rp+ items are better remembered in comparison to the Nrp baseline performance (i.e., items from categories that did not receive retrieval practice). What is particularly interesting, however, is that retrieval performance for exemplars from practised categories that did not receive retrieval practice (i.e., Rp– items, such as rugby, cricket, robin, and mallard) are more poorly recalled than Nrp items. Thus, despite the fact that Rp– items and Nrp items are treated in the same manner (at least, in respect of having received no retrieval practice), Rp– item performance is reliably poorer by virtue of being, in this case, semantically related to Rp+ items (Figure 2.1).

M. C. Anderson and Spellman (1995) have argued that the mechanism underlying Rp– item performance is inhibitory; that is, an active form of forgetting that is quite different in nature from the passive forms of forgetting associated with decay and interference. By using an independent cue technique (i.e., novel cues during the final test phase of the retrieval practice paradigm), Anderson and Spellman showed that Rp– items remained significantly more poorly recalled than Nrp items. The rationale for this modification is that, if retrieval-induced forgetting is caused by non-inhibitory means (say, associative interference), the provision of novel cues at test should prove sufficient to create a completely new retrieval route by which Rp– items could still be accessed. In other words, if the typical retrieval-induced forgetting effect is due to the associative blocking of the original route, the use of a novel cue should allow any such blocking to be circumvented. If, as Anderson and Spellman have argued, the exemplars themselves are inhibited (i.e., not the retrieval route), these items should remain unavailable to conscious inspection irrespective of whether original or novel cues are employed at final test.

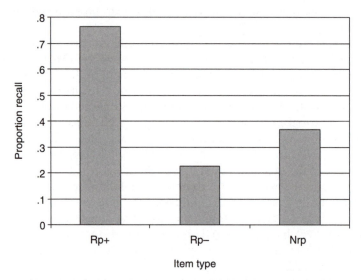

Figure 2.1 The effects of selective retrieval practice on memory. Retrieval-induced forgetting is measured by comparing recall of unpracticed items from practiced categories (i.e., Rp– items) with recall of items from unpracticed categories (i.e., Nrp items). If fewer Rp– items are recalled than Nrp items then retrieval-induced forgetting is present (i.e., (Rp–) – Nrp). Rp+ = practiced items from practiced category. Rp– = unpracticed items from practiced category. Nrp = unpracticed items from unpracticed category. From Macrae and MacLeod (1999, Experiment 1).

This is exactly what happens; despite the use of novel cues, Rp– items remain more poorly recalled than Nrp items (see also Saunders & MacLeod, 2006).

It is worth noting, however, that non-inhibitory explanations have also been offered to account for this effect. Most notable amongst these is the strategy disruption hypothesis which argues that the retrieval practice procedure forces the rememberer to use a recall order that is different from the order in which the items were originally learned. The resultant disruption to the temporal sequencing of information may, in turn, contribute to retrieval-induced forgetting (see Dodd, Castel, & Roberts, 2006; C. M. MacLeod, Dodd, Sheard, Wilson, & Bibi, 2003). While few of us would argue against the notion that non-inhibitory mechanisms have the potential to contribute to retrieval-induced forgetting, much of the available empirical evidence regarding these effects supports an inhibitory account (see e.g., Bajo, Gómez-Ariza, Fernandez, & Marful, 2006; Bäuml & Kuhbandner, 2003; Dunn & Spellman, 2003; Johnson & Anderson, 2004; M. D. MacLeod & Saunders, 2005; Saunders & MacLeod, 2006; Veling & Knippenberg, 2004).

Most recently, a study by Storm, Bjork, Bjork, and Nestojko (2005) provides compelling evidence for an inhibitory account of this effect. Their innovation was to use what they called an 'impossible retrieval task' within the standard retrieval practice paradigm; that is, where participants are cued to recall exemplars that do not exist from half of the presented categories (e.g., a metal beginning Mu___). For the other categories, participants were required to engage in retrieval practice for *new* exemplars (i.e., exemplars that belonged to the category but had not actually been presented in the original study phase). Retrieval-induced forgetting effects emerged following retrieval practice on extra-list (i.e., new) exemplars (see also Bäuml, 2002). More interesting from our point of view, however, is that retrieval-induced forgetting *also* emerged following the impossible retrieval practice procedure. If associative blocking is responsible for retrieval-induced forgetting, we might not have expected this kind of forgetting to have emerged here because blocking would have been impossible. Blocking could not have occurred because there were, in fact, no members of the previously studied categories to retrieve and therefore become strengthened as a result of the selective retrieval practice procedure. If, however, retrieval-induced forgetting is due to inhibitory means, we would still expect such forgetting effects to emerge, irrespective of whether the retrieval attempt was successful or not. Indeed, Storm and colleagues speculate that the more difficult one makes the impossible retrieval task, the stronger the retrieval-induced forgetting given that, in the search for possible targets, more potential competing responses are likely to be actively inhibited.

If we now turn our attention to the issue of whether this kind of retrieval inhibition can fulfil our criteria for a flexible updating mechanism, we might also expect to find evidence that such forgetting effects are transitory. The constantly changing nature of our goal-directed behaviour means that information inhibited at one moment in time may actually be required at some later time. Thus, such inhibitory effects could be expected to be apparent one moment but gone the next. In exploring this possibility, M. D. MacLeod and Macrae (2001) demonstrated that the critical factor in determining the presence of retrieval-induced forgetting is when the selective retrieval practice procedure actually takes place in relation to the final test. Using a set of personality traits concerning two fictitious individuals (Bill and John), MacLeod and Macrae showed that retrieval-induced forgetting effects emerged even when the original information is 24 hours old; that is presentation followed by a 24-hour delay, followed by retrieval practice, filler task, and then final test. If, however, a 24-hour delay is inserted between the retrieval practice phase and the final test (i.e., presentation, retrieval practice, 24-hour delay, filler task, and then final test), retrieval-induced forgetting dissipates (see also Saunders & MacLeod, 2002). Although there may be a variety of retrieval conditions under which this kind of forgetting may become more permanent (see M. D. MacLeod & Saunders, 2008, for a discussion), the notion that there may be a form of temporary forgetting under executive control is of considerable interest. We explore these issues further in the remainder of this chapter in which we consider some of the parameters that determine when such forgetting effects are likely to emerge and some of the unanticipated costs associated with this otherwise adaptive mechanism. We do this by considering two real-life situations: learning and exam revision, and the interviewing of eyewitnesses to crimes.

LAST-MINUTE REVISION AND EXAM PERFORMANCE

How many times have we found ourselves cramming for exams in the last half-hour before sitting a test? Inevitably, because such revision is time-limited, only some of the information relevant to the exam can be covered – other material will inevitably be neglected. Last-minute cramming of this sort would seem to be a reasonable strategy to adopt if the information that is refreshed happens to come up in the exam. But what happens in the event that the exam prompts for related information that one did not have time to refresh? Might we be worse off than if we had not engaged in last-minute revision at all? Could such a revision strategy set up the kinds of conditions likely to give rise to retrieval-induced forgetting? Or, does the fact that one is highly motivated to perform well in the test overcome any problems typically associated with retrieval-induced forgetting?

If we are correct about the effects of retrieval inhibition, we might expect that performance on related but unpractised material (i.e., information that had not been subject to retrieval practice prior to an exam) will be more poorly recalled than if students had not performed any last-minute revision. To test this possibility, Macrae and MacLeod (1999, Study 2) informed participants that they were to be tested on a series of facts about two fictitious islands (Tok and Bilu). Each of these islands had ten associated facts (e.g., *the main cash crop on Tok is maize; Bilu's only major export is copper*). The descriptions of the islands carried the sort of information that one would typically expect to learn for an impending examination. Following the initial presentation of facts about both islands, participants were given a standard retrieval practice procedure in which they were cued to retrieve half of the facts about one of the islands (e.g., *Bilu's only major export is c___*).

Despite the fact that participants were very familiar with the idea of being tested and that they had been informed in advance that they would be tested on these items later, a typical pattern of retrieval-induced forgetting nevertheless emerged. Thus, it would seem that, despite our best intentions, we may actually forget the very information we wish to remember. Importantly, a non-relevant retrieval practice condition (i.e., where participants were cued to retrieve non-relevant information such as the capital cities of countries – 'The capital city of Cuba is H___') provided a between-subjects baseline which showed that the retrieval-induced forgetting observed was not due to movement in the Nrp baseline but rather to a real drop in Rp– item recall performance. Specifically, Rp– items were significantly more poorly recalled than either the non-relevant retrieval practice condition or the Nrp baseline. Thus, it would seem that we may be better served by not engaging in last-minute revision as this may set up exactly the kinds of conditions likely to promote the forgetting of related material. But is this always the case?

Integration effects and the inevitability of retrieval-induced forgetting

These kinds of forgetting effects are not inevitable. There are a number of ways in which unintended forgetting can be minimized. In particular, it has been argued that, by increasing the richness of the connectivity between items (i.e., increased integration), one can minimize the risk of unintended forgetting (M. C. Anderson & McCulloch, 1999). Indeed, even simple instructions to 'integrate information' can prove sufficient to reduce although not entirely eliminate retrieval-induced forgetting. Anderson and McCulloch have argued that these effects are due to the protection or 'inoculation' properties of having integrated material in memory. Dunn and Spellman (2003) have similarly shown that such integration effects are also likely to occur in the social world. Having manipulated memory for traits associated with particular stereotypes (e.g., Asian-Americans are *intelligent*, *diligent*, and *reserved*; Feminists are *strong*, *loud*, and *bitter*, etc), Dunn and Spellman found that the extent to which participants believed a particular stereotype to hold true significantly moderated the extent of retrieval-induced forgetting. Stereotypes are, in fact, highly structured knowledge frameworks against which information can subsequently be integrated. It would seem that the more one believes in a particular stereotype, the more likely the information that constitutes that stereotype will be highly integrated and, as a result, prove less susceptible to retrieval inhibition.

More recently, integration effects have been explored within an education and learning setting. Carroll, Campbell-Ratcliffe, Murnane, & Perfect (2007) considered whether experts would be less vulnerable to the effects of retrieval-induced forgetting than would novices. In other words, could higher levels of expertise protect against this kind of active forgetting? The basic notion here is that individuals are considered experts because of the ways in which information about a particular knowledge domain is organized and presumably integrated. Using fourth-year psychology students as 'experts' and first-year psychology students as 'novices', Carroll and colleagues examined memory for items of information presented in clinical case studies from psychology textbooks depicting behaviour and symptoms typically associated with schizophrenia and autism. The case studies, however, were free of such clinical labels and, as a result, participants had to draw upon their own psychological expertise to enable a diagnosis to be made. Following a selected retrieval practice procedure on some of the items associated with one of the cases, they found that retrieval-induced forgetting emerged only for novices. Expertise appears to offer some degree of protection against the effects of retrieval inhibition.

Anderson and McCulloch (1999), however, point out a potential paradox in this line of argument. Specifically, they make the point that, as we become more expert, we should become *less* adept at retrieving information from this knowledge domain because of the higher level of competition from related memories. As a result, one might expect experts to have an even greater need for an adaptive forgetting mechanism that reduces competition from related memories at retrieval. In other words, experts could be expected to show *bigger* retrieval-induced forgetting effects than would novices. But this is clearly not the case – otherwise we could expect experts to be less able to retrieve facts from their field of expertise than novices!

This apparent paradox is likely to have something to do with pre-existing schemata. Expertise, in a sense, involves the integration of a host of facts about a certain knowledge domain. The richness of this knowledge framework, in turn, is a function of the interconnectedness between items of information. Thus, when we say that someone has achieved 'expert' status, it is probably more a case of adding additional information to an already existing framework – a framework in which the nature of the connections between pieces of information can be more fully explored and, as a result, more potential routes identified by which information might ultimately be accessed. Recent work in our own labs, however, would suggest that such knowledge structures are not the only way by which retrieval-induced forgetting can be minimized. Rather, it would appear that the way in which the material is learned (i.e., the actual process of encoding) may prove to be just as important.

Spacing effects and retrieval-induced forgetting

The spacing of retrieval attempts has long been recognized as a means of promoting memory performance (Crowder, 1976). Specifically, memory is significantly improved when the information to be learned is presented on more than one occasion (i.e., spaced or distributed learning) in comparison to the same amount of time spent learning the material but on a single occasion (i.e., massed learning). More recent studies have confirmed this pattern of effects (see, e.g., Cepeda, Pashler, Vul, Wixted, & Rohrer, 2006; Krug, Davis, & Glover, 1990; Russo, Parkin, Taylor, & Wilks, 1998; Verkoeijen, Rikers, & Schmidt, 2005). It is important to note, however, that the critical factor in these effects may have less to do with spacing per se than with the relationship between spacing and retention interval (Greene, 1992). On the whole, massed items tend to be better remembered after short retention intervals whereas distributed items tend to be better remembered after longer retention intervals (Balota, Duchek, & Paullin, 1989). The critical question for us here, however, is whether the spacing of retrieval practice during initial learning might confer some protection against the detrimental effects of retrieval-induced forgetting.

To explore this possibility, we recently conducted a study in which participants were presented with 20 facts about two fictitious planets called 'Minocoswell' and 'Rupplenair'. Each fact was presented on a separate card and there were ten facts related to each planet. On each of the cards, one word in the sentence was underlined (e.g., 'The most popular drink on Rupplenair is sherry'). Participants were told to try to remember the underlined words. Some participants learned the facts under 'massed' conditions (i.e., items were presented at the rate of one card per 12 seconds). Learning in this condition was considered massed because there was less than 1 second separation between each successive presentation. Other participants learned the same facts but under 'distributed' conditions. Here, each card was presented for a period of 4 s before moving on to the next item. After participants had seen all 20 cards, all the items were presented in the same order for a second time, and then a third time. The learning in this condition was considered distributed because there were intervening items. We also ran a third condition in which the same items were re-presented. Specifically, participants were presented with a particular item for 4 s and then an additional copy of that item for a further 4 s, followed by a third copy of that item also for 4 s. Thus, participants in all three conditions saw each card for the equivalent amount of time. The re-presented condition differed from the distributed condition only in respect of items not being separated by different items, and differed from the massed condition in that items were presented on three occasions and not on a single occasion (Figure 2.2). Following this learning phase, participants followed the standard retrieval practice procedure in which they were provided with a hint about the target item to be recalled (e.g., '*the most popular drink on Rupplenair is s____*'). Counterbalancing throughout ensured that each of the words appeared equally often as Rp+, Rp–, or Nrp items. Following retrieval practice, participants completed an 8-minute distractor task which was followed by a final test of memory in which participants were encouraged to recall all the items originally presented.

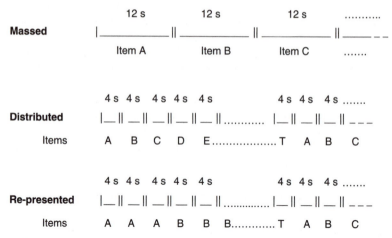

Figure 2.2 Schematic diagram of order of presentation and duration of items during presentation phase of a modified retrieval practice paradigm.

Retrieval practice rates were comparable across all learning conditions: massed 87%, distributed (89%), and re-presented (86%). Consistent with findings in the literature, a clear learning advantage emerged for the total number of items recalled (i.e., Rp+, Rp– and Nrp) in the distributed condition (73%) in comparison to either the massed (60%) or the re-presented conditions (61%). There was also a significant interaction between item type and learning condition (p < .001). Simple effects analysis revealed that retrieval-induced forgetting occurred in both the massed and re-presented conditions but failed to emerge in the distributed condition (Figure 2.3). Although we need to be cautious about over-interpreting the results from this modest study, there would appear to be some justification for believing that learning conditions may be an important determinant of susceptibility to retrieval-induced forgetting.

Of particular interest here is to consider what it is about distributed practice that might create resistance to retrieval-induced forgetting. There are at least three candidates that are worthy of further exploration: the first has simply to do with the strength of the representation. Distributed learning entails that the encoded information has to be brought back into conscious awareness and each time this happens, the process of retrieval is likely to strengthen the representation. The memory trace for each item is likely to have been strengthened each time an item is lost from working memory and subsequently refreshed. As a result, we might have expected all twenty items to have been similarly strengthened and therefore represent a source of strong competition at retrieval. Given that we know that taxonomically strong exemplars are more likely to be subject to inhibitory control than are taxonomically weak exemplars (M. C. Anderson et al., 1994), we might expect stronger retrieval-induced forgetting effects to have emerged in the distributed

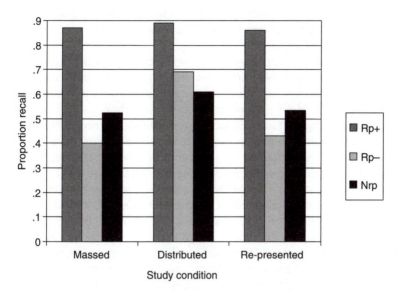

Figure 2.3 The effects of type of study on retrieval-induced forgetting. Participants learned facts via either (1) massed study whereby each item was presented for 12 seconds, or (2) distributed study whereby each item appeared for 4 seconds three times each but each presentation was interleaved with other items, or (3) re-presentation whereby each item was presented three times for 4 seconds in succession. The type of study that participants engaged in during learning affected retrieval-induced forgetting for Rp– items; massed study and re-presentation led to impaired recall for Rp– facts whereas distributed study led to improved recall for Rp– facts.

condition than in either the massed or re-presented conditions where items would not have been strengthened to the same degree. Given the current pattern of results, this would seem an unlikely explanation.

The second is that distributed practice is likely to have created encoding conditions in which there is greater potential for contextual drift. Changes to the encoding context, in turn, will increase the likelihood of multiple unique contexts being encoded and thereby provide multiple retrieval routes by which target information can ultimately be accessed. In this particular study, however, such contextual changes during encoding were likely to have been kept to a minimum. Distributed learning conditions over longer time periods or expanded study (i.e., where the interval between retrieval attempts is gradually increased), however, may offer protection against retrieval inhibition. The third candidate concerns the potential to integrate material during encoding. One possible explanation for this may lie in M. C. Anderson and McCulloch's (1999) observation that it actually takes very little encouragement for people to integrate material. Indeed, many of the participants in their studies reported having integrated spontaneously. In our study, it is possible that the distributed nature of the presentation of items allowed or even encouraged participants to integrate material. During massed and re-presented conditions, the opportunity to engage in spontaneous integration would have been more limited.

Despite the fact that spacing effects on memory performance have been known for some considerable time, there is still much to be done in teasing out why they are so effective in promoting memory performance. We also need to consider more closely the interaction between retention interval and spaced learning. Over longer retention intervals, for instance, the degree of protection from retrieval inhibition may be moderated by the extent to which the spaces between learning are of equivalent duration or whether they are gradually increased. These are important empirical questions that are worthy of further investigation – not only from a theoretical point of view but also in terms of developing effective educational programmes. Clearly, if we are to better understand the effects of spacing on memory, we need to explore whether participants are actively engaged in integration – the process of creating inter-connections between items. By understanding how interconnectedness pro-tects against retrieval-induced forgetting and the conditions likely to promote integration, we can try to ensure that, when faced with those occasions when we least want forgetting to occur, we have some notion of how to avoid retrieval-induced forgetting. In the next section, we provide an example of how this approach may ultimately lead to improved eyewitness performance.

UNINTENDED FORGETTING AND EYEWITNESS MEMORY

Post-event questioning has been identified as a source of potentially deleteri-ous effects on memory. Leading questions are known to influence how wit-nesses remember an incident. The use of the definite article (i.e., 'the'), for example, has been associated with an increase in errors in testimony (Loftus & Zanni, 1975), as have changes in the use of verbs in questions (Loftus & Palmer, 1974). More recently, psychological research has attempted to under-stand the mechanisms by which post-event questioning can alter what we remember about an event. Post-event questioning can be considered a memorial task which requires the rememberer to recollect an incident and to retrieve relevant details in response to each question. The positive con-sequences of this kind of questioning include facilitating the subsequent remembering of a retrieved memory (e.g., R. A. Bjork & Bjork, 1992). This, in turn, may also facilitate remembering for previously retrieved details over the months or years that it might take to bring a case to court. Unfortunately, while the positive consequences of questioning may aid the initial police investi-gation, there may also be a number of unintended negative consequences.

Recently, concern has been expressed regarding the effects of non-exhaustive police questioning (Saunders & MacLeod, 2002). Given that, in most cases, the interviewer is unlikely to have been present at the incident, the questions asked about the incident are likely to probe memory for a subset of things known about that event; that is, it is unlikely that a witness will be asked about every single detail that he/she remembers about that particular event. Thus, the structure of most police interviews effectively constitutes a selective retrieval task which, as we have argued earlier, is likely to set up exactly the kinds of conditions most likely to give rise to retrieval-induced forgetting for non-probed-for items. In an eyewitness paradigm, Shaw, Bjork, and Handal (1995) demonstrated that repeated questioning for half of the items from a particular category (e.g., textbooks or sweatshirts) resulted in improved memory for probed-for items but impaired memory for unprobed-for items.

While Shaw and colleagues' findings are consistent with retrieval-induced forgetting, they were unable to exclude other explanations for the observed recall pattern. In particular, participants were more likely to recall questioned items first and, as a result, more likely to report the remaining non-questioned items last, thereby suggesting that the earlier output of the stronger questioned items could have blocked the recall of weaker non-questioned items. As output interference is a product of the order in which items are recalled and not a function of selective retrieval practice, it cannot be concluded with any certainty that selective questioning had been responsible for the pattern of forgetting observed.

More conclusive evidence that selective questioning can initiate retrieval-induced forgetting effects in eyewitness settings emerged from two studies by M. D. MacLeod (2002). In the first study, participants viewed a slide sequence showing a series of items that had been stolen from two houses during a burglary. Participants were subsequently questioned about half of the stolen items from one of the houses. This selective questioning procedure was found to initiate retrieval-induced forgetting for the remaining non-questioned items from the house that had been the target of the selective retrieval practice. In the second study, participants viewed a series of slides concerning two women making bogus charity calls at houses. Prior pilot work had indicated that the two women were easily identifiable by the colour of their hair (i.e., blonde or brunette), which suggested that each suspect implicitly formed a discrete category. After viewing the slides, participants were questioned about half of the descriptor information concerning one of the women. Again, selective questioning was found to lead to retrieval-induced forgetting for the non-questioned descriptor information (see also Migueles & Garcia-Bajos, 2007, for a similar finding). In both studies, output interference was excluded as a possible explanation for the pattern of memory performance observed, thereby suggesting that selective questioning may be responsible for activating inhibitory processes that subsequently inhibit or suppress non-questioned details. These studies raise the intriguing possibility that the procedures used to elicit eyewitness testimony may, in fact, lead to the unintentional forgetting of other related material.

In real-world situations, selective retrieval about a witnessed event is also likely to be a function of inquisitive family members, friends, solicitors, and even other witnesses. For example, in the minutes prior to the arrival of the police following an incident, witnesses are highly likely to talk to one another about what each had seen happen. This kind of co-witness discussion has been found to be a potent source of suggestion whereby a witness can unwittingly incorporate details from another witness's inaccurate verbal description of an event into their own account (Gabbert, Memon, & Allan, 2003). It would seem that post-event co-witness discussion may also be a source of incomplete retrieval which, in turn, may lead to inhibition of non-retrieved details concerning an incident. Thus, there is potential for retrieval inhibition to have occurred even before a witness has been questioned by the police. Cuc, Koppel, and Hirst (2007), for example, have demonstrated that simply listening to another individual engage in selective retrieval can lead to retrieval-induced forgetting in the listener. Most importantly, retrieval-induced forgetting was found not only for listening to selective retrieval of word-pairs, but also for listening to incomplete retrieval of stories, and also in uncontrolled free-flowing conversation. This socially shared retrieval-induced forgetting effect appears to be most likely to occur when a listener is monitoring the speaker for accuracy thereby suggesting that the listener is also retrieving information concurrently with the speaker (e.g., when an eyewitness is listening to another witness re-tell their story or perhaps even when a police interviewer is listening to an eyewitness). While the possibility that hearing a co-witness describe an event may lead to retrieval-induced forgetting has not been directly examined, the finding that free-flowing conversation can result in the inhibition of non-retrieved information in a listener would suggest it is plausible.

Errors of omission via the inhibition of non-questioned details may also have implications for errors of commission, such as exposure to misleading post-event information. Witnesses may be subject to misleading information from many sources, such as other witnesses, police and the media – all of which have been found to influence eyewitness memory (see Davis & Loftus, 2007, for discussion). Specifically, the presence of misinformation in post-event sources can lead individuals to report misleading information in place of original and correct information.

Misinformation effects are typically studied using a three-phase paradigm whereby participants encode an event (e.g., usually via a visual slide sequence, video, or verbal narrative), receive misleading information embedded within a set of questions that probes memory for the witnessed event, and then complete a forced-choice recognition test. Participants who report the misleading item in preference to the original item are said to have been misled (e.g., Loftus et al., 1978). While various accounts have been put forward to explain misinformation effects such as destructive updating (Loftus et al., 1978) and source monitoring (Lindsay & Johnson, 1989), the possibility that post-event questioning itself may actually be the vehicle by which misinformation is incorporated into memory has remained largely overlooked.

Given that selective questioning is known to initiate retrieval-induced forgetting for non-questioned details from questioned events (M. D. MacLeod, 2002; Shaw et al., 1995), it would seem likely that the incomplete nature of questioning in the misinformation paradigm may give rise to conditions likely to produce retrieval inhibition for non-questioned details. We have argued elsewhere (M. D. MacLeod & Saunders, 2008) that, if an original item has been inhibited and, therefore, unavailable to conscious inspection, participants may be more likely to select misleading information subsequently introduced about that item in preference to the original. Thus, incomplete questioning may give rise to two unintended negative consequences: errors of omission (i.e., retrieval-induced forgetting) and commission (i.e., misinformation effects).

To investigate whether retrieval-induced forgetting might facilitate the reporting of misinformation, Saunders and MacLeod (2002) modified the standard retrieval practice paradigm so as to allow misinformation to be incorporated following selective retrieval practice. After reading two narratives about separate burglaries, participants responded to selective questioning for half of the items from one of the narratives. On completing this phase, participants engaged in a free recall task for all items from both narratives. This served as a manipulation check for the presence of retrieval-induced forgetting. Having established that retrieval-induced forgetting had occurred, participants then entered the misinformation phase of the study whereby they answered some questions concerning non-target scene-setting details from the narratives. Contained in one of the questions was a piece of misleading information about either an Rp+ item (i.e., an item that had previously been the subject of retrieval practice), or an Rp– item (i.e., a non-questioned item from the questioned narrative), or an Nrp item (i.e., a non-questioned item from non-questioned narrative). Finally, participants completed a forced-choice recognition test whereby they had to choose between the original, misleading or a novel item for the critical item and between the original item and two novel items for non-critical items.

Our findings suggest that misinformation effects were more likely to emerge when misleading information was introduced about an Rp– item; that is, items that were subject to retrieval-induced forgetting. Conversely, when misinformation was presented about items that had not been subject to retrieval-induced forgetting (i.e., Rp+ and Nrp items), the level of misinformation reported in the final test did not differ from that of a control group who had received non-relevant retrieval practice in place of relevant selective questioning (Figure 2.4).

If retrieval-induced forgetting promotes the likelihood of misinformation effects, we might expect that such effects are likely to occur only when retrieval inhibition remains active. One method of manipulating the presence of retrieval-induced forgetting is via the insertion of a delay between selective questioning and the manipulation check (i.e., recall task). As M. D. MacLeod and Macrae (2001) have previously demonstrated, the effects of

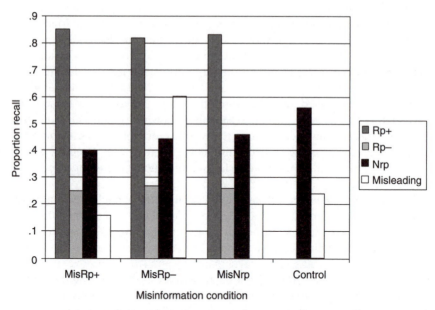

Figure 2.4 Retrieval-induced forgetting facilitates the reporting of misinformation. Misinformation is more likely to be reported when it is presented about an item subjected to retrieval-induced forgetting (i.e., Rp– item) than when it is introduced about items that are not subjected to retrieval-induced forgetting (i.e., Rp+, Nrp, and Control items). MisRp+ = misinformation presented about Rp+ item. MisRp– = misinformation presented about Rp– item. MisNrp = misinformation presented about Nrp item. Control = misinformation presented about Control item. From Saunders and MacLeod (2002, Experiment 1).

retrieval-induced forgetting can dissipate over time. Thus, we might expect misinformation effects to emerge when misleading information is presented shortly after selective questioning; that is, while the original item has been inhibited. To examine this, we manipulated the delay between the selective questioning and misinformation phases by inserting a 24-hour delay either before or after the selective questioning procedure. Retrieval-induced forgetting and misinformation effects were evident only when the delay occurred prior to selective questioning. When there was a 24-hour delay following the selective questioning procedure, retrieval-induced forgetting had dissipated and misinformation failed to emerge. Given that suggestibility is apparent only while retrieval-induced forgetting remains active, there is strong inference that the temporary unavailability of the original item in memory increases the likelihood of an individual being misled under misinformation conditions.

While these studies suggest that retrieval-induced forgetting increases the likelihood of misinformation effects occurring, it does not demonstrate conclusively that inhibitory processes are responsible. To address this issue, we adapted the independent cue technique (cf. M. C. Anderson & Spellman,

1995) and applied it to the modified misinformation paradigm (M. D. MacLeod & Saunders, 2005). Consistent with an inhibitory account, retrieval-induced forgetting remained evident despite the use of novel retrieval cues. Furthermore, misinformation effects occurred wherever misleading information had been introduced about an inhibited item. Specifically, we found misinformation effects not only for Rp– items (i.e., first-order inhibition) but also for Nrp items that were semantically related to Rp+ (i.e., cross-category inhibition) and also Rp– items (i.e., second-order inhibition). Conversely, Nrp items that were semantically dissimilar to both Rp+ and Rp– items were neither inhibited nor susceptible to misinformation (Figure 2.5). This pattern of results strongly suggests that retrieval inhibition is a potent factor in creating the conditions necessary for misinformation effects to emerge.

Our final point is that post-event questioning may also have implications for the confidence expressed by a witness in the accuracy of their memory and that this may ultimately affect how jurors interpret the reliability of their testimony (see Cutler, Penrod, & Dexter, 1990; Cutler, Penrod, & Stuve, 1988). Others have argued that witness confidence can account for as much as 50% of the variance in jurors' judgments of eyewitness accuracy (e.g., Wells, Lindsay, & Ferguson, 1979), which strongly suggests that jurors believe that confident witnesses are also accurate witnesses. While witnesses who are

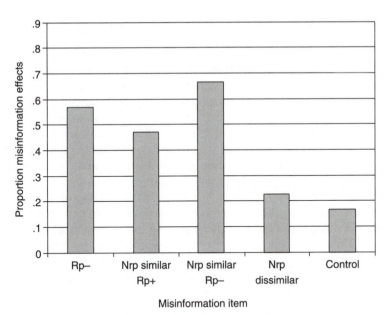

Figure 2.5 The effects of inhibition on the reporting of the original item after exposure to misinformation. Misinformation is more likely to be reported when misleading post-event information is presented on inhibited items (i.e., Rp–, Nrp similar Rp+, and Nrp similar Rp–) than when presented about non-inhibited items (i.e., Nrp dissimilar, Control). From M. D. MacLeod and Saunders (2005).

accurate and confident may not necessarily pose a problem for the legal system, witnesses who are confident but inaccurate may lead juries to place too much weight upon erroneous testimony. Shaw (1996), for example, demonstrated that participants are more confident in consistently incorrect and misleading responses following questioning than in the absence of questioning and that this confidence inflation is still evident 48 hours after questioning. Similarly, participants who engage in reflective thought which can be considered a form of self-generated questioning (e.g., *'did I choose the right person from the lineup?'*) were also more confident in giving consistently inaccurate and misleading responses than those participants who did not engage in reflective thought. Thus, internal and external post-event questioning seems to increase the retrieval fluency of inaccurate responses whereby questioned participants become more confident in their responses despite the inaccuracy of their memories (see also Odinot, Wolters, & Lavender, 2009). A critical question for us, therefore, is whether self-generated questions about a sub-set of items known about a witnessed event might also give rise to retrieval-induced forgetting.

CONCLUSIONS

The benefits of possessing an infallible memory are generally considered to be beyond doubt. Yet it is clear from this chapter that it is only because memory is 'imperfect' (i.e., fallible) that we can go about our daily lives in a purposive adaptive manner. Without the kind of temporary forgetting revealed by the retrieval practice paradigm, purposive remembering would become a desirable though elusive goal. Our chapter demonstrates, however, that such forgetting is not inevitable. Rather, it is possible to protect against the effects of retrieval inhibition by integrating material and also ensuring the most effective learning conditions (i.e., distributed rather than massed practice) although, as we discussed, these may be related. Finally, we considered that this otherwise adaptive forgetting mechanism may sometimes result in unintended consequences such as promoting the reporting of misinformation. Where misleading information is introduced about an item that has been inhibited, witnesses are more likely to retrieve the misinformation than the original. The sunny side of this story, however, is that, by improving our understanding of the conditions most likely to give rise to such forgetting effects, we may be better placed to minimize the unintended consequences of unintended forgetting.

References

Anderson, J. R., & Schooler, L. L. (2000). The adaptive nature of memory. In E. Tulving & F. I. M. Craik (Eds.), *The Oxford handbook of memory* (pp. 557–582). New York: Oxford University Press.

Anderson, M. C. (2003). Rethinking interference theory: Executive control and the mechanisms of forgetting. *Journal of Memory and Language, 49*, 415–445.

Anderson, M. C., Bjork, R. A., & Bjork, E. L. (1994). Remembering can cause forgetting: Retrieval dynamics in long-term memory. *Journal of Experimental Psychology: Learning, Memory and Cognition, 20*, 1063–1087.

Anderson, M. C., & McCulloch, K. C. (1999). Integration as a general boundary condition on retrieval-induced forgetting. *Journal of Experimental Psychology: Learning, Memory and Cognition, 25*, 608–629.

Anderson, M. C., & Spellman, B. A. (1995). On the status of inhibitory mechanisms in cognition: Memory retrieval as a model case. *Psychological Review, 102*, 68–100.

Bajo, M. T., Gómez-Arizza, C. J., Fernandez, A., & Marful, A. (2006). Retrieval-induced forgetting in perceptually driven memory tests. *Journal of Experimental Psychology: Learning, Memory and Cognition, 32*, 1185–1194.

Balota, D. A., Ducheck, J. M., & Paullin, R. (1989) Age-related differences in the impact of spacing, lag and retention interval. *Psychology and Aging, 4*, 3–9.

Bäuml, K.-H. (2002). Semantic generation can cause episodic forgetting. *Psychological Science, 13*, 356–360.

Bäuml, K.-H., & Kuhbandner, C. (2003). Retrieval-induced forgetting and part-list cuing in associatively structured lists. *Memory and Cognition, 31*, 1188–1197.

Bjork, E. L., Bjork, R. A., & Anderson, M. C. (1998). Varieties of goal-directed forgetting. In J. M. Golding & C. M. MacLeod (Eds.), *Intentional forgetting* (pp. 103–137). Mahwah, NJ: Lawrence Erlbaum Associates, Inc.

Bjork, E. L., Bjork, R. A., & MacLeod, M. D. (2006). Types and consequences of forgetting: Intended and unintended. In L.-G. Nilsson & N. Ohta (Eds.), *Memory and society: Psychological perspectives* (pp. 134–159). London: Psychology Press.

Bjork, R. A. (1989). Retrieval inhibition as an adaptive mechanism in human memory. In H. L. Roediger & F. I. M. Craik (Eds.), *Varieties of memory and consciousness: Essays in honor of Endel Tulving* (pp. 309–330). Hillsdale, NJ: Lawrence Erlbaum Associates, Inc.

Bjork, R. A. & Bjork, E. L. (1992). A new theory of disuse and an old theory of stimulus fluctuation. In A. F. Healy, S. M. Kosslyn, & R. M. Shiffrin (Eds.), *From learning processes to cognitive processes: Essays in honor of William K. Estes* (Vol. 2, pp. 35–67). Hillsdale, NJ: Lawrence Erlbaum Associates, Inc.

Carroll, M., Campbell-Ratcliffe, J., Murnane, H., & Perfect, T. (2007). Retrieval-induced forgetting in educational contexts: Monitoring, expertise, text integration, and test format. *European Journal of Cognitive Psychology, 19*, 580–606.

Cepeda, N. J., Pashler, H., Vul, E., Wixted, J. T., & Rohrer, D. (2006). Distributed practice in verbal recall tasks. A review and quantitative synthesis. *Psychological Bulletin, 132*, 354–380.

Crowder, R. G. (1976). *The principles of learning and memory*. Oxford: Lawrence Erlbaum Associates.

Cuc, A., Koppel, J., & Hirst, W. (2007). Silence is not golden: A case for socially shared retrieval-induced forgetting. *Psychological Science, 18*, 727–733.

Cutler, B. L., Penrod, S. D., & Dexter, H. R. (1990). Juror sensitivity to eyewitness identification evidence. *Law and Human Behavior, 14*, 185–191.

Cutler, B. L., Penrod, S. D., & Stuve, T. E. (1988). Juror decision making in eyewitness identification cases. *Law and Human Behavior, 12*, 41–55.

Davis, D., & Loftus, E. F. (2007) Internal and external sources of misinformation in adult witness memory. In M. P. Toglia, J. D. Read, D. F. Ross, & R. C. L. Lindsay

(Eds.), *Handbook of eyewitness psychology: Vol. 1. Memory for events* (pp. 195–237). Mahwah, NJ: Lawrence Erlbaum Associates, Inc.

Dodd, M. D., Castel, A. D., & Roberts, K. E. (2006). A strategy disruption component to retrieval-induced forgetting. *Memory and Cognition, 34*, 102–111.

Dunn, E. W., & Spellman, B. A. (2003). Forgetting by remembering: Stereotype inhibition through rehearsal of alternative aspects of identity. *Journal of Experimental Social Psychology, 39*, 420–433.

Gabbert, F., Memon, A., & Allan, K. (2003). Memory conformity: Can eyewitnesses influence each other's memories for an event? *Applied Cognitive Psychology, 17*, 533–544.

Greene, R. L. (1992). Repetition paradigms. In R. L. Greene (Ed.), *Human memory: Paradigms and paradoxes* (pp. 132–152). Hillsdale, NJ: Lawrence Erlbaum Associates, Inc.

James, W. (1890). *Principles of psychology*. New York: Holt.

Johnson, H. (1994). Processes of successful intentional forgetting. *Psychological Bulletin, 116*, 274–292.

Johnson, S. K., & Anderson, M. C. (2004). The role of inhibitory control in forgetting semantic knowledge. *Psychological Science, 15*, 448–453.

Krug, D., Davis, T. B. & Glover, J. A. (1990). Massed versus distributed repeated reading: A case of forgetting helping recall? *Journal of Educational Psychology, 82*, 366–371.

Lindsay, D. S., & Johnson, M. K. (1989). The eyewitness suggestibility effect and memory for source. *Memory and Cognition, 17*, 349–358.

Loftus, E. F., Miller, D. G., & Burns, H. J. (1978). Semantic integration of verbal information into a visual memory. *Journal of Experimental Psychology: Human Learning and Memory, 4*, 19–31.

Loftus, E. F., & Palmer, J. C. (1974). Reconstruction of automobile destruction: An example of the inter-action between language and memory. *Journal of Verbal Learning and Verbal Behavior, 13*, 585–589.

Loftus, E. F., & Zanni, G. (1975). Eyewitness testimony: The influence of the wording of a question. *Bulletin of the Psychonomic Society, 5*, 86–88.

MacLeod, C. (1989). Directed forgetting affects both direct and indirect tests of memory. *Journal of Experimental Psychology: Learning, Memory and Cognition, 15*, 13–21.

MacLeod, C. M., Dodd, M. D., Sheard, E. D., Wilson, D. E., & Bibi, U. (2003). In opposition to inhibition. In B. H. Ross (Ed.), *The psychology of learning and motivation, 43* (pp. 163–214). San Diego, CA: Academic Press.

MacLeod, M. D. (1999). Why did it happen to me? The role of social cognition processes in adjustment and recovery from criminal victimization and illness. *Current Psychology, 18*, 18–31.

MacLeod, M. D. (2002). Retrieval-induced forgetting in eyewitness memory: Forgetting as a consequence of remembering. *Applied Cognitive Psychology, 16*, 135–149.

MacLeod, M. D., Bjork, E. L., & Bjork, R. A. (2003). The role of retrieval-induced forgetting in the construction and distortion of memories. In B. Kokinov & W. Hirst (Eds.), *Constructive memory* (pp. 55–68). NBU Series in Cognitive Science. Sofia: New Bulgarian University Press.

MacLeod, M. D., & Macrae, C. N. (2001). Gone but not forgotten: The transient nature of retrieval-induced forgetting. *Psychological Science, 12*, 148–152.

MacLeod, M. D., & Saunders, J. (2005). The role of inhibitory control in the production of misinformation effects. *Journal of Experimental Psychology: Learning, Memory and Cognition, 31*, 964–979.

MacLeod, M. D., & Saunders, J. (2008). Retrieval inhibition and memory distortion: Negative consequences of an adaptive process. *Current Directions in Psychological Science, 17*, 26–30.

Macrae, C. N., & MacLeod, M. D. (1999). On recollections lost: When practice makes perfect. *Journal of Personality and Social Psychology, 77*, 463–473.

Migueles, M., & Garcia-Bajos, E. (2007). Selective retrieval and induced forgetting in eyewitness memory. *Applied Cognitive Psychology, 21*, 1157–1172.

Odinot, G., Wolters, G., & Lavender, T. (2009). Repeated partial eyewitness questioning causes confidence inflation but not retrieval-induced forgetting. *Applied Cognitive Psychology, 23*, 90–97.

Ribot, T. A. (1887). *Diseases of memory: An essay in the positive psychology.* New York: Appleton-Century-Crofts.

Russo, R., Parkin, A. J., Taylor, S. R., & Wilks, J. (1998). Revising current two-process accounts of spacing effects in memory. *Journal of Experimental Psychology: Learning, Memory and Cognition, 24*, 161–172.

Saunders, J., & MacLeod, M. D. (2002). New evidence on the suggestibility of memory: The role of retrieval-induced forgetting in misinformation effects. *Journal of Experimental Psychology: Applied, 8*, 127–142.

Saunders, J., & MacLeod, M. D. (2006). Can inhibition resolve retrieval competition through the control of spreading activation? *Memory and Cognition, 34*, 307–322.

Shaw J. S. III (1996). Increases in eyewitness confidence resulting from postevent questioning. *Journal of Experimental Psychology: Applied, 2*, 126–146.

Shaw, J. S. III, Bjork, R. A., & Handal, A. (1995). Retrieval-induced forgetting in an eyewitness-memory paradigm. *Psychonomic Bulletin and Review, 2*, 249–253.

Storm, B. C., Bjork, E. L., Bjork, R. A., & Nestojko, J. (2006). Is retrieval success necessary for retrieval-induced forgetting? *Psychonomic Bulletin and Review, 13*, 1023–1027.

Veling, H., & Knippenberg, A. V. (2004). Remembering can cause inhibition: Retrieval-induced inhibition as cue-independent process. *Journal of Experimental Psychology: Learning, Memory and Cognition, 30*, 315–318.

Verkoeijen, P. P. J. L., Rikers, R. M. J. P., & Schmidt, H. G. (2005). Limitations to the spacing effect. Demonstration of an inverted u-shaped relationship between interrepetition spacing and free recall. *Experimental Psychology, 52*, 257–263.

Wells, G. L., Lindsay, R. C. L., & Ferguson, T. J. (1979). Accuracy, confidence, and juror perceptions in eyewitness identification. *Journal of Applied Psychology, 64*, 440–448.

3 More than just a memory

The nature and validity of working memory in educational settings

Darren S. Levin, S. Kenneth Thurman
and Marissa H. Kiepert

Since its origins in the 1960s cognitive revolution, "short-term" or "primary" memory has developed into the more sophisticated concept of working memory, in which information is not only retained for a brief period of time, but is also manipulated and closely involved in higher order processing activities such as comprehension, problem solving, and reasoning. While the dominant model of working memory has been Baddeley and Hitch's multiple-component model (1974; Baddeley, 2000, 2007), there are several other theoretical views including Cowan's embedded-processes model (1988, 1999, 2005) and Ericsson and Kintsch's long-term working memory theory (1995). Assessments of working memory in children and adults are typically grounded or validated in light of a particular theoretical viewpoint. Research with children has focused on the relationship of working memory to academic achievement. This chapter reviews how working memory has been defined, assessed, and measured in experimental and applied (i.e., educational) settings with children. In light of this review, it raises serious questions regarding the ecological validity of much current research into the measurement of working memory in the classroom.

MODELS OF WORKING MEMORY

How working memory is defined, assessed, and measured in laboratory or applied settings is guided by and closely related to a particular theoretical framework of working memory; moreover, how researchers define, assess, and measure working memory has implications for its applicability in real-world situations. Thus, it is necessary to briefly present several theoretical views of working memory prior to discussing how this construct is used in educational settings.

Baddeley and Hitch's multicomponent model

The dominant theory of working memory is the multicomponent Baddeley and Hitch model which was promulgated in 1974, and later revised by Baddeley (2000, 2007). This model defines working memory as "a limited capacity temporary storage system that underpins complex human thought" (Baddeley, 2007, p. 7). In contrast to Atkinson and Shiffrin's (1968) "modal model" which depicted short-term memory as a temporary but unitary store of information, Baddeley and Hitch (1974) proposed a multicomponent system to account for several of the inconsistencies found between the modal model and existing data. Baddeley (2007) suggests that the modal model could not account for (1) evidence that short-term and long-term memory could not be neatly distinguished based on codes (i.e., semantic, phonetic, and visual), (2) findings from studies indicating that short-term memory could be severely disrupted, yet the transfer of information to long-term memory remained largely unaffected, and (3) data showing that concurrent tasks could selectively interfere with the uptake of information into long-term memory.

Baddeley and Hitch's (1974) original model of working memory consisted of three components, each of which is responsible for different tasks. The "central executive" is the attentional control, decision-making system and is supported by two temporary storage subsystems (or "slave systems") that are domain specific. The first slave system, the "phonological loop," has received the most empirical investigation and support. The function of the phonological loop is to store and manipulate speech-based information through a subvocal rehearsal process known as articulatory control. The second slave system, the visuospatial sketchpad, stores and manipulates visual and spatial information. In 2000, Baddeley extended this model to include a third temporary storage subsystem known as the episodic buffer. This fourth component was proposed to account for data indicating that visual and phonological information are combined in some way (e.g., Logie, Della Sala, Val Wynn, & Baddeley, 2000; Saito, Logie, Morita, & Law, 2008), and helps explain data that could not be supported solely by these two existing slave systems. Thus, the episodic buffer was added as a subsystem that formed an interface between the other components and long-term memory (Baddeley, 2007).

Early research on the model focused heavily on the phonological loop. Initial laboratory evidence supporting the existence of a phonological loop includes:

- the *irrelevant speech* effect: the effect occurring when subject performance on remembering printed verbal items is disrupted by irrelevant spoken material presented at the same time (Colle & Welsh, 1976),
- the *word length* effect: a phenomenon in which memory span coincides with the spoken length of the word such that memory span for long words is smaller than for short (Baddeley, Thomson, & Buchanan, 1975),

- the *phonological similarity* effect: the effect that occurs when similar sounding words impair immediate serial recall (Conrad & Hull, 1964), and
- *articulatory suppression*, which occurs when the prevention of the subvocal rehearsal processes severely disrupts performance on a memory list and also abolishes the word length effect (Baddeley, Lewis, & Vallar, 1984).

The concept of a phonological loop has not gone unchallenged, however. To date, the theoretical underpinnings of the phonological loop continue to be researched and have produced interesting developments in our understanding of language acquisition and processing (see Baddeley, 2007 for review).

The visuospatial sketchpad, researched to a lesser degree than the phonological loop, is also empirically supported. Evidence for the visuospatial sketchpad comes from studies on visual imagery (e.g., Baddeley, Grant, Wight, & Thompson, 1975) and more recently from neuropsychology research using brain-imaging techniques (e.g., Jonides et al., 1993; Smith & Jonides, 1997; Della Sala & Logie, 2002). Recent reviews of the advancements of the visuospatial sketchpad are given by Logie (1995, 2003), and Fletcher and Henson (2001).

Despite being at the core of the model, attempts to analyze the central executive came later than developments on these two subcomponents. However, great strides have been made in understanding the functions of the central executive since Baddeley's first attempt in 1986, which comprised only a single book chapter. Review of recent developments in research on the central executive can be found in Baddeley (2007).

Other models of working memory have emerged in response to criticisms of Baddeley and Hitch's multicomponent theory. Two of the most influential are Cowan's embedded-processes model and Ericsson and Kintsch's long-term working memory theory.

Cowan's embedded-processes model

Cowan's embedded-processes model of working memory (1988, 1999, 2005) has been developing since 1988, although the term "embedded processes" did not appear until 1999. One of the most notable differences between Cowan's model of working memory and Baddeley's model is in the *level* of analysis: Cowan uses more generic terms to explain working memory rather than explicit terms favored by Baddeley. For example, rather than supporting specific slave systems, Cowan's model uses vaguer terminology such as "activated memory," which according to him is a more all-embracing term. Activated memory is not limited to phonological or visual-spatial information, but can include representations of tactile sensory information, which is lacking from Baddeley's model, even with the inclusion of an episodic buffer (Cowan, 2005).

Two key elements play a role in Cowan's model (1988, 1999, 2005). The first is activated memory, or sensory and categorical features from long-term memory that are currently in an activated state. The second element is the focus of attention, which is a portion of the activated memory that is in conscious awareness and of limited capacity. It functions to form new episodic links between items that are activated at the same time and which are subsequently integrated into long-term memory. Like Baddeley, Cowan (2005) suggests that the central executive controls, at least in part, the focus of attention through orienting responses that can either attract attention when information is new or interesting, or counteract the central executive when information is not novel. Recently Cowan (2005) has asserted that working memory is "a set of processes that hold a limited amount of information in a readily accessible state for use in an active task" (p. 39). However, there are clear conceptual similarities between the rival theories and Cowan has stated that: "Practically, there may be only subtle (though potentially important) differences between a distinct-buffers view and a more integrated approach" (2005, p. 43).

Ericsson and Kintsch's long-term working memory theory

Another rival to the multicomponent view is Ericsson and Kintsch's (1995) theory of long-term working memory (LT-WM). Unlike the models just discussed, LT-WM is meant to describe a specific *instance* of working memory capacity. Specifically, LT-WM theory accounts for the extensive working memory capacity often displayed by experts and skilled performers as well as the large working memory demands made by text comprehension. Like Cowan's model, LT-WM theory developed in response to Baddeley's model, or rather, the inadequacies of Baddeley's model. In particular, Ericsson and Kintsch (1995) made the case that Baddeley's model (1986) left unexplained the working memory processes of highly skilled activities (such as piano playing, typing, and reading). It is noteworthy, however, that the LT-WM theory of Ericsson and Kintsch was formulated in 1995, before Baddeley added the episodic buffer as the fourth component of his model in 2000 – a component he deemed necessary to help account for "the temporary storage of material in quantities that seemed clearly to exceed the capacity of either the verbal or visual-spatial peripheral subsystems. This shows up particularly clearly in the retention of prose passages" (Baddeley, 2003, p. 202).

In their theory, Ericsson and Kintsch (1995) refer to the temporary storage of information (the traditional view of working memory) as short-term working memory (or ST-WM), which differs from LT-WM in "the durability of the storage it provides and the need for sufficient retrieval cues in attention for access to information in long-term memory" (Ericsson & Kintsch, 1995, p. 211). In highly skilled activities retrieval cues in ST-WM make accessible relevant information in long-term memory. Thus, Ericsson and Kintsch stress the importance of efficient and reliable storage of information, as well as its organization.

ASSESSMENT OF WORKING MEMORY

The theories of working memory described above provide the foundations and theoretical underpinnings for the design of empirical (i.e., experimental) working memory tasks. Empirical working memory tasks attempt to delineate *how* humans use the basic functions of working memory to solve problems and adapt to their environments. In addition, such empirical findings provide data that support, refute, or otherwise shape the original theories. Such is the typical evolution of knowledge (Kuhn, 1962); each step shapes the previous step allowing for theory modification and evolution.

With regard to working memory, experimental findings have allowed for further construct development and the differentiation of working memory from short-term memory and verbal working memory from visual-spatial working memory. As empirical support is established for theoretical and empirical working memory task validity, working memory tasks are further developed for educational practice, most notably to predict or establish link-ages between working memory and academic achievement such as general reasoning ability (e.g., Kyllonen & Christal, 1990), reading comprehension (e.g., Coltheart, 1987), arithmetic problem solving (e.g., Logie, Gilhooly, & Wynn, 1994), vocabulary acquisition (e.g., Gathercole & Baddeley, 1993), and learning disabilities (e.g., Reid, Hresko, & Swanson, 1996) (all as cited in Roid, 2003, p. 43). The previous section provided a history of the theoretical underpinnings of empirical working memory tasks. In this section, we explore the empirical tasks themselves, as well as the educationally relevant assessments that have evolved from them and are currently used in educational settings. In doing so, we wish to emphasize the breadth and depths of empirical working memory tasks, and thus their potential contributions to educational applications. However, we also underscore the chasm that actually exists between empirical and educational assessment practices, and therefore, the specific educational conclusions that can be drawn regarding the interpretation of educational working memory tasks.

In empirical assessment of working memory, respondents are typically required to combine memory for a sequence of items while simultaneously processing other information. This activity is increased over successive trials until criteria errors are committed (Gathercole & Alloway, 2008). Conventionally, many of the empirical assessments of working memory have been referred to as "span tasks," including reading span, digit span, listening span, computation span, counting span, and other types of visual-spatial spans.

Laboratory assessment of verbal working memory

Reading span tasks

Modern empirical assessment of working memory can be traced to Daneman and Carpenter's (1980) landmark study, which used a reading span test that assessed college students' use of both processing and storage capacity. Sets of sentences of approximately the same length were printed on cards, which were then read aloud by the students at a normal reading pace. Students were unable to view their previously read sentences. Presentation of a blank card signaled to the students to recite the last word of each sentence that was shown on the cards. Longer sets of sentences were presented in ensuing sets, until students failed all trials within a given set. Reading span was calculated based on the largest list size of perfectly recalled final words.

Tirre and Peña (1992) expanded on Daneman and Carpenter's test by presenting sentences on a computer screen. In their task, respondents, who were US Air Force personnel, were required to answer "True" or "False" to each sentence before proceeding; this ensured meaningful processing and provided a measure of knowledge which was also correlated with working memory. Unlike the previous studies, respondents in de Jong's (1998) study were children who were required to read sentences ranging from four to seven words. All these studies directly related working memory to reading skills, but Friedman and Miyake (2004) concluded that reading span tasks may be mediated by variables other than working memory capacity, such as time of processing.

Digit, letter, and word span tasks

Digit span tasks typically require the respondent to listen to verbally presented digits, and then recall them either in the same order in which they are presented (digits forward) or in backwards order (digits backward). Ramsay and Reynolds (1995) reviewed 27 articles on the separate scaling of the Digits Forward and Digits Backward subtests of the Test of Memory and Learning. Using factor analysis, Ramsay and Reynolds concluded that, despite similarities, the two tasks reflect different abilities. Similarly, Reynolds (1997) confirmed that the two tasks differ in that digits backward span requires the use of transformation (i.e., working memory), whereas the digits forward span does not. Despite Reynolds' warning that "separate scaled scores for forward and for backward memory span tasks should be provided routinely on any standardized assessment" (1997, p. 39), raw scores on the two tasks continue to be summed on some commercially available assessments of working memory to produce a single standard score.

There is a multitude of other span tasks that are derived from the digits forward/backward tasks, such as letter spans, number–letter combinations, and various word spans. All of these require participants to respond selectively according to certain criteria: for instance, the letters in alphabetical order or words according to prescribed categories (e.g., body parts followed by non-body parts).

Listening span tasks

Listening span tests are analogous to reading span tests in that they typically require a respondent to listen to a series of sentences and then recall the last word spoken in each sentence. Listening span tests have the advantage of not taxing reading skills which may be suspect in some children with educational disabilities. There are many varieties of listening span test, including the cloze procedure and knowledge verification procedures described below.

Siegel and Ryan (1989) explored working memory differences in children with a reading, math, or attention disability using a cloze procedure (Savage, Lavers, & Pillay, 2007). Children were verbally presented with a set of sentences in which the last word in each sentence was missing. After each sentence the children were required to say the missing word and subsequently verbally recall all the missing words in the set. Example sentences from Seigel and Ryan include: "In summer it is very ____"; "People go to see monkeys in a ____"; "With dinner we sometimes eat bread and ____." In this case, the child was then required to repeat the words that he or she had chosen (i.e., hot, zoo, butter).

Under the knowledge verification procedure, a respondent is required to answer a question about sentences (e.g., by responding "true" or "false"; "yes" or "no") before being asked to recall the last word of the sentence. For example, Gathercole and Pickering (2000a) asked students to listen to a pair of sentences and judge the veracity of each spoken sentence (e.g., Oranges live in water) before recall. Whereas the cloze procedure has been used to establish a linkage between working memory and a reading disability (e.g., Siegel & Ryan, 1989), studies that have used a knowledge verification procedure have generally not supported such a link (e.g., Gathercole & Pickering, 2000b; Stothard & Hulme, 1992).

Computation span test

Based on the Operation Word task used by Turner and Engle (1989), de Jong (1998) employed the computation span test to distinguish differences in memory processing and storage. Analogous to the reading span tests employed in the same study (de Jong, 1998), each computation span test item required the child to first read and solve aloud a simple mathematical computation (e.g., $3 + 1$) immediately before listening to a single digit spoken by the test administrator. Each computation consisted of either the addition or subtraction of 1 from a number less than 10, and the correct answer was always less than 10. After the digit was presented, the child was required to immediately begin the next computation, so as to minimize the possibility of rehearsal. As the number of computations increased from two to seven, so the list of numbers that had to be stored also increased.

Counting span task

In the same study, de Jong (1998) used a counting span test based on Case, Kurland, and Goldberg's (1982) design. The counting span test requires respondents to retain and reproduce a series of digits while counting. In de Jong's design, a card was presented to each child, on which an irregular pattern of green and yellow dots was printed. Each child was required to count aloud the number of green dots on each card; these numbers were to be stored and subsequently recalled in the correct order.

Assessment of visual-spatial working memory

Pentland, Anderson, Dye, and Wood (2003, pp. 144–145) define nonverbal memory as a "process that relates to the encoding and retrieval of spatial representations" and suggest that "nonverbal memory is more precisely defined in terms of a synthesis of visual and spatial (visuo-spatial) informa-tion." They suggest that, whereas the visual processing system processes object properties such as shape and color, the spatial processing unit assesses properties such as location and size (Pentland et al., 2003).

Historically, assessing visual-spatial working memory has been more chal-lenging than assessing verbal working memory, due to the relative difficulty of designing tasks that are pure measures of visual-spatial constructs (Pickering, 2001). For example, verbal mediation is often used by respondents when per-forming many tasks of visual-spatial working memory (Pulos & Denzine, 2005). Two measures that are relatively free of verbal mediation, however, are the Corsi Block Test (Milner, 1971) and the Visual Patterns Test, devised by Wilson, Scott, and Power (1987), developed by Logie and Pearson (1997), and normed by Della Sala, Gray, Baddeley, Allamano, and Wilson (1999).

The Corsi Block Test (CBT) was designed in the early 1970s to be used in neuropsychology practice, and is an extension of the Cube Imitation Test, developed by Knox (1913) to diagnose "mental retardation" in early twentieth-century immigrants to the United States (Vecchi & Richardson, 2001). The CBT typically consists of wooden pegs arranged in a nonsym-metrical pattern, which are attached to a wooden board. The examiner taps specific blocks in a predetermined sequence (usually at the rate of 1 block per second), and upon cue, the respondent repeats the sequence. By increasing the number of blocks tapped, the examiner controls for the difficulty of the task (Pickering, 2001). Although the Corsi Block Test has been used extensively to assess individuals suspected of neuropsychological deficits, standardization of the assessment has been lacking (Kessels, van Zandvoort, Postma, Kappelle, & de Haan, 2000). In fact, Berch, Krikorian, and Huha (1998) identified significant variations in their review of 38 empirical studies utilizing the CBT. Such variations were associated with physical charac-teristics such as the color of the board, number of blocks positioned on the board, block size, block placement, and display area. Also noted in their

review were significant administrative differences, for example, pointing procedure, block-tapping rate, starting point, trials per level, discontinue criterion, and block-tapping sequences. By using a computerized version of the
CBT, Vandierendonck, Kemps, Fastame, and Szmalec (2004) investigated the
CBT's potential load on working memory and concluded that the "findings
are clear and fit in well with the working memory framework of Baddeley and
Hitch (1974)."

Whereas the CBT is purported to measure visual and spatial working
memory, the Visual Patterns Test (VPT) is designed to be a "purer" assessment of visual working memory (Della Sala et al., 1999). The VPT consists of
crossword puzzle-like grids (without the numbers) that increase in the number
of cells from four (i.e., a 2×2 matrix) to 30 (i.e., a 5×6 matrix). In each grid,
the individual cells are either black or white. Each grid is displayed on a card,
which is presented to the respondent for 3 seconds. When removed from view,
the respondent is asked to reproduce the grid by marking the cells in an
empty grid of the same size as that presented. Scoring is based on the number
of correctly filled cells in the most complex pattern accurately recalled.

Star Counting Test

Based on Baddeley and Hitch's (1974) working memory model and Norman
and Shallice's (1986) theory of central executive functioning, the Star Counting Test was "directly aimed at measuring the ability to activate, modulate, and
inhibit processes of working memory" (de Jong, 1998, p. 84). For example, de
Jong and Das-Smaal (1995) used nine rows of three to five stars in each item.
A number was inserted at the beginning of the item, and plus and minus signs
were inserted between some stars. The child was instructed to begin counting
starting with the number presented at the beginning of the item, and count
the stars from left to right, and top to bottom. However, the plus sign indicated to count the subsequent stars in forward sequence, whereas the minus
sign clued the respondent to continue counting the subsequent stars in a
backward order. Empty spaces took the place of some stars to prevent the
child from counting by fives. Although the SCT does load on working memory skills, the authors concluded that SCT is "probably not a completely pure
measure of working memory capacity" due to its demand of attention,
counting speed, and sustained effort (de Jong, & Das-Smaal, 1995, p. 89).

Direction Span Test

Lecerf and Roulin (2006) designed the Direction Span Test (DST) to distinguish visual-spatial short-term memory from visual-spatial working memory.
A 5×5 computerized matrix was presented on a computer monitor to each
respondent. Directional arrows appeared randomly, one at a time, in different
cells, which were to be encoded by the respondent. On tasks of short-term
memory (Location Span Test), respondents were instructed to memorize the

cells that contained the arrows. On tasks of working memory (DST), respondents were instructed to memorize the cells that were *pointed at* by the directional arrow. These two tasks were both subjected to different manipulations (e.g., encoding time, interval time, and order of presentation). Use of the DST established further support for the differentiation of short-term visual-spatial memory from visual-spatial working memory, and that encoding time, but not interval time, can enhance performance on visual-spatial working memory tasks.

Other spatial tasks

Shah and Miyake (1996) and Handley, Capon, Copp, and Harper (2002) also concluded that spatial and verbal working memory represent distinct systems, utilizing different pools of resources. Both studies incorporated a reading span test derived from Daneman and Carpenter (1980) and a spatial span task. The spatial span for both studies required participants to view normal and mirror-imaged capitalized English letters. However, the letters were rotated to various degrees, and the respondent was required to quickly and effectively judge which letter was normal, and which was a mirror image. Furthermore, the respondent was subsequently asked to recall the orientations of the images in the correct order in which they appeared.

Educational applications of working memory

Of the many instruments that are available to measure working memory, the Wechsler Intelligence Scale for Children – Fourth Edition (WISC-IV), the Woodcock–Johnson III Tests of Cognitive Abilities (WJ III COG), and the Stanford–Binet Intelligence Scales, Fifth Edition (SB5) are the most widely used today (Leffard et al., 2006). The following is a brief review of subtests that measure working memory, and, although not exhaustive, represents widely used subtests that have been distinguished by literature review and expert consensus (i.e., Flanagan, Ortiz, & Alfonso, 2007; Leffard et al., 2006) to measure working memory.

Wechsler assessments

The Wechsler Intelligence Scale for Children – Fourth Edition (WISC-IV) and the Wechsler Adult Intelligence Scale – Third Edition (WAIS-III) both include subtests that purport to measure working memory. Whereas the WISC-IV is normed for children aged 6.0–16.11, the WAIS-III is normed for individuals aged 16.0–89.0. The WISC-IV technical manual defines working memory as "the ability to actively maintain information in conscious awareness, perform some operation or manipulation with it, and produce a result" (Wechsler, 2003, p. 8). The WISC-IV test developers indicate that the Baddeley model of working memory serves as the basis for the working memory assessments (Leffard et al., 2006), and furthermore that working memory on these assessments can be assessed with three separate subtests: Digit Span, Letter–Number Sequencing, and Arithmetic. The Digit Span subtest is composed of Digits Forward and Digits Backward. The numbers cued increase for both tasks, and the tasks are terminated when the respondent fails a specific number of trials according to established criteria. Of significant mention is that the Digits Forward "involves rote learning and memory, attention, encoding, and auditory processing" whereas Digits Backward involves "working memory, transformation of information, mental manipulation, and visual-spatial imaging" (Wechsler, 2003, p. 16). Because Digits Backward (but not Digits Forward) emphasizes working memory and transformation of information, the Digit Span subtest does not appear to separate working memory from short-term memory. Thus, although the clinician can statistically separate respondents' performance on these tasks, interpreting the entire subtest as a construct of working memory is inadvisable. A similar issue regarding construct validity exists for the Arithmetic subtest, albeit for different reasons. On this subtest, the respondent is verbally presented with arithmetic problems to solve within a specified time limit without the use of paper or pencil. This subtest involves mental manipulation, concentration, attention, short- and long-term memory, numerical reasoning ability, and mental alertness (Wechsler, 2003, p. 17). Furthermore, Groth-Marnat, Kaufman, and Sattler also suggest that Arithmetic "may involve sequencing, fluid reasoning, and logical reasoning" (as cited in Wechsler, 2003, p. 17). It is worth noting that "working memory" is absent in both of these descriptions. Because of the many different cognitive domains that may be used on these tasks, Leffard et al. (2006) warn that the Arithmetic subtest is a "less pure" measure of working memory, and should therefore not be used as a measure of working memory.

The Letter–Number Sequencing task best exemplifies a valid working memory task from the Wechsler series. This subtest requires the respondent to listen to a series of letters and numbers, and then recall the numbers in ascending order and the letters in alphabetical order until he or she fails a specific number of trials according to criteria. Because of the transformations skills required of the respondent, higher-order processing demands are thus required (Leffard et al., 2006), especially when compared to those skills required for the Digit Span task.

The Woodcock–Johnson III Tests of Cognitive Abilities (WJ III COG)

The Woodcock–Johnson III Tests of Cognitive Abilities (WJ III COG) were designed and developed to measure broad and narrow abilities according to the Cattell–Horn–Carroll theory (see Carroll, 1993; Mather & Woodcock, 2001) of cognitive abilities. Mather and Woodcock (2001) define working memory as the narrow "ability to hold information in mind for a short time while performing some operation on it" (as cited in Leffard et al., 2006, p. 237). Two subtests of the WJ III COG, the Auditory Working Memory and Numbers Reversed, are aggregated to reflect the working memory Clinical Cluster. The Auditory Working Memory subtest requires the respondent to listen to a series of nouns and numbers, and to then repeat the nouns in the same order followed by the numbers in the same order. The Numbers Reversed subtest is analogous to the Digits Backward task of the Wechsler scales. Both working memory subtests on the WJ III COG are normed for persons aged 4 to 90 years.

Stanford–Binet Intelligence Scales, Fifth Edition (SB5)

In the Stanford–Binet Intelligence Scales, Fifth Edition (SB5), Roid (2003, p. 137) defines working memory as "a class of memory processes in which diverse information in short-term memory is inspected, sorted, or transformed." The Last Word subtest was adapted from Daneman and Carpenter's (1980) seminal work. On levels 1–3, the respondent is required to repeat brief phrases and sentences. However, levels 1–3 appear to assess short-term memory only, as opposed to levels 4–6, which appear to more accurately reflect working memory. On levels 4–6, the respondent is required to provide brief responses to sentences (i.e., "yes" or "no") before recalling the last word in each sentence. The questions and their subsequent answers thus serve as the "transformation" requirement of working memory.

In order to provide a nonverbal alternative to traditional working memory tasks, the Block Span task was adapted from the original Corsi Block Test, developed by Knox (1913). On this task, the examiner taps a series of blocks with a separate block in a specified order. Then, the respondent taps the same blocks in the same order. On later tasks, the examiner taps specified blocks that are located in either red or yellow rows, and the respondent must tap the same blocks in order, but in one row (e.g., yellow) before the other row (e.g., red). Similar to the Last Word task, early levels of the Block Span task (i.e., 1–2) appear to assess short-term memory only, whereas levels 3–6 require the additional demands of working memory. As such, great care must be used when interpreting the SB5 subtests that purport to measure both verbal and nonverbal working memory, as respondents' scores may actually be more reflective of short-term memory. These two subtests are normed for individuals aged 2 to 85 years.

Differential Ability Scales, Second Edition (DAS-II)

Revised in 2007, the Differential Ability Scales, Second Edition (DAS-II) contains a working memory cluster for the Early Years Battery (Upper Level) and the School-Age Battery. For both batteries, the working memory cluster score is composed of two subtests: Recall of Sequential Order, and Recall of Digits Backward. In the Recall of Sequential Order subtest, the respondent is presented with an oral list of body parts, and is required to verbally sequence the list in order from the highest part on the body to the lowest. Older children are also presented with non-body parts, and must sequence the body parts (again from highest to lowest) followed by the non-body parts. The Recall of Digits Backward subtest is analogous to the Digits Backward task of the Wechsler scales. The two working memory subtests on the DAS-II are normed for children aged 5.0–17.11. Although the DAS-II was not developed to directly reflect current Cattell–Horn–Carroll (CHC) theory, "the factor structure of the DAS-II fits the seven-factor CHC model well" (Elliott, 2007, p. 13), and the working memory subtests were included in the current edition to reflect the general importance of research in the area of working memory.

Wide Range Assessment of Memory and Learning, Second Edition (WRAML2)

In addition to the six Core Subtests, the Wide Range Assessment of Memory and Learning Second Edition (WRAML2) includes two optional subtests that specifically address working memory: Verbal Working Memory and Symbolic Working Memory. Both subtests are normed for individuals aged 5–90. The Verbal Working Memory subtest requires respondents to complete two distinct, but related tasks. Respondents are verbally presented with a list of words that include animals and non-animals. The respondent is first asked to repeat the list, recalling all the animals followed by the non-animals. Then, after hearing another list, the respondent is asked to recall the animals in order of their typical sizes (smallest to largest), followed by the non-animals in any order. Respondents over 14 years of age are asked to verbally list the non-animals in relative size as well.

On the Symbolic Working Memory subtest, respondents are verbally presented with a series of random numbers, and are required to point out the numbers in ascending order on a stimulus card. Respondents are also verbally presented with random numbers–letters, and then asked to point out the numbers followed by the letters in correct order on another stimulus card. These two subtests are normed for individuals aged 9–85 years and older.

Working Memory Test Battery for Children (WMTB-C)

The Working Memory Test Battery for Children (WMTB-C) assesses working memory in children aged 5 to 15 (Pickering & Gathercole, 2001). Three of the nine subtests on the WMTB-C directly measure working memory: Listening Recall, Counting Recall, and Backward Digit Recall tasks. These subtests reflect the empirical and educational tasks described throughout this chapter. The other six subtests address the visual-spatial sketchpad and the phonological loop.

By examining the relationships between working memory tasks used in empirical research and tasks used in actual educational practice (delineated

Table 3.1 Relationship between empirical support, laboratory, and educational assessment of working memory

Task	Relevant empirical assessment	Educational application
Reading span tasks	Daneman & Carpenter (1980, 1983) Daneman & Green (1986) Masson & Miller (1983) Tirre and Peña (1992) de Jong (1998) Friedman & Miyake (2004)	SB5: Last Word[a] WMTB-C: Listening Recall
Listening span tasks	Siegel & Ryan (1989) Gathercole & Pickering (2000a, 2000b) Stothard & Hulme (1992)	
Computation span tasks	Turner & Engle (1989) de Jong (1998)	
Counting span tasks	de Jong (1998) Case, Kurland, & Goldberg (1982)	WMTB-C: Counting Recall
Corsi Block Test/Cube Imitation Test	Vandierendonk, Kemps, Fastame, & Szmalec (2004)	SB5: Block Span[a]
Visual Patterns Test		
Direction Span Test	Lecerf & Roulin (2006)	
Other spatial tasks	Shah & Miyake (1996) Handley, Capon, Copp, & Harper (2002)	
Digit span tasks and derivatives	Ramsay & Reynolds (1995) Reynolds (1997)	Wechsler: Digit Span[b] Wechsler: Letter Number Sequencing Wechsler: Arithmetic[c] WJ: Auditory WM WJ: Numbers Reversed DAS-II: Recall of Sequential Order DAS-II: Recall of Digits Backward WRAML2: Verbal Working Memory WRAML2: Symbolic Working Memory CMS: Sequences WMTB-C: Backward Digit Recall

a Working memory tapped on later items only.
b Working memory tapped on Digits Backward only.
c Additional constructs tapped other than working memory.

in Table 3.1) a number of conclusions can be drawn. First, of the 15 most widely used subtests in educational practice, 11 are based either directly or indirectly on digit span tasks, leaving results derived from the majority of the empirical studies unaccounted for in educational assessment. Second, the Digit Span subtest (WISC-IV, WAIS-III), arguably the most widely used subtest purporting to measure working memory, contains many items (i.e., Digits Forward) that reflect memory span, not working memory. This was included on the WISC-IV (2003) despite Reynolds' (1997) caveats published six years previously. Third, the Arithmetic subtest (WISC-IV, WAIS-III) likely loads on other cognitive factors to such an extent that Leffard et al. (1996) caution that it does not accurately measure working memory. Fourth, both working memory subtests on the SB5 may or may not reflect working memory, depending on which particular items are presented to the respondent. Fifth, of the 15 subtests described, only the Block Span (SB5) addresses visual-spatial working memory (and as just mentioned, only depending on specific items presented). Sixth, many of the educational subtests were derived from empirical studies that used adult subjects, raising concerns regarding the developmental applicability of such tasks.

By using these subtests during the educational assessment of working memory, our conclusions regarding children's cognitive skill sets are compromised. Furthermore, and perhaps more importantly, such educational assessments may not accurately assess the day-to-day demands of working memory, especially related to children's learning within educational milieus.

ECOLOGICAL VALIDITY

In the first section of this chapter we examined the various models of working memory before focusing on the various measures employed and their potential problems, and then considering their application both in laboratory studies and in the domain of assessment. Before we consider the application of working memory to elementary classrooms, it is first necessary to address the issue of ecological validity.

The notion of ecological validity grows from the early work of Brunswik (1943, 1956). Brunswik's (1956) concern was with the over-generalization of perceptual cues in the laboratory to the real-world performance. Brunswik's view of ecological validity focused on how well a cue predicted a perceptual state in the environment. Brunswik's basic assertion was that generalizability depends not only on the representativeness of the sample but also on the representativeness of the cues presented in perceptual experiments. Over time the use of the term "ecological validity" has experienced some shift from Brunswik's original conceptualization to which certain authors have objected (e.g., Araujo, Davids, & Passos, 2007; Hammond, 1999). Be this as it may, these newer concepts of ecological validity are more to the point of the current discussion.

For example, Bronfenbrenner (1979) suggested that developmental researchers had to have greater concern with the study of human development in real-life situations. He espoused the view that research had to take place in both representative as well as natural settings. Similarly, Neisser (1976) has suggested that "cognitive psychologists must make a greater effort to understand cognition as it occurs in the ordinary environment and in the context of purposeful activity" (p. 7). More recently other authors (e.g., Savage et al., 2007 and Thurman & Kiepert, 2008) have made similar assertions regarding the study of working memory. Thurman and Kiepert stress that "with respect to applied cognitive research [including studies of working memory], the issue of ecological validity is particularly paramount because the success of an intervention oftentimes relies on our understanding of a child's functioning in everyday life" (p. 269). Similarly, Savage et al. (2007) assert that "empirically, the most popular current measures of WM [working memory] . . . can be criticized on a range of theoretical grounds including . . . the lack of ecological validity" (p. 197). Pickering (2006) has recently pointed out that in spite of the concerns expressed regarding ecological validity, working memory function is still assessed primarily using things like nonsense words, numbers or other equally meaningless information. The previous section of this chapter further validates Pickering's point.

Another view of ecological validity likens the construct to predictive validity. For example, Sbordone (1996) has suggested that ecological validity is characterized as a "functional and predictive relationship" between a person's test performance and their behavior in real-world settings (p. 16). To make such predictions it is necessary to understand the constructs being studied, in this case working memory, in the natural environment. In fact, Isquith, Gioia, and Espy (2004) have asserted that, when considering the assessment of executive function in young children, "the child's everyday environments, both at home and at school or day care, are important venues for observing routine manifestations of executive functions" (p. 406). Such observations typically culminate in the process of collecting and quantifying behavioral data that accurately reflect the construct under study. For example, the Behavior Rating Inventory of Executive Functioning (BRIEF) (Gioia, Isquith, Guy, & Kenworthy, 2000) may be an effective tool for measuring children's executive functions as they are manifested in children's natural environments. Used in this way, observational data help ensure the ecological validity of the constructs under study, as well as the generalizability and applicability of the construct to the targeted populations within their natural environments. Moreover, this approach is likely to enhance the power of these types of assessments for predicting real-world function (Thurman & McGrath, 2008).

Verisimilitude and veridicality

Ecological validity is relevant for applied cognitive research in general, and for understanding how children use working memory in academic settings. The concept of verisimilitude reflects an aspect of ecological validity, and refers to how closely the demands required by an experiment or assessment tool resemble the demands required of the individual in day-to-day functioning (Frazen & Wilhelm, 1996). This is an especially salient issue when drawing conclusions based on traditional educational assessments of working memory. As others (e.g., Gathercole & Alloway, 2008) discuss and as we have pointed out in the previous section, multifarious span tasks have been commonly used to assess working memory in research and educational settings. For example, many of the commercially available educational assessments of working memory are replete with tasks requiring backward digit recall and derivatives of it. However, one would be hard pressed to demonstrate when, if ever, students are actually required to perform such a task within classroom settings. As such, it appears that the vast majority of the ways that working memory has been conceptualized, measured, and assessed lack verisimilitude. Although we acknowledge that working memory is used to a substantial degree during the active processes of learning, we also suggest that there seems to be a schism between working memory's theoretical, empirical, and educational underpinnings and the way in which it is actually used, especially within the educational milieu. There is little doubt regarding the predictive power of working memory on academic achievement. A plethora of studies (see Gathercole & Alloway, 2008) convincingly demonstrates this relationship. However, with regard to verisimilitude, we suggest that it may be more ecologically valid to examine the behavioral manifestations of working memory, rather than the underlying construct, so that realistic, practical, and ecologically valid interventions can be designed and implemented, with (potentially) long-lasting, positive behavioral and academic consequences.

Table 3.2 provides some classroom examples requiring the use of working memory skills. Examination of Table 3.2 should provide the reader with

Table 3.2 Examples of the use of working memory skills in the classroom[a]

Subtraction problems requiring borrowing, especially when done mentally

Following a multi-step command in the proper order

Writing a complex sentence

Identifying rhyming words after listening to a four-line passage

Comprehending a read passage

Word decoding and supplying its meaning

Writing a spelling word after its oral presentation

Translating a passage from English to French

a The authors would like to thank Dr. Catherine Fiorello for some of these examples.

insight into how the tasks used to measure working memory in the laboratory and during educational assessments (see Table 3.1) contrast with the use of working memory skills in the classroom. These examples we hope are helpful to researchers and practitioners in meeting the challenge of understanding and assessing working memory in an ecologically valid manner.

Consideration needs to be given not only to whether assessments contain items that are similar to those in the classroom environment (Frazen & Wilhelm, 1996), but also to whether actual *performance (i.e., obtained scores)* on the assessments predicts performance of actual classroom tasks that require working memory. Furthermore, it is important to determine whether or not working memory skills are used and applied in a similar manner to the way they manifest in classroom learning tasks. Thus, although the approaches espoused by Isquith et al. (2004) specifically address the issue of verisimilitude, an assessment's construct validity, generalizability, and practicality must be further explored. Assessment approaches must also be interpreted within the context of the settings, people, and situational circumstance in which the behaviors are exhibited. It is possible, for example, that a child might appear to have a working memory deficit in the classroom when, in fact, his/her behavior might be a function of other more situational variables. By not controlling or addressing these variables, hypotheses that what has been observed is due to specific neurocognitive variables may be mitigated. By addressing these issues during educational assessment, however, more ecologically valid conclusions regarding working memory can be formulated.

Because working memory abilities increase with development, assessment tools used to measure working memory must respect the changing demands of a child's environment as he or she matures (Anderson, 2002; Silver, 2000). As Anderson (2002) suggests, assessments of cognitive abilities (including executive functioning) must be "suitable for children and valid for specific developmental stages" (p. 75). Being cognizant of age appropriateness of assessment tasks is critical for assuring ecological validity. As previously discussed, many studies of working memory have used adults rather than children in their experimental procedures, thus attenuating any conclusions that may be generalized to children's skill sets. Moreover, the demands required by an assessment tool must be reflective of specific, relevant, and everyday environmental demands that are salient from the child's perspective, and not necessarily from the perspective of the researcher. When interpreting ecologically valid working memory assessment results, any and all inconsistencies must be addressed. For example, observations that a student often "forgets" teachers' questions while taking notes yet easily "recalls" sequences of chemistry laboratory skills while conducting experiments will need to be rectified. By approaching working memory assessment in this way, proper construct measurement is ensured, rather than merely describing and documenting observed behaviors at specific moments of time or place.

Not only must assessments depict real-world events, but they must also *predict* behavioral functioning in authentic situations. This issue, termed veridicality, reflects the significance of correlational power: the greater the correlation between working memory assessment and performance of real-world tasks, the greater is our ability to predict, and therefore plan appropriate interventions. For example, behaviors exhibited in isolated testing situations by individuals with central nervous system lesions may not be particularly strong predictors of a person's ability to carry out activities of daily living in their natural environments (Chaytor & Schmitter-Edgecombe, 2003).

CONCLUSIONS

Understanding working memory is essential in designing effective classroom instruction. Thus, when empirically and educationally assessing working memory, it is essential to consider the verisimilitude and veridicality of an assessment instrument. By approaching working memory assessment in this way, we establish as much congruence as possible between the cognitive demands of the assessment environment and those found in the natural environment (Frazen & Wilhelm, 1996). In accordance with previous studies with children (Gioia & Isquith, 2004; Isquith et al., 2004), Chaytor, Schmitter-Edgecombe, and Burr (2006) also stress the importance of assessing cognitive demands in the environment with the purpose of obtaining ecologically valid assessment of executive functions. It is hoped that in doing so, researchers and educators can maximize authentic data-driven decisions, and therefore plan more appropriate, effective, and efficient interventions for the children they serve. Recently, Thurman and McGrath (2008) have provided insight into the techniques for assessing children in the natural environment. They suggest that environmentally based assessment practices are essential for assuring ecological validity.

Although a plethora of findings indicates that working memory deficits are associated with poor academic performance, there is less agreement on the actual components of these deficits that might be responsible for this suppression of performance (Gathercole, Lamont, & Alloway, 2006). Consequently, greater understanding of working memory is needed within the classroom context and would result in an increased degree of ecological validity especially in light of data that suggest that teachers may not have a good understanding of working memory (Fiorello, Thurman, Zavertnick, Sher, & Coleman in press).

References

Anderson, P. (2002). Assessment and development of executive function during childhood. *Child Neuropsychology, 8*, 71–82.

Araujo, D., Davids, K., & Passos, P. (2007). Ecological validity, representative design and correspondence between experimental task constraints and behavior setting: Comment on Rogers, Kadar, and Costall (2005). *Ecological Psychology*, *19*, 69–78.

Atkinson, R. C., & Shiffrin, R. M. (1968). Human memory: A proposed system and its control processes. In K. W. Spence & J. T. Spence (Eds.), *The psychology of learning and motivation: Advances in research and theory* (Vol. 2, pp. 89–195). New York: Academic Press.

Baddeley, A. D. (1986). *Working memory*. London: Oxford University Press.

Baddeley, A. (1996). Exploring the central executive. *Quarterly Journal of Experimental Psychology, 49A*, 5–28.

Baddeley, A. (2000). The episodic buffer: A new component of working memory? *Trends in Cognitive Sciences, 4*, 417–423.

Baddeley, A. (2003). Working memory and language: An overview. *Journal of Communication Disorders, 36*, 189–208.

Baddeley, A. D. (2007). *Working memory in thought and action*. New York: Oxford University Press.

Baddeley, A. D., Grant, S., Wight, E., & Thompson, N. (1975). Imagery and visual working memory. In P. M. A. Rabbitt & S. Dornic (Eds.), *Attention and performance V* (pp. 205–217). Hillsdale, NJ: Lawrence Erlbaum Associates, Inc.

Baddeley, A. D., & Hitch, G. J. (1974). Working memory. In G. Bower (Ed.), *The psychology of learning and motivation* (Vol. 8, pp. 47–90). New York: Academic Press.

Baddeley, A. D., Lewis, V. J., & Vallar, G. (1984). Exploring the articulatory loop. *Quarterly Journal of Experimental Psychology, 36*, 233–252.

Baddeley, A. D., Thomson, N., & Buchanan, M. (1975). Word length and the structure of short-term memory. *Journal of Verbal Learning and Verbal Behavior, 14*, 575–589.

Berch, D. B., Krikorian, R., & Huha, E. M. (1998). The Corsi block-tapping task: Methodological and theoretical considerations. *Brain and Cognition, 38*, 317–338.

Bronfenbrenner, U. (1979). *The ecology of human development: Experiments by nature and design*. Cambridge, MA: Harvard University Press.

Brunswik, E. (1943). Organismic achievement and environmental probability. *Psychological Review, 50*, 255–272.

Brunswik, E. (1956). *Perception and the representative design of psychological experiments*. Berkeley: The University of California Press.

Carroll, J. B. (1993). *Human cognitive abilities: A survey of factor-analytic studies*. New York: Cambridge University Press.

Case, R., Kurland, D. M., & Goldberg, J. (1982). Operational efficiency and the growth of short-term memory span. *Journal of Experimental Child Psychology, 33*, 386–404.

Chaytor, N, & Schmitter-Edgecombe, M. (2003). The ecological validity of neuropsychological tests: A review of the literature on everyday cognitive skills. *Neuropsychology Review, 13*, 181–197.

Chaytor, N, Schmitter-Edgecombe, M., & Burr, R. (2006). Improving the ecological validity of executive function assessment. *Archives of Clinical Neuropsychology, 21*, 217–227.

Colle, H. A., & Welsh, A. (1976). Acoustic masking in primary memory. *Journal of Verbal Learning and Verbal Behavior, 15*, 17–31.

Conrad, R., & Hull, A. J. (1964). Information, acoustic confusion and memory span. *British Journal of Psychology, 55*, 429–432.

Cowan, N. (1988). Evolving conceptions of memory storage, selective attention, and their mutual constraints within the human information processing system. *Psychological Bulletin, 104*, 163–191.

Cowan, N. (1999). An embedded-processes model of working memory. In A. Miyake & P. Shah (Eds.), *Models of working memory: Mechanisms of active maintenance and executive control* (pp. 62–101). Cambridge, UK: Cambridge University Press.

Cowan, N. (2005). *Working memory capacity*. New York: Psychology Press.

Daneman, M., & Carpenter, P. A. (1980). Individual differences in working memory and reading. *Journal of Verbal Learning and Verbal Behavior, 19*, 450–466.

Daneman, M., & Carpenter, P. A. (1983). Individual differences in integrating information between and within sentences. *Journal of Experimental Psychology: Learning, Memory, and Cognition, 9*, 561–584.

Daneman, M., & Green, I. (1986). Individual differences in comprehending and producing words in context. *Journal of Memory and Language, 25*, 1–18.

de Jong, P. F. (1998). Working memory deficits of reading disabled children. *Journal of Experimental Child Psychology, 70*, 75–96.

de Jong, P. F., & Das-Smaal, E. A. (1995). Attention and intelligence: The validity of the star counting test. *Journal of Educational Psychology, 87*, 80–92.

Della Sala, S., Gray, C., Baddeley, A., Allamano, N., & Wilson, L. (1999). Pattern span: A tool for unwelding visuo-spatial memory. *Neuropsychologia, 37*, 1189–1199.

Della Sala, S., & Logie, R. H. (2002). Neuropsychological impairments of visual and spatial working memory. In A. D. Baddeley, M. D. Kipelman, & B. A. Wilson (Eds.), *Handbook of memory disorders* (2nd ed., pp. 271–292). Chichester: Wiley.

Elliott, C. D. (2007). *Examiner's manual. Differential ability scales, Second Edition.* San Antonio, TX: Harcourt Assessment.

Ericsson, K. A., & Kintsch, W. (1995). Long-term working memory. *Psychological Review, 102*, 211–245.

Fiorello, C. A., Thurman S. K., Zevertnik, J., Sher, R., & Coleman, S. (in press). A comparison of teachers' and school psychologists' views of the importance of CHC abilities in the classroom. *Psychology in the Schools*.

Flanagan, D. P., Ortiz, S. O., & Alfonso, V. C. (2007). *Essentials of cross-battery assessment* (2nd ed.). Hoboken, NJ: Wiley.

Fletcher, P., & Henson, R. (2001). Frontal lobes and human memory: Insights from functional neuroimaging. *Brain, 124*, 849–881.

Frazen, M. D., & Wilhelm, K. L. (1996). Conceptual foundations of ecological validity in neurological assessment. In R. J. Sbordone & C. J. Long (Eds.), *Ecological validity of neuropsychological testing* (pp. 91–112). Delray Beach, FL: GR Press/St. Lucie Press.

Friedman, N. P., & Miyake, A. (2004). The reading span test and its predictive power for reading comprehension ability. *Journal of Memory and Language, 51*, 136.

Gathercole, S. E., & Alloway, T. (2008). Working memory and classroom learning. In S. K. Thurman & C. A. Fiorello (Eds.), *Applied cognitive research in k-3 classrooms* (pp. 17–40). New York: Routledge.

Gathercole, S. E., Lamont, E., & Alloway, T. P. (2006). Working memory in the classroom. In S. J. Pickering (Ed.), *Working memory and education* (pp. 220–241). New York: Academic Press.

Gathercole, S. E., & Pickering, S. J. (2000a). Assessment of working memory in six- and seven-year-old children. *Journal of Educational Psychology, 92*, 377–390.

Gathercole, S. E., & Pickering, S. J. (2000b). Working memory deficits in children with low achievements in the national curriculum at 7 years of age. *British Journal of Educational Psychology, 70,* 177–194.

Gioia, G. A., & Isquith, P. K. (2004). Ecological assessment of executive function in traumatic brain injury. *Developmental Neuropsychology, 25,* 135–158.

Gioia, G. A., Isquith, P. K., Guy, S. C., & Kenworthy, L. (2000). *The Behavior Rating Inventory of Executive Function.* Lutz, FL: Psychological Assessment Resources.

Hammond, K. (1999). *Ecological validity: Then and now.* Retrieved February, 2008, from http://www.brunswik.org/notes/essay2.html

Handley, S. J., Capon, A., Copp, C., & Harper, C. (2002). Conditional reasoning and the tower of Hanoi: The role of spatial and verbal working memory. *British Journal of Psychology, 93,* 501–518.

Isquith, P. K., Gioia, G. A., & Espy. K. A. (2004). Executive function in preschool children: Examination through everyday behavior. *Developmental Neuropsychology, 26,* 403–422.

Jonides, J., Smith, E. E., Koeppe, R. A., Awh, E., Minoshima, S., & Mintun, M. (1993). Spatial working memory in humans as revealed by PET. *Nature, 363,* 623–625.

Kessels, R. P. C., van Zandvoort, M. J. E., Postma, A., Kappelle, L. J., & de Haan, E. H. F. (2000). The Corsi block-tapping task: Standardization and normative data. *Applied Neuropsychology, 7,* 252–258.

Knox, H. A. (1913). The differentiation between moronism and ignorance. *New York Medical Journal, 98,* 564–566.

Kuhn, T.S. (1962) *The structure of scientific revolutions.* Chicago: University of Chicago Press.

Lecerf, T., & Roulin, J. (2006). Distinction between visuo-spatial short-term-memory and working memory span tasks. *Swiss Journal of Psychology/Schweizerische Zeitschrift für Psychologie/Revue Suisse de Psychologie, 65,* 37–54.

Leffard, S. A., Miller, J. A., Bernstein, J., DeMann, J. J., Mangis, H. A., & McCoy, E. L. B. (2006). Substantive validity of working memory measures in major cognitive functioning test batteries for children. *Applied Neuropsychology, 13,* 230–241.

Logie, R. H. (1995). *Visuo-spatial working memory.* Hove, UK: Lawrence Erlbaum Associates Ltd.

Logie, R. H. (2003). Spatial and visual working memory: A mental workspace. In D. Irwin and B. Ross (Eds.), *Cognitive vision: The psychology of learning and motivation* (Vol. 42, pp. 37–78). San Diego, CA: Academic Press.

Logie, R. H., Della Sala, S., Wynn, V., & Baddeley, A. D. (2000). Visual similarity effects in immediate verbal serial recall. *Quarterly Journal of Experimental Psychology A: Human Experimental Psychology, 5,* 626–646.

Logie, R. H., & Pearson, D. G. (1997). The inner eye and the inner scribe of visuo-spatial working memory: Evidence from developmental fractionation. *European Journal of Cognitive Psychology, 9,* 241–257.

Masson, M. E., & Miller, J. A. (1983). Working memory and individual differences in comprehension and memory of text. *Journal of Educational Psychology, 75,* 314–318.

Mather, N., & Woodcock, R. W. (2001). *Examiner's manual. Woodcock-Johnson III Tests of Cognitive Abilities.* Itasca, IL: Riverside.

Milner, B. (1971). Interhemispheric differences in the localisation of psychological processes in man. *British Medical Bulletin, 27,* 272–277.

Neisser, U. (1976). *Cognition and reality: Principles and implications of cognitive psychology*. San Francisco: W. H. Freeman and Company.

Norman, D. A., & Shallice, T. (1986). Attention to action: Willed and automatic control of behavior. In G. E. Schwartz, R. J. Davidson, & D. Shapiro (Eds.), *Consciousness and self-regulation: Advances in research and theory* (Vol. 4, pp. 1–18). New York: Plenum Press.

Pentland, L. M., Anderson, V. A., Dye, S., & Wood, S. J. (2003). The nine box maze test: A measure of spatial memory development in children. *Brain and Cognition, 52*, 144–154.

Pickering, S. J. (2001). The development of visuo-spatial working memory. *Memory, 9*, 423–432.

Pickering, S. J. (2006). Assessment of working memory in children. In S. J. Pickering (Ed.), *Working memory and education* (pp. 242–273). New York: Academic Press.

Pickering, S., & Gathercole, S. (2001). *Working Memory Test Battery for Children*. San Antonio, TX: The Psychology Corporation.

Pulos, S., & Denzine, G. (2005). Individual differences in planning behavior and working memory: A study of the Tower of London. *Individual Differences Research, 3*, 99–104.

Ramsay, M. C., & Reynolds, C. R. (1995). Separate digits tests: A brief history, a literature review, and a re-examination of the factor structure of the test of memory and learning (TOMAL). *Neuropsychology Review, 5*, 151–171.

Reynolds, C. R. (1997). Forward and backward memory span should not be combined for clinical analysis. *Archives of Clinical Neuropsychology, 12*, 29–40.

Roid, G. H. (2003). *Examiner's manual. Stanford-Binet Intelligence Scales, Fifth Edition*. Itasca, IL: Riverside.

Saito, S., Logie, R. H., Morita, A., & Law, A. (2008). Visual and phonological similarity effects in verbal immediate serial recall: A test with Kanji materials. *Journal of Memory and Language, 59*, 1–17.

Savage, R., Lavers, N., & Pillay, V. (2007). Working memory and reading difficulties: What we know and what we don't know about the relationship. *Educational Psychology Review, 19*, 185.

Sbordone, R. J. (1996). Ecological validity: Some critical issues for neuropsychologists. In R. J. Sbordone & C. J. Long (Eds.), *Ecological validity of neuropsychological testing* (pp. 15–41). Delray Beach, FL: GR Press/St. Lucie Press.

Shah, P., & Miyake, A. (1996). The separability of working memory resources for spatial thinking and language processing: An individual differences approach. *Journal of Experimental Psychology: General, 125*, 4–27.

Siegel, L. S., & Ryan, E. B. (1989). The development of working memory in normally achieving and subtypes of learning disabled children. *Child Development, 60*, 973–980.

Silver, C. H. (2000). Ecological validity of neurological assessment of childhood traumatic brain injury. *Journal of Head Trauma Rehabilitation, 15*, 973–988.

Smith, E. E., & Jonides, J. (1997). Working memory: a view from neuroimaging. *Cognitive Psychology, 33*, 5–42.

Stothard, S. E., & Hulme, C. (1992). Reading comprehension difficulties in children: The role of language comprehension and working memory skills. *Reading and Writing: An Interdisciplinary Journal, 4*, 245.

Thurman, S. K., & Kiepert, M. H. (2008). Issues and concerns in conducting applied cognitive research. In S. K. Thurman & C. A. Fiorello (Eds.), *Applied cognitive research in k-3 classrooms* (pp. 265–288). New York: Routledge.

Thurman, S. K., & McGrath, M. C. (2008). Environmentally based assessment practices: Viable alternatives to standardized assessment for assessing emergent literacy skills in young children. *Reading and Writing Quarterly: Overcoming Learning Difficulties, 24*, 7–24.

Tirre, W. C., & Peña, C. M. (1992). Investigation of functional working memory in the reading span test. *Journal of Educational Psychology, 84*, 462–472.

Turner, M. L., & Engle, R. W. (1989). Is working memory capacity task dependent? *Journal of Memory and Language, 28*, 127–154.

Vandierendonck, A., Kemps, E., Fastame, M. C., & Szmalec, A. (2004). Working memory components of the Corsi blocks task. *British Journal of Psychology, 95*, 57–79.

Vecchi, T., & Richardson, J. T. E. (2001). Measures of visuospatial short-term memory: The Knox cube imitation test and the Corsi blocks test compared. *Brain and Cognition, 46*, 291–294.

Wechsler, D. (2003). *Examiner's manual: Wechsler Intelligence Scale for Children – Fourth Edition*. San Antonio, TX: Harcourt Assessment.

Wilson, J. T. L., Scott, J. H., & Power, K. G. (1987). Developmental differences in the span of visual memory for pattern. *British Journal of Developmental Psychology, 5*, 249–255.

Applications to law

The application of psychology to memory issues in law represents both one of the earliest and most recent areas of applied research in psychology. Research began in Europe around the turn of the twentieth century into such issues as whether witnesses whose accounts were likely to be reliable could be identified through tests (Gross, 1898) and the suggestibility of children as witnesses (Binet, 1900). This research contributed to the *Aussage* movement which used 'event tests' – unexpected incidents staged in front of an unsuspecting audience – to demonstrate the frequent unreliability of even sworn accounts given by the witnesses (Sporer, 1982). The *Aussage* tradition crossed the Atlantic with the appointment of a leading proponent, Münsterberg, to a position at Harvard. His book *On the witness stand* (Münsterberg, 1908) represented the first extended account in English of the existing research on the reliability and consistency of witnesses and also discussed related issues such as false confessions and the detection of deception in witnesses and defendants. However, while the breezy and bombastic tone of the book (it was written initially as a series of press articles) made for a popular success, it had little impact on judicial process and interest in the topic languished with the author's death in 1916.

The growth of cognitive psychology in the 1970s led to a renewed interest in applied issues in general and witness reliability on particular. In the United States, the work of Elizabeth Loftus highlighted the role of reconstructive processes in remembering and in particular the role of post-event misinformation. Loftus's work demonstrated that post-event misinformation – information which an eyewitness subsequently reads or hears from others – is readily incorporated into the witness's account without their knowledge or awareness (Loftus, 1979). In the United Kingdom, much early research focused on understanding mistaken identification following a number of sensational miscarriages of justice based on confident but inaccurate identifications of suspects by witnesses (Davies & Griffiths, 2008). However, the public role of psychologists in the applied arena took rather different forms in the two countries. In the United States psychologists such as Loftus increasingly began to be admitted as expert witnesses in criminal trials to comment on the general reliability of witness testimony, whereas in the United Kingdom, experts were less involved in the courts and more in an advisory role in relation to training police officers and regulating their procedures (Bull, Bustin, Evans, & Gahagan, 1983).

The three contributions to this section of the book represent cutting-edge research on contemporary controversies concerning memory and the law. The 'recovered memories' debate was the talking point of applied memory research in the 1990s. The idea, originally espoused by Freud, that witnesses could recover memories of traumatic events from their childhood without any apparent awareness in adulthood sprang into sudden prominence in the wake of the Franklin trial in California (Maclean, 1993). The chief prosecution witness, Eileen Franklin, testified that her father had been responsible for an unsolved murder of a young girl some 20 years previously, but that she had repressed all memories of having witnessed the shocking event until a revelation when she saw her own daughter in circumstances which brought back the scene of the crime. A psychiatrist, Lenore Terr, testified for the prosecution that such recovered memories of traumatic events were a frequent feature of professional practice, while for the defense, Elizabeth Loftus argued that there was nothing in Ms Franklin's account which could not have been found in contemporary newspaper reports; indeed, some errors in her testimony could be directly attributable to these reports. The jury found George Franklin guilty but this was eventually reversed on appeal. Subsequent research by Loftus and others demonstrated that witnesses could be persuaded to accept and adopt as true, fictional events from their past suggested to them by experimenters (Loftus, 1993), while others have sought to furnish accounts of memories recovered by persons without apparent previous awareness, for which there is other corroborative evidence for their accuracy (Cheit, 2008).

The debate within psychology as to the truth or falsity of such memories reached the covers of weekly magazines and was aired in courts of law. Today, an uneasy consensus has emerged that some recovered memories are true, some false and some a mixture, but there has been no scientific way of differentiating true from false memories (Davies & Dalgleish, 2001). In their contribution, Elke Geraerts, Linsey Raymaekers, and Harald Merckelbach describe recent research examining the content of true and false memories. They have found a number of strong predictors of the credibility of a memory: true recovered memories tend to emerge spontaneously and come as a surprise to the person concerned; false memories on the other hand are typically recovered slowly in a piecemeal fashion as the person strives to remember, often instigated by suggestive therapeutic techniques.

A second area of contemporary controversy concerns the reliability of children's testimony. Traditionally, courts in the United Kingdom and the United States have taken a skeptical view of the reliability of children's evidence, reflected in procedural rules which excluded or restricted their testimony. In the last 20 years, growing concerns over the extent of sexual and physical abuse of children have led to calls for a change in attitude toward children's evidence by the courts. The case for some relaxation of the rules was greatly strengthened by experimental research demonstrating that when appropriate questioning was employed, children were capable of providing accurate and reliable accounts of experiences they had witnessed (Rudy & Goodman, 1981). However, the issue of suggestibility, first highlighted by Binet a century ago, continues to be a source of concern, particularly for pre-school children, and there have been several apparent miscarriages of justice caused by the uncritical acceptance of the testimony of very young children (Ceci & Bruck, 1995). Children, like all vulnerable witnesses, are capable of making mistakes if interviewing procedures are overly leading.

The second contribution concerns one of the most cited theories of child abuse: the child sexual abuse accommodation syndrome or CSAAS (Summit, 1983). This states that it is common for abused children not to disclose abuse, to deny it occurred if asked and, if it is eventually disclosed, to recant subsequently. While influential in both the child abuse literature and the courts, CSAAS has lacked a credible basis in systematic research. Kamala London and Sarah Kulkofsky describe the results of a major review of the literature which concludes that, while many children do fail to disclose spontaneously, when presenting for forensic interviews, most will do so if asked directly and that recantation is not a common feature of abuse investigations. Their conclusions could have important implications for the way children suspected of being abused should be interviewed and how the courts should view their evidence.

The final contribution concerns an area of continuing controversy – mistaken identification – and examines new evidence that witnesses may encode surprisingly little identity information on the basis of a casual interaction with a stranger. Change blindness was first observed by vision scientists who discovered that people are often oblivious to major changes in their perceptual environment from one moment to the next. Levin, Simons, Angelone, and Chabris (2002) demonstrated that this was not only a laboratory phenomenon but extended to the real world: around a third or more of unwitting participants will not notice when the stranger they have been talking to has changed identity when they disappear briefly from sight. Cara Laney and Elizabeth Loftus review fresh research on change blindness in a forensic setting and explore the implications of these startling findings for the reliability of eyewitness identification.

References

Binet, A. (1900). *La suggestibilité* [On suggestibility]. Paris: Schleicher.
Bull, R., Bustin, R., Evans, P., & Gahagan, D. (1983). *Psychology for police officers*. Chichester: Wiley.
Ceci, S. J., & Bruck, M. (1995). *Jeopardy in the courtroom: A scientific analysis of children's memory*. Washington, DC: American Psychological Association.
Cheit, R. (2008). The recovered memory project: 33 other cases of corroborated

recovered memory. Retrieved 7 January 2009 from: www.brown.edu/Departments/ Taubman_Center/Recovmem/arch_other.html

Davies, G. M., & Dalgleish, T. (2001). *Recovered memories: Seeking the middle ground.* Chichester: Wiley.

Davies, G. M., & Griffiths, L. (2008) Eyewitness identification and the English courts: A century of trial and error. *Psychiatry, Psychology and Law, 15*, 435–449.

Gross, H. (1898) *Kriminalpsychologie* [Criminal Psychology]. Leipzig: Vogel. (English translation downloadable at http://manybooks.net/titles/grosshanetext98crmsy10. html)

Levin, D. T., Simons, D. J., Angelone B. L., & Chabris, C. F. (2002). Memory for centrally attended changing objects in an incidental real-world change detection paradigm. *British Journal of Psychology, 93*, 289–302.

Loftus, E. F. (1979) *Eyewitness testimony.* Cambridge, MA: Harvard University Press.

Loftus, E. F. (1993). The reality of repressed memories. *American Psychologist, 48*, 518–537.

Maclean, H. N. (1993) *Once upon a time.* New York: Harper-Collins.

Münsterberg, H. (1908). *On the witness stand: Essays on psychology and crime.* New York: McClure.

Rudy, L., & Goodman, G. S. (1991). Effects of participation on children's reports: Implications for children's testimony. *Developmental Psychology, 27*, 527–538.

Sporer, S. L. (1982). A brief history of the psychology of testimony. *Current Psychological Reviews, 2*, 323–340.

Summit, R. C. (1983). The Child Sexual Abuse Accommodation syndrome. *Child Abuse and Neglect, 7*, 177–193.

4 Mechanisms underlying recovered memories

Elke Geraerts, Linsey Raymaekers and Harald Merckelbach

What would it be like to remember *each thing* that ever occurred to you? Although no such person has yet been found, there are some people with an astonishing autobiographical memory. Consider the example of AJ, a 42-year-old woman from California (Parker, Cahill, & McGaugh, 2006). AJ remembers every day of her life, since her teens, in extraordinary detail. When you mention any date over several decades to her, she is immediately able to mentally travel back to that day, imagining where she was, what she was doing, and what made the news that day. Just as though it happened yesterday. AJ reports that her personal memories are vivid, like "a running movie that never stops" (p. 35). You might think that having such an outstanding memory would be wonderful. AJ, however, says that it comes with a price. For example, when unpleasant things happen to her, AJ wants to forget, but she just cannot. She finds the continuous remindings very distracting and they "seem to rule her life" (p. 35). Clearly, AJ's experience of life is very different from most people's, and shows that a perfect memory can be troublesome: AJ is able to remember many happy times in life, but she is also often reminded of bad times.

Would you prefer AJ's memory over your own? Maybe forgetting is not all negative. For many years now, researchers have been pointing out that forgetting may actually serve a useful function (Bjork, 1989). Schacter (2001), for example, argues that forgetting has an adaptive purpose, preventing us from storing mundane, confusing or out-of-date memories. We want to remember our current phone number, not an old one, and where we parked our car today, not yesterday. We all agree about that. An important question is whether we can also forget more emotional experiences. That is, can people forget an emotionally traumatic event like childhood sexual abuse (CSA)? Can such memories be blocked from consciousness and is it possible that we might recall them many years later?

This issue has led to a controversy within the fields of psychology and psychiatry for many years now. Especially the authenticity of these so-called recovered memories has often been a reason for discussion (for reviews, see e.g., Brewin, 2007; Wright, Ost, & French, 2006). On one side of this debate, there are scholars and clinicians who claim that the most traumatic memories can be pushed out of consciousness. For example, Brown and colleagues stated: "approximately a third of sexually abused victims report some period of their lives where they did not remember anything about the abuse and later recovered the memory of abuse" (Brown, Scheflin, & Hammond, 1998, p. 196). On the other side of the debate are researchers who have long studied the fallibility and suggestibility of memory. They maintain that traumatic memories are imprinted in memory and are rarely, if ever, forgotten. Also, they point out that there are clear reasons to be cautious in interpreting recovered memories. Human memory is fallible and when people remember, they may engage in reconstructing an experienced event, thereby adding things to memory that may not have taken place. Moreover, people often confuse the sources of their memories, frequently failing to distinguish things that they have for instance imagined or seen in a film, from things that truly happened to them. The dangers of such confusion grow when people participate in certain forms of therapy aimed at recovering memories. The use of such techniques as hypnosis, guided imagery, dream interpretation, and other highly suggestive treatments may create a situation in which it may be difficult for a person to discriminate fact from fiction (Loftus & Davis, 2006; McNally, 2003).

Unlike most controversies in psychology, this one has spread far beyond the clinic and laboratory: It has influenced legislation and outcomes in civil suits and criminal trials. Famous cases of recovered memory have received intense media attention because of their legal implications. Also, fictionalized cases often appear in films or books with a recovered memory as a main plot device.

The purpose of this chapter is to discuss how studies on forgetting and false memories are relevant to the debate surrounding recovered memories. Moreover, we will review recent research examining the cognitive functioning of people reporting recovered CSA memories.

FORGETTING MEMORIES

As argued above, without a way of screening out unwanted thoughts, memories, and associations, the sheer volume of information available to us would be overwhelming. The idea that not all of our forgetting is an accident but may be related to our motives and intentions is known as motivated forgetting. One convenient way to study this is with a method known as the directed forgetting procedure, in which participants are instructed to forget recently encoded materials.

There are two variants of the directed forgetting procedure that researchers have employed, and each gets at somewhat different psychological processes (for reviews, see Anderson, 2005; Golding, 2005). In a typical procedure using *item method directed forgetting*, subjects view a series of words, to be encoded for a later memory test. Immediately following each word, subjects receive an instruction prompting them to either continue to remember the word, or to forget it. After the list is completed, subjects are given a test of all to-be-remembered *and* to-be-forgotten words. Typically, final test performance for to-be-forgotten words is dramatically impaired, relative to to-be-remembered items, which are recalled quite well. Most theorists attribute item method forgetting to an encoding deficit. Subjects may rehearse the words until they receive an instruction to either remember or forget the word. At this point, they either terminate encoding and rehearsal, or continue to rehearse the word if they have received an instruction to remember the word (Basden, Basden, & Gargano, 1993). This illustrates one way in which people are able to exercise voluntary control over what they allow into memory: People strategically regulate whether a stimulus is given the elaborative processing necessary to maintain it.

In contrast to the item method, *list method directed forgetting* presents the forget instruction halfway through the list. The instruction is unexpected and therefore subjects are likely to continue their best efforts to encode the words until the forget instruction is given. A final test is then given and subjects are asked to disregard the earlier instruction to forget, and to remember as much as they can. In this procedure, it is unlikely that subjects rely on a strategy in which they do not profoundly encode the words in the first part of the list. That is, they do not receive any mention that they will have to forget anything until the entire first half of the list has been presented, and therefore have no motive to not encode items as effectively as possible. This suggests that this procedure does not rely on motivated encoding deficits, but rather a retrieval deficit (Basden et al., 1993). Consistent with this idea, list method directed forgetting effects typically dissipate when recognition memory is tested, showing that forgotten items remain intact in memory. Accordingly, this method shows that when people are no longer inclined to remember recently encountered and well-encoded events, they can take mental action to lower the accessibility of those events.

Is there any evidence that such processes can be engaged to forget autobiographical memories? Barnier and colleagues (2007) examined this issue by exploring whether subjects would show directed forgetting of such memories. They asked subjects to generate a personal memory in response to each of 24 different cue words. The cue words were designed to elicit neutral, positive and negative autobiographical memories (e.g., park, love, accident). Importantly, after the first 12-item word list was presented, subjects either received an instruction to forget the previous items, as they were simply practice, or that they should remember them, as they might be asked to recall the memories later on. Subjects then generated another 12 memories in response to 12 new cue words. Next, subjects were asked to list all of the memories that they had generated from both lists. In several experiments, Barnier et al. found reliable and strong directed forgetting effects. These effects occurred for neutral, positive, and negative memories. Hence, it seems that directed forgetting effects can take place for autobiographical memories, or at least for our ability to remember that we have recently thought about particular memories.

Several studies have begun to investigate directed forgetting in people with posttraumatic stress disorder and acute stress disorder (for a review, see Geraerts & McNally, 2008), as well as recovered memories of abuse (see later on in this chapter). Also, several other paradigms have been developed to examine how people attempt to push unwanted memories out of awareness (for a review, see Anderson, 2005).

Natural repressors

Research on motivated forgetting has shown that people are able to push unwanted memories out of mind. Are there also people who are so skilled at pushing memories out of mind that they would be particularly good at forgetting unhappy experiences in life? It seems so: "Repressors," people possessing a so-called repressive coping style, tend to recall fewer negative events from their lives (Myers & Brewin, 1994). Typically, repressors tend to report low levels of anxiety and stress even when physiological measures indicate strong emotional reactions to a certain person or situation.

To examine whether repressors are skilled at inhibiting retrieval, Myers, Brewin, and Power (1998) used a directed forgetting procedure in which subjects studied pleasant or unpleasant words. Repressors were more adept than nonrepressors at using retrieval inhibition to block recall of recently studied unpleasant words, even though there were no differences between the two groups in blocking recall of pleasant words.

Apart from forgetting unpleasant words in the laboratory, repressors have also been found to be superior to nonrepressors in intentionally suppressing personal emotional events from their past. Barnier, Levin, and Maher (2004) made use of a thought suppression paradigm (see Wegner, Schneider, Carter, & White, 1987) to examine this issue. In the first phase, repressors and non-repressors were instructed to identify a recent event that made them either proud or embarrassed in a so-called imagining period. After this period, they were told either to avoid thinking about this event or to think of anything at all. Finally, in the expression period, subjects were instructed to think of anything. Subjects monitored occurrence of the target thought throughout these periods. For the proud event, all subjects avoided target thoughts when instructed to suppress them. However, for the embarrassing event, repressors reported fewer thoughts than nonrepressors, even when *not* instructed to suppress them. Moreover, irrespective of instructions, repressors failed to show the post-suppression rebound effect typically found in this paradigm. That is, repressors did not show an increase in thoughts related to the embarrassing event after having suppressed this event.

It seems like repressors are natural suppressors, skilled in avoiding negative thoughts about an embarrassing event. But does such a repressive coping style come with a cost? May natural repressors experience more unwanted intrusions in the days after having intentionally avoided such thoughts? That's the conclusion a recent study in our laboratory reached (Geraerts,

Merckelbach, Jelicic, & Smeets, 2006a). Repressors were instructed to keep a 7-day diary reporting their positive and negative intrusions, after having suppressed these intrusions in the laboratory, just as in the study of Barnier et al. Again, repressors showed fewer negative intrusions than nonrepressors in the laboratory session. Over the 7-day period, however, they reported the *highest* number of negative intrusions. These results seem to suggest that repressive coping might indeed be adaptive in the short run, leading to fewer unwanted thoughts. In the long run, though, having a repressive coping style seems maladaptive, increasing the frequency of intrusions even more. So, it seems doubtful that a repressive coping style is the most sensible way for coping with emotionally negative events.

FALSE MEMORIES

The literature reviewed above clearly shows that people can forget unwanted memories. Apart from these errors of omission, memory is also subject to commission errors. A growing body of research shows that memory more closely resembles a synthesis of experiences than a replay of a videotape (Schacter, 2001). In the most dramatic errors of commission, people may even come to believe memories of experiences that never occurred. In some cases these false memories pertain to traumatic events, such as childhood abuse.

At first sight, the idea that someone would remember a traumatic experience that has never occurred seems rather implausible. Yet, people have recollected all sorts of unlikely events. To name just a few examples: There are individuals who claim to have recovered memories of satanic ritual abuse (Scott, 2001), previous lives (Peters, Horselenberg, Jelicic, & Merckelbach, 2007), and even abduction by space aliens (Clancy, 2005). Most of these memories have surfaced with the help of mental health professionals.

The controversy regarding the possibility of such false memories, especially memories of CSA, has sparked great interest in memory distortion among cognitive psychologists. These psychologists have conducted at least three types of relevant studies. The first began to appear before the debate over false memories, whereas the other two emerged in response to it. The first type of study relates to how misinformation given to subjects after they witness an event may distort their memory for details of the event. Loftus has shown that giving witnesses misleading information after an event can distort their memory reports of that event. The so-called *misinformation effect* occurs when subjects believe they have seen items that were misleadingly suggested (for a review, see Loftus, 2005).

The second type of false memory study involves the creation of false memories of having encountered certain stimuli. For over a decade now, researchers have been examining how people develop false memories in the laboratory. A study by Roediger and McDermott (1995) inspired many of these experiments. Reviving a task introduced by Deese (1959), they conducted a study that involved what has come to be known as the Deese–Roediger–McDermott (DRM) paradigm. Their work showed that it is amazingly easy to foster false memories among college students in the laboratory. In their experiments, subjects studied a list of words that are strong semantic associates of a word not presented on the list – the *critical lure*. This lure captures the gist or essence of the entire list. For example, one list contained words related to the topic of sleep, such as *bed*, *rest*, *awake*, *tired*, and *dream*. However, the word *sleep* was not mentioned. Roediger and McDermott tested whether subjects would "remember" having heard words that had been only suggested, not presented (i.e., the critical lures), like *sleep*. Intriguingly, on subsequent tests, many of their subjects falsely recalled and recognized having seen these critical lures. Subsequent DRM studies have shown how easily false memories develop in the laboratory and how long lasting they can be (for a review, see Gallo, 2006).

Implanting a false detail or suggesting a word, however, seems a far cry from implanting an entirely false memory of an emotional experience in a person's past. With this restriction in mind, the third type of false memory study examined whether it is possible to implant false autobiographical memories. By using the suggestion that the critical information originated from well-informed family members, investigators succeeded in getting people to incorrectly believe that they had experienced a childhood event had occurred when in fact it never happened. Examples include being lost in a shopping mall for an extended period of time, being hospitalized overnight, and spilling a punch bowl at a family wedding (Hyman, Husband, & Billings, 1995; Loftus & Pickrell, 1995). In each of these studies a significant minority of subjects came to accept all or part of the suggestion and claimed it as their own experience. Would people also fall sway to suggestion if the falsely suggested event were highly emotional? The answer seems to be yes, as shown in one study that persuaded one-third of subjects that as children they had almost drowned and had to be rescued by a lifeguard (Heaps & Nash, 2001). Another research group made about half of their subjects believe that they had experienced awful events as children, such as being a victim of a vicious animal attack (Porter, Yuille, & Lehman, 1999). Taken together, these studies demonstrate the power of this type of suggestion. It has led many subjects to believe or sometimes even remember in detail events that did not occur. Across many studies that now have utilized this procedure, an average of about 30% of subjects have created either partial or complete false memories (Lindsay, Hagen, Read, Wade, & Garry, 2004).

Another clever technique for planting false memories involves the use of fake photographs. Wade, Garry, Read, and Lindsay (2002) showed subjects a doctored photograph that was made up of a real photograph of the subject and a relative pasted into a prototype photograph of a hot-air balloon. Family members confirmed that the event never occurred. Subjects were instructed to tell everything they could remember. By the end of the experiment, which entailed three interviews, about half of the subjects had recalled, partially or clearly, the false hot-air balloon ride. Recently, research showed that the use of fake photographs could also lead subjects to believe negative events such as having been hospitalized as a child (Raymaekers, 2005).

These studies and many more like them clearly show that people can develop false beliefs and memories for events that did not happen to them. But might such false beliefs and memories have repercussions on attitudes and behavior? Studies from Bernstein and colleagues (Bernstein, Laney, Morris, & Loftus, 2005) may provide some clues: They falsely suggested to their subjects that they had become ill after eating a certain food (e.g., hard-boiled eggs, strawberry ice cream) when they were children and found that this false suggestion increased subjects' confidence that the critical event had occurred. Moreover, these false beliefs had consequences for their subjects, including decreased self-reported preference for the target food and an increased anticipated behavioral avoidance of the target food.

So, these studies demonstrate that false beliefs can influence attitudes. A recent study conducted in our laboratory examined whether false beliefs or memories can also produce real changes in *behavior* (Geraerts, Bernstein, Merckelbach, Linders, Raymaekers, & Loftus 2008a). We falsely suggested to subjects that, as children, they had become ill after eating egg salad. After this manipulation, a significant minority of our subjects came to believe they had experienced this event. More importantly, this newfound auto-biographical belief was accompanied by a significantly lower consumption of egg salad sandwiches, both immediately and 4 months after the false suggestion.

Clearly, a large collection of studies on the creation of false memories has conclusively shown that misinformation can distort memory reports, non-presented stimuli can be lured into memory, and suggestions may get people to incorrectly believe they experienced a childhood event when they actually did not. To what extent are these conclusions relevant to the question of whether people develop false memories of traumatic events? Objections to laboratory demonstrations of the misinformation effect as irrelevant to the real world of psychotherapy have less force nowadays than they originally did as researchers have responded to these objections by showing that it is possible to implant false memories of a diversity of experiences. Moreover, and ironically, the most impressive demonstrations of the creation of false memories have arisen in clinical settings, not in the laboratory. If one considers that trivial manipulations in the laboratory can create memory distortion, these effects may be even more pronounced in the context of suggestive therapy in which therapist and patient join forces in an attempt to uncover memories of abuse over many sessions and with the aid of techniques such as guided imagination and hypnosis.

RECOVERED MEMORIES IN THE LABORATORY

One outstanding aspect of the recovered memory debate has been the absence of any research on cognitive functioning of people reporting recovered memories. Until recently, scholars on both sides of the debate have argued their case by relying on evidence from either clinical experience, surveys of abuse survivors, or studies with college students (McNally, 2003). Laboratory studies on the cognitive functioning of people reporting recovered memories have been surprisingly lacking. Are these individuals better at forgetting trauma-related material relative to individuals who have always remembered their abuse, and can we observe such increased forgetting skills in the laboratory? Conversely, are such individuals more likely to create false memories in the laboratory? Recently, laboratories at Harvard and Maastricht Universities have tried to answer these questions.

Directed forgetting

Some clinical theorists like Terr (1991) maintain that sexually abused children cope by developing an avoidant encoding style that enables them to disengage their attention from threatening cues, thereby impairing their memory for these cues. If people reporting recovered memories have indeed acquired this cognitive style, then this should be evident in the laboratory. As the item method directed forgetting (see above) taps encoding abilities, McNally and colleagues examined the ability of people with recovered CSA memories to forget trauma-related words (McNally, Clancy, & Schacter, 2001). Subjects were shown a series of words on a computer screen, one at a time. Each word appeared for 2 seconds and was replaced by a cue instructing the subject either to remember or to forget the previous word. Three categories of words were used: trauma-related (e.g., *abuse*), positive (e.g., *sociable*), and neutral (e.g., *banister*). Immediately after this encoding phase, subjects were asked to write down as many words as they could remember, regardless of the original instructions to forget or remember. Interestingly, McNally et al. found *normal* memory functioning in the recovered memory group. That is, they recalled to-be-remembered words more often than to-be-forgotten words, regardless of word valence. Moreover, they showed neither worse nor better memory for trauma-related words relative to control subjects without a history of abuse. So, people with recovered memories did not exhibit the predicted superior ability to avoid the encoding of material related to abuse.

Might their reported forgetting of childhood abuse be attributed to superior retrieval inhibition instead of avoidant encoding? To examine this possibility, both McNally's and our laboratory used the list method directed forgetting procedure (see above). Subjects were told they were taking part in an emotional judgment task, with no hint that they had to remember words. After presentation of the first list, we told them that what they had done until then had been just practice; they could forget about those words. The second word list was then presented for which subjects were asked to rate the emotionality of each word. In a surprise recall task, subjects were asked to recall as many words as possible from *both* lists. Both laboratories found that subjects recalled more words from the second list than from the first list which had been followed by the forget instruction. Also, all groups recalled trauma words more often than positive words. Interestingly, people reporting recovered CSA memories did not exhibit superior forgetting of trauma versus positive words, relative to control subjects (Geraerts, Smeets, Jelicic, Merckelbach, & van Heerden, 2006b; McNally, Clancy, Barrett, & Parker, 2004). This finding suggests that people with recovered memories are not superior at inhibiting retrieval of trauma-related words. So, again no support for the idea that people with recovered memories of CSA are better forgetters of trauma cues than are people who report either never forgetting their abuse or never having been abused.

Creating false memories

Might it be the case then that scholars do have a point in arguing that at least some recovered memories might be false recollections, often induced by suggestive therapeutic techniques? Is it that people reporting recovered memories – or at least some of them – may be more prone to developing false memories, and is this evident in the laboratory? To address this possibility, McNally's laboratory and ours used the DRM paradigm (see above) to elicit false memories in people reporting recovered memories. In doing so, we tested the idea that people reporting recovered CSA memories would be more prone to falsely remembering and recognizing non-presented words. That is, they would have more difficulty differentiating between what they really saw and what they imagined. As hypothesized, we found that, as a group, people with recovered CSA memories more often falsely recalled and recognized the non-presented critical lures, relative to people with continuous CSA memories, and people with no history of abuse. Importantly, this was true for both neutral and trauma-related word lists (Clancy, Schacter, McNally, & Pitman, 2000; Geraerts, Smeets, Jelicic, van Heerden, & Merckelbach, 2005).

What do these findings tell us about the authenticity of reports of recovered abuse memories? Several researchers have suggested that deficits in source monitoring may lead to false memories. People with such deficits are prone to making incorrect judgments about the origins or sources of information (Johnson, Hashtroudi, & Lindsay, 1993). Relating this to the DRM paradigm, when subjects think of the critical lure at study because it automatically comes to mind, they later on must differentiate between memories of internally generated thoughts of the lures and memories of the studied words. The above results suggest that at least some individuals with recovered memories may have a source-monitoring deficit for all types of material, whether the content is neutral or trauma-related (see also, McNally, Clancy, Barrett, & Parker, 2005). They may be more likely to accept an internally generated thought as being a genuine memory. So, it seems plausible that at least some of those with recovered memories developed false memories of abuse via a subtle interaction between already existing source-monitoring difficulties and suggestive therapeutic techniques.

A step outside the laboratory

This kind of work in the laboratory may lead one to conclude that recovered memories are sometimes fictitious. On the other hand, work outside the laboratory has also shown that the opposite may happen, that recovered memories may reflect genuine abuse events. Schooler and colleagues (e.g., Schooler, Bendiksen, & Ambadar, 1997; Shobe & Schooler, 2001) published several case descriptions of individuals who experienced the discovery of apparently long-forgotten memories of abuse, memories that were all recovered outside the context of therapy. Importantly, corroborative information was found for these cases. In some of these cases something fascinating was found: The partners of the women who reported a recovered memory experience mentioned that their spouses had talked about the abuse, *prior* to the alleged recovered memory experience. Schooler et al. proposed that such cases demonstrate a forgot-it-all-along (FIA) mechanism, which can lead to the forgetting of prior instances of recollecting a past event. During the recovered memory experience, the traumatic event may be recalled in a qualitatively different way from past occasions of remembering it. For example, more completely, more episodically, or as abuse per se, rather than as some more innocent category of childhood event. As such a recollection is often paired with shock and surprise, individuals' assessment of their prior knowledge may be affected. They might reason, "If I am this shocked and surprised now, then I must have completely forgotten about the experience" (p. 283). Hence, these case studies put forward the possibility that at least some recovered memories reflect genuine abuse episodes about which people simply forgot their prior thoughts.

Forgetting prior remembering

Is it possible that some people with recovered memories are not truly recalling the abuse event for the first time in years, but are forgetting prior cases of thinking about it? If so, how would this forgetting of prior recall come about? To explore this possibility, we (Geraerts, Arnold, Lindsay, Merckelbach, Jelicic, & Hauer, 2006c) investigated whether people reporting recovered memories were more likely to underestimate their prior remembering. In an FIA task, we asked subjects with recovered or continuous memories of abuse to generate an autobiographical memory from their childhood in response to each of 25 cue phrases describing common childhood events (e.g., being home alone, going to the dentist). For some events, they were asked to focus on emotionally positive aspects of the event, but for others, they were instructed to concentrate on the negative aspects. Two months later subjects returned to the laboratory and generated the same memories. This time, however, subjects were instructed to retrieve the events in the same emotional frame as before for some events, but for other events they were instructed to retrieve the event in the opposite emotional frame. So, for example, if they had recalled "being home alone without parents" in a positive light during the first visit (e.g., having lots of freedom), they recalled the same event again, but focused on the negative aspects (e.g., being afraid of a thunderstorm or feeling lonely). Finally, subjects returned to the laboratory for a third time 2 months later and recalled all of the events yet again. Now subjects had to recall each event in the same emotional frame in which they had recalled it during their first visit. Critically, after recalling each of the memories, subjects told the experimenter whether or not they had recalled that same memory during the second visit. Would people be able to remember having recalled the event during the second visit? Would this depend on whether it was recalled in the same "emotional context" both then and now?

Interestingly, when the emotional framing on the final visit differed from the one on the second visit, subjects showed a pronounced tendency to forget having remembered the event during that second visit, relative to when the emotional framing remained the same. So, simply shifting the way that people thought about the very same memory (whether positively or negatively) from one occasion to the next made them forget thinking about the memory before. Strikingly, this tendency was significantly greater for people reporting recovered memories than it was for people reporting continuously available memories, or people without any history of abuse.

So it seems that one reason why people may have a recovered memory experience is that they simply forget having remembered the event before, just as was observed in the case studies reported by Schooler et al. (1997). They may forget prior cases of remembering if, for example, the mental context when they are having their recovered memory experience differs dramatically from the mental context on prior occasions in which they thought of the event. By this view, it's not that people have forgotten the event all those years, it's that they simply can't remember having remembered, due to retrieval failures.

TWO TYPES OF RECOVERED MEMORY EXPERIENCES

When we review these laboratory findings, we can see different interpretations of recovered memories. People with recovered memories show an increased tendency toward false memory formation. In contrast, they also show pronounced underestimation of prior remembering. How can these phenomena be integrated? Careful inspection of the precise type of recovered memory experiences may provide an answer. As we interviewed many people with recovered memories, we were able to identify two qualitatively different types of recovered memory experiences. In one type, people come to realize that they are abuse survivors, commonly attributing current life difficulties to their forgotten memories of CSA. In this type of recovered memory experience, abuse events are mostly slowly recalled over time, often instigated by suggestive therapeutic techniques such as guided imagery, dream interpretation, and hypnosis. In the other type of recovered memory experience, people are unexpectedly reminded of events that they believe they had not thought about for many years. Mostly, individuals recollect the abuse when encountering salient retrieval cues (e.g., a book or movie in which CSA is clearly depicted, being in the same setting as where the abuse happened, or events involving the person's children). This kind of recollection clearly differs from the one in which the person is gradually recalling the abuse, often in the course of suggestive therapy. If so, one expects it to be easier to find corroborative evidence for spontaneously recovered memories than for memories recovered through suggestive therapy.

To examine this issue, we invited to the laboratory subjects who had always remembered the abuse, had a recovered memory of it that took place during suggestive therapy, or had a recovered memory spontaneously, outside of therapy (Geraerts, Schooler, Merckelbach, Jelicic, Hauer, & Ambadar, 2007). After filling out a questionnaire about their memory of the abuse events, subjects were queried systematically about sources of corroboration. Independent raters, who were blind to the group that a subject was assigned to, then used this information to seek objective evidence, by interviewing other people who could potentially corroborate the event. A memory was considered corroborated if either (a) another individual reported learning about the abuse within a week after it happened, (b) another individual reported having been abused by the same perpetrator, or (c) the perpetrator admitted to committing the abuse. Strikingly, memories that were recovered spontaneously, outside of therapy, were corroborated at a rate (37%) that was quite comparable to that observed for people with continuously accessible memories of abuse (45%). In contrast, memories recovered through suggestive therapy could not be corroborated (0%). Although the lack of corroboration does not imply that these recovered memories are false, it does recommend caution in interpreting memories recovered in suggestive therapy.

Differing origins of recovered memory experiences

The foregoing findings suggest that recovered memories may originate in different ways for people who recollect the abuse event spontaneously, and for those who recall it through suggestive therapy. We hypothesized that memories recalled through suggestive therapy may be more likely to be the product of suggestion, a possibility consistent with (but not demanded by) the lack of corroboration. People recalling memories spontaneously, by contrast, may have recalled the event previously, but may have simply forgotten the fact that they have recalled it before. To examine these possibilities we tested people with spontaneously recovered memories, people with memories recovered through suggestive therapy, and people with continuously available memories on a simplified version of the above-mentioned forgot-it-all-along task (Geraerts et al., 2009). Strikingly, only those subjects who had recovered their memories spontaneously showed exaggerated forgetting of prior remembering; subjects who recovered their memories in suggestive therapy or subjects with continuous memories showed no such pattern. When tested on a simple false memory task (DRM task), however, only people who recovered their memories in suggestive therapy showed exaggerated false memory formation; neither the spontaneously recovered group nor people with continuous access to their memories showed such a pattern.

This double dissociation strongly supports the idea that memories recovered in suggestive therapy and recovered spontaneously may have fundamentally different origins. As a group, people who report having recovered their memories in suggestive therapy generally show a pronounced tendency to incorrectly claim that they have experienced events when they have demonstrably not experienced them as measured by the DRM test. To the extent that this pattern on the DRM task is indicative of a broader deficit in monitoring the source of one's memories, this finding suggests that such reports of recovered memories should be viewed with a cautious eye, as they may reflect an interaction of suggestive therapy with pre-existing source-monitoring deficits. In contrast, people who believe they have spontaneously recovered a memory of CSA show no evidence at all of heightened susceptibility to the creation of false memories. This group does, however, show a pronounced tendency to forget prior incidences of remembering when those prior retrievals have taken place in a different retrieval context. So, even when prior accessibility of simple events studied in the laboratory can be objectively demonstrated, this group, as a whole, was significantly more likely to deny having remembered those events on previous occasions. These findings suggest that this group, as a whole, may simply be failing to remember their prior thoughts about a *genuine* incidence of CSA.

The data so far do not explain *why* some people might show greater susceptibility to forgetting prior remembering. Why is this the case? One possibility is that people with authentic abuse experiences may engage in thought suppression in order to limit intrusive reminders of these unwanted experiences. If so, then the difference between people with spontaneously recovered memories and those with continuously available abuse memories may be attributable to individual differences in the ability to suppress intrusive reminders. This hypothesis has recently received support in our laboratory. We asked people to imagine and describe the most positive and most anxious autobiographical memory that they had experienced over the previous two years (Geraerts, McNally, Jelicic, Merckelbach, and Raymaekers, 2008b). Following this, they were asked to suppress all thoughts about the events for several minutes. If a thought about the event did come to mind, however, they had to indicate this by means of pressing a joystick. After this suppression period, subjects were allowed to think of anything, including the positive or negative event, and again were asked to indicate thoughts of the target event (i.e., expression period). Interestingly, the spontaneously recovered memory group showed significantly fewer intrusions of the anxious event during this suppression period as well as the expression period. Moreover, when asked to keep a diary recording intrusions of either the positive or negative event for 7 days after the experiment, the spontaneously recovered group showed significantly fewer intrusions than the other groups. These findings suggest that people with authentic abuse events may learn to consistently suppress reminders of those events, causing them to forget their prior thoughts of the event. A subsequent recovery experience is then more likely to be judged as novel, creating the experience of discovering a memory for the first time (FIA phenomenon).

CONCLUSIONS

The debate about recovered memories of childhood abuse has received a lot of attention, in part because of concern that some proportion of recovered memory experiences is false. Accordingly, cognitive researchers have examined how people may forget certain experiences on the one hand, and how people may come to remember events that have not happened to them on the other hand. Research on the cognitive functioning of people reporting recovered CSA memories has yielded evidence for at least two types of recovered memory experiences, each with their specific origin.

False recovered memories might arise when people participate in prolonged periods of trying to recollect an abuse event, instigated by highly suggestive memory recovery techniques. False memories of abuse have indeed been induced by such procedures, emphasizing the role of suggestion and source-monitoring errors in shaping what people believe has happened to them. As shown in Henkel (2004), repeated retrieval attempts can make us confuse what we imagined for what we saw, and what was suggested to us, for what we experienced. When a suggestive therapist is convinced of the existence of repressed abuse memories, and when a client starts to remember certain events, it may become difficult to appreciate that the memory may not be real, particularly when it provides a convenient explanation for current symptomatology.

Indeed, memories of CSA that are recovered in suggestive therapy appear, in general, to be less easy to corroborate than are memories that are recovered spontaneously, outside of therapy. Although the lack of corroboration does not indicate that a recovered memory is false, research suggests that people recovering memories under such circumstances are in fact more suggestible. This raises the possibility that some of these recovery events may not reflect real abuse, but rather the unwitting result of overly suggestive therapeutic techniques. Other types of therapy that do not involve suggestion are not necessarily subject to this concern (see e.g., Andrews et al., 1999). Thus, some cases of recovered memories may in fact be false memories that are, in effect, unwittingly implanted by therapists who actually intend to help the patient.

On the other hand, some recovered memories of sexual abuse have proven to be real events that can be corroborated, sometimes even with a confession from the perpetrator. Indeed, memories recovered spontaneously appear to be as corroboratable as continuously accessible memories, suggesting that many of these experiences reflect real abuse events. People recovering memories under these circumstances exhibit an especially pronounced tendency to forget their prior experiences of remembering, and also show superior ability to suppress thoughts about anxious autobiographical memories.

Research on cognitive mechanisms underlying recovered memories has advanced our understanding on the validity of recovered memory reports and how such memories come about. Now that the recovered memory debate is decreasing in intensity and divergence (see, e.g., Davies & Dalgleish, 2001), it will be important that research findings on recovered memories are applied in the justice system and in clinical practice. Exciting future research on recovered memories on a wide range of empirical and theoretical fronts will only continue to advance our understanding of questions that are – at least for now – left unanswered.

Acknowledgment

Elke Geraerts and Linsey Raymaekers were supported by grants from the Netherlands Organization for Scientific Research (NWO 451 07 004 and NWO 400 06 024, respectively).

References

Anderson, M. C. (2005). The role of inhibitory control in forgetting unwanted memories: A consideration of three methods. In C. MacLeod & B. Uttl (Eds.), *Dynamic cognitive processes* (pp. 159–190). Tokyo: Springer-Verlag.

Andrews, B., Brewin, C. R., Ochera, J., Morton, J., Bekerian, D. A., Davies, G. M., & Mollon, P. (1999). Characteristics, context and consequences of memory recovery among adults in therapy. *British Journal of Psychiatry, 175*, 141–146.

Barnier, A. J., Conway, M. A., Mayoh, L., Speyer, J., Avizmil, O., & Harris, C. B. (2007). Directed forgetting of recently recalled autobiographical memories. *Journal of Experimental Psychology: General, 136*, 301–322.

Barnier, A. J., Levin, K., & Maher, A. (2004). Suppressing thoughts of past events: Are repressive copers good suppressors? *Cognition and Emotion, 18*, 513–531.

Basden, B. H., Basden, D. R., & Gargano, J. G. (1993). Directed forgetting in implicit and explicit memory tests: A comparison of methods. *Journal of Experimental Psychology: Learning, Memory and Cognition, 19*, 603–616.

Bernstein, D. M., Laney, C., Morris, E. K., & Loftus, E. F. (2005). False beliefs about fattening foods can have healthy consequences. *Proceedings of the National Academy of Sciences, 102*, 13724–13731.

Bjork, R. A. (1989). Retrieval inhibition as an adaptive mechanism in human memory. In H. L. Roediger III & F. I. M. Craik (Eds.), *Varieties of memory and consciousness: Essays in honor of Endel Tulving* (pp. 309–330). Hillsdale NJ: Lawrence Erlbaum Associates, Inc.

Brewin, C. R. (2007). Autobiographical memory for trauma: Update on four controversies. *Memory, 15*, 227–248.

Brown, D., Scheflin, A. W., & Hammond, D. C. (1998). *Memory, trauma treatment, and the law*. New York: Norton.

Clancy, S. A. (2005). *Abducted: How people come to believe they were kidnapped by aliens*. Cambridge, MA: Harvard University Press.

Clancy, S. A., Schacter, D. L., McNally, R. J., & Pitman, R. K. (2000). False recognition in women reporting recovered memories of sexual abuse. *Psychological Science, 11*, 26–31.

Davies, G. M., & Dalgleish, T. (Eds.). (2001). *Recovered memories: Seeking the middle ground*. Chichester: John Wiley & Sons.

Deese, J. (1959). On the prediction of occurrence of particular verbal intrusions in immediate recall. *Journal of Experimental Psychology, 58*, 17–22.

Gallo, D. A. (2006). *Associative illusions of memory. False memory research in DRM and related tasks*. New York: Psychology Press.

Geraerts, E., Arnold, M. M., Lindsay, D. S., Merckelbach, H., Jelicic, M., & Hauer, B. (2006c). Forgetting of prior remembering in persons reporting recovered memories of childhood sexual abuse. *Psychological Science, 17*, 1002–1008.

Geraerts, E., Bernstein, D. M., Merckelbach, H., Linders, C., Raymaekers, L., & Loftus, E. F. (2008a). Lasting false beliefs and their behavioral consequences. *Psychological Science, 19*, 749–753.

Geraerts, E., Lindsay, D. S., Merckelbach, H., Jelicic, M., Raymaekers, L., Arnold, M. M., & Schooler, J. S. (2009). Cognitive mechanisms underlying recovered memory experiences of childhood sexual abuse. *Psychological Science, 20*, 92–98.

Geraerts, E., & McNally, R. J. (2008). Forgetting unwanted memories: Directed forgetting and thought suppression methods (invited review). *Acta Psychologica, 127*, 614–627.

Geraerts, E., McNally, R. J., Jelicic, M., Merckelbach, H., & Raymaekers, L. (2008b). Linking thought suppression and recovered memories of childhood sexual abuse. *Memory, 16*, 22–28.

Geraerts, E., Merckelbach, H., Jelicic, M., & Smeets, E. (2006a). Long term consequences of suppression of intrusive thoughts and repressive coping. *Behaviour Research and Therapy, 44*, 1451–1460.

Geraerts, E., Schooler, J. W., Merckelbach, H., Jelicic, M., Hauer, B. J. A., & Ambadar, Z. (2007). The reality of recovered memories: Corroborating continuous and discontinuous memories of childhood sexual abuse. *Psychological Science, 18*, 564–567.

Geraerts, E., Smeets, E., Jelicic, M., Merckelbach, H., & van Heerden, J. (2006b). Retrieval inhibition of trauma-related words in women reporting repressed or recovered memories of childhood sexual abuse. *Behaviour Research and Therapy, 44*, 1129–1136.

Geraerts, E., Smeets, E., Jelicic, M., van Heerden, J., & Merckelbach, H. (2005). Fantasy proneness, but not self-reported trauma is related to DRM performance of women reporting recovered memories of childhood sexual abuse. *Consciousness and Cognition, 14*, 602–612.

Golding, J. M. (2005). Directed forgetting tasks in cognitive research. In A. Wenzel & D. C. Rubin (Eds.), *Cognitive methods and their application to clinical research* (pp. 177–196). Washington, DC: American Psychological Association.

Heaps, C. M., & Nash, M. (2001). Comparing recollective experience in true and false autobiographical memories. *Journal of Experimental Psychology: Learning, Memory and Cognition, 27*, 920–930.

Henkel, L. A. (2004). Erroneous memories arising from repeated attempts to remember. *Journal of Memory and Language, 50*, 26–46.

Hyman I. E., Husband, T. H., & Billings, F. J. (1995). False memories of childhood experiences. *Applied Cognitive Psychology, 9*, 181–195.

Johnson, M. K., Hashtroudi, S., & Lindsay, D. S. (1993). Source monitoring. *Psychological Bulletin, 114*, 3–28.

Lindsay, D. S., Hagen, L., Read, J. D., Wade, K. A., & Garry, M. (2004). True photographs and false memories. *Psychological Science, 15*, 149–154.

Loftus, E. F. (2005). Planting misinformation in the human mind: A 30-year investigation of the malleability of memory. *Learning and Memory, 12*, 361–366.

Loftus, E. F., & Davis, D. (2006). Recovered memories. *Annual Review of Clinical Psychology, 2*, 469–498.

Loftus, E. F., & Pickrell, J. E. (1995). The formation of false memories. *Psychiatric Annals, 25*, 720–725.

McNally, R. J. (2003). *Remembering trauma.* Cambridge, MA: Belknap Press/Harvard University Press.

McNally, R. J., Clancy, S. A., Barrett, H. M., & Parker, H. A. (2004). Inhibiting retrieval of trauma cues in adults reporting histories of childhood sexual abuse. *Cognition and Emotion, 18*, 479–493.

McNally, R. J., Clancy, S. A., Barrett, H. M., & Parker, H. A. (2005). Reality monitoring in adults reporting repressed, recovered, or continuous memories of childhood sexual abuse. *Journal of Abnormal Psychology, 114*, 147–152.

McNally, R. J., Clancy, S. A., & Schacter, D. L. (2001). Directed forgetting of trauma cues in adults reporting repressed or recovered memories of childhood sexual abuse. *Journal of Abnormal Psychology, 110*, 151–156.

Myers, L. B., & Brewin, C. R. (1994). Recall of early experience and the repressive coping style. *Journal of Abnormal Psychology, 103*, 288–292.

Myers, L. B., Brewin, C. R., & Power, M. J. (1998). Repressive coping and the directed forgetting of emotional material. *Journal of Abnormal Psychology, 107*, 141–148.

Parker, E. S., Cahill, L., & McGaugh, J. L. (2006). A case of unusual autobiographical remembering. *Neurocase, 12*, 35–49.

Peters, M. J. V., Horselenberg, R., Jelicic, M., & Merckelbach, H. (2007). The false fame illusion in people with memories about a previous life. *Consciousness and Cognition, 16*, 162–169.

Porter, S., Yuille, J. C., & Lehman, D. R. (1999). The nature of real, implanted, and fabricated memories or emotional childhood events. Implications for the recovered memory debate. *Law and Human Behavior, 23*, 517–537.

Raymaekers, L. (2005). Using doctored photographs to study false memories for neutral/positive and negative events. Maastricht University: Bachelor thesis.

Roediger, H. L. III, & McDermott, K. B. (1995). Creating false memories: Remembering words not presented in lists. *Journal of Experimental Psychology: Learning, Memory, and Cognition, 21*, 803–814.

Schacter, D. L. (2001). *How the mind forgets and remembers. The seven sins of memory.* Boston: Houghton Mifflin.

Schooler, J. W., Bendiksen, M. A., & Ambadar, Z. (1997). Taking the middle line: Can we accommodate both fabricated and recovered memories of sexual abuse? In M. Conway (Ed.), *False and recovered memories* (pp. 251–292). Oxford: Oxford University Press.

Shobe, K. K., & Schooler, J. W. (2001). Discovering fact and fiction: Case-based analyses of authentic and fabricated memories of abuse. In G. M. Davies & T. Dalgleish (Eds.), *Recovered memories: Seeking the middle ground* (pp. 95–151). Chichester: John Wiley & Sons.

Scott, S. (2001). *The politics and experience of ritual abuse: Beyond disbelief.* Buckingham, UK: Open University Press.

Terr, L. C. (1991). Childhood traumas: An outline and overview. *American Journal of Psychiatry*, *148*, 10–20.

Wade, K., Garry, M., Read, J. D., & Lindsay, D. S. (2002). A picture is worth a thousand lies. Using false photographs to create false childhood memories. *Psychonomic Bulletin and Review*, *9*, 597–603.

Wegner, D. M., Schneider, D. J., Carter, S. R., & White, T. I. (1987). Paradoxical effects of thought suppression. *Journal of Personality and Social Psychology*, *53*, 5–13.

Wright, D. B., Ost, J., & French, C. C. (2006). Recovered and false memories. *Psychologist*, *19*, 352–355.

5 Factors affecting the reliability of children's forensic reports

Kamala London and Sarah Kulkofsky

Child maltreatment is a major societal problem. In the United States, over four million cases of child maltreatment are investigated each year (Pipe, Lamb, Orbach, & Cederborg, 2007a). Propelled by a rash of high-profile infamous childcare and satanic ritualistic abuse cases from the 1980s and 1990s, a corpus of research has emerged to outline the interview contexts that help and hinder children's reports of past events. In this chapter, we review contemporary research findings on factors affecting the reliability of children's forensic reports. In the first half of the chapter, we review the literature on autobiographical memory and suggestibility. In the second half of the chapter, we review contemporary research findings regarding whether and how sexually abused children tend to tell others about the abuse.

AUTOBIOGRAPHICAL MEMORY

Understanding children's ability to provide complete and accurate reports of past events in forensic contexts requires an understanding of children's developing memory systems. Crucially important in this regard is research on the development of *autobiographical memory*. Autobiographical memory refers to memory about personally experienced events. Some authors specify that autobiographical memories are only those memories that are long-lasting and centrally involve the self (e.g., Nelson, 1993b; Nelson & Fivush, 2004). Memories of personally experienced events that may be more likely to be forgotten or do not centrally involve the self are sometimes referred to as *event memories* or *episodic memories*. Autobiographical memories and more general event memories appear to rely on the same underlying neurological systems (Nelson & Fivush, 2004) and thus appear only to differ in the meaning or significance of the event. Thus, research on both autobiographical memory and event memory is relevant here.

The research on the development of autobiographical memory has shown that by around 2 years of age, as children begin to develop stable self-concepts and the language of narrative, they begin to show the ability to talk about past events (Nelson & Fivush, 2004). At this young age, however, children's reports often require a great deal of adult prompting. Children's responses to open-ended prompts such as "Tell me what happened" tend to include very little detail (Fivush, 1993). Throughout early childhood children's ability to provide detailed and elaborate accounts of past events continues to improve so that by about age 6, children are able to provide more complete and elaborate accounts of past events (Fivush, Haden, & Adam, 1995; Hamond & Fivush, 1991).

Many studies of children's autobiographical memory focus on naturally occurring events, and thus memory accuracy cannot be assessed since the researchers themselves do not know what happened. However, maternal reports tend to confirm the accuracy of children's statements (e.g., Fivush, Gray, & Fromhoff, 1987). Other work using staged events for which statements can be verified has also shown high rates of accuracy (e.g., Leichtman, Pillemer, Wang, Koreishi, & Han, 2000). As such, young children's spontaneous recall of personally experienced past events is often characterized as accurate albeit incomplete.

However, the enthusiasm for the accuracy of children's spontaneous statements should be tempered to some degree. It is certainly not the case that all spontaneous statements made by young children are accurate. In particular, if the child is interviewed about confusing events or events that run counter to their knowledge, then the accuracy of the child's report may be compromised. For example, Ornstein and colleagues (Ornstein, Merrit, Baker-Ward, Furtado, Gordon, & Principe, 1998) had children experience a mock medical examination in which some common features (such as listening to the child's heart) were omitted and atypical features (such as wiping the child's belly button with alcohol) were added. When children were interviewed about the event after a 12-week delay, 42% of 4-year-olds and 74% of 6-year-olds spontaneously reported that at least one of the common features was part of the examination although it was not. Similarly, Goodman and colleagues (Goodman, Quas, Batterman-Faunce, Riddelsburger, & Kuhn 1994) interviewed children about a painful genital catheterization procedure. Among the children who were 3 to 4 years old, 23% of free recall statements were incorrect. Finally, Kulkofsky, Wang, and Ceci (2008) had preschool-aged children engage in a pizza-baking activity that included a number of unusual, non-schematic elements (e.g., the pizza was baked in a refrigerator). At one week 24% of children's free recall statements were classified as incorrect. Thus, although children in the above studies were largely accurate, children's spontaneous statements are not completely error-free. Given that in forensic settings young children are often interviewed about events that may be ambiguous and may not fit their current knowledge base, these findings may be particularly concerning.

In addition to often being incomplete, young children's recall of personal memories are also dominated by scripts. Scripts are generalized accounts of what *usually* happens in a given situation (Nelson, 1993a). For example, an adult's script for going to a restaurant may include waiting to be seated, reviewing the menu, ordering the meal, eating, and paying the bill. Very young children show better performance in reporting scripted information compared to information about specific events (Hudson & Nelson, 1986). Further, young children have more difficulty distinguishing between specific episodes of repeated events (Farrar & Goodman, 1992). When forensic interviewers are interested in a single novel event, children's reliance on scripts may not prove problematic; however, in the context of child maltreatment cases, children often are interviewed about repeated events. Thus, children's reliance on scripts in these contexts may create difficulties in obtaining complete and accurate accounts of specific episodes.

Finally, although children are able to report memories of childhood experiences, and may report memories of younger ages than adults are able to recall (Fivush & Schwarzmueller, 1999), there does appear to be a limit to how early in childhood children can remember. Specifically, children show difficulty with remembering events that occurred prior to the onset of language. For example, Peterson and Rideout (1998) interviewed young children about a visit to an emergency room that occurred when children were between 13 and 34 months old. Eighteen months later, only children who were 25 months and older at the time of the injury were able to verbally recall any details of the event, even though at the time of the interview these children had the requisite verbal ability to do so. Similarly, Bauer, Wenner, and Kroupina (2002) interviewed 3-year-olds about a previous experience in the lab when they were between 13 and 20 months of age. Only children who had been 20 months of age spontaneously provided verbalizations that indicated memory for the event, although children at all age groups showed non-verbal evidence of memory. In a related study, Simcock and Hayne (2002) exposed children who were 27, 33, and 39 months old to a novel event and then tested their memories 6 months and 1 year later. At both the initial exposure and at the memory interviews parents reported children's vocabulary, including their vocabulary that was pertinent to the novel event. At both the 6-month and 1-year tests, no child used words to describe the event that had not been part of the child's vocabulary at the time of the original event. Taken together, these results suggest that later verbal recall of an event is, in part, dependent on children's language ability at the time of encoding.

When children participate in the forensic arena, they frequently are asked to provide details about events that occurred months or even years ago. This raises concerns about how well children can remember events after a significant delay. The results of a number of studies of children's memories of unique naturalistic events (e.g., hurricanes, medical procedures, trips to Disneyland) indicate that, although there is forgetting, preschool and school-aged children do accurately recall details about personally experienced events with delays of months and even years (e.g., Bahrick, Parker, Fivush, & Levitt, 1998; Hammond & Fivush, 1991). For example, Peterson and colleagues (e.g., Peterson, 1996; Peterson & Bell, 1996; Peterson & Whalen, 2001) examined children's long-term memory for emergency room visits. Children (ages 2 to 13 years) were interviewed as soon after the visit as possible and then, depending on the study, they were interviewed 6 months to 5 years later. Preschoolers reported fewer details than older children did, but even 3-year-olds (but not 2-year-olds) recalled some central information about highly salient events.

The research on autobiographical memory development suggests that in general young children's spontaneous reports of personally experienced past events are largely accurate although they can be quite sparse. However, accuracy is impaired when children are asked to recall confusing or ambiguous events and children's reliance on scripts may lead to further memory errors. Finally, there is a limit to how far back children can remember, and thus, the veracity of memories recalled before the onset of language should be considered suspect.

SUGGESTIBILITY

Since the 1980s a great deal of developmental research has focused on the issue of *suggestibility*. Ceci and Bruck (1993) defined suggestibility as "the degree to which children's encoding, storage, retrieval, and reporting of events can be influenced by a range of social and psychological factors" (p. 404). This broad definition of suggestibility allows for information that is presented both before and after an event to taint children's recall, and further allows for the possibility that children's reports may be inaccurate even without any underlying memory impairment. That is, children may accept an interviewer's suggestion while knowing that the suggestion is not correct.

While the literature implies that children's spontaneous reports are largely accurate, reports that emerge as a result of suggestive interviewing techniques tend to be error-prone. In the classic sense, suggestive techniques involve asking leading questions. Studies of actual investigative interviews indicate that forensic interviewers frequently ask children leading questions (Ceci, Kulkofsky, Klemfuss, Sweeney, & Bruck, 2007a). Moreover, extensive training programs designed to teach best practices for interviewing young witnesses do not appear to be effective in reducing the number of leading questions interviewers ask (Sternberg, Lamb, Davies, & Westcott, 2001a). Leading questions are even used when interviewers are using a scripted interview protocol, although using an interview protocol does appear to reduce the number of suggestive utterances and increase the amount of information that is obtained from non-suggestive means (e.g., Orbach, Hershkowitz, Lamb, Sternberg, Esplin, & Horowitz, 2000). Leading questions are likely used, particularly with young children, because, as noted above, their spontaneous reports are often skeletal in nature and provide very little detail about the specific event. However, in general children are less accurate when answering direct questions compared to open-ended questions (Ornstein et al., 1998; Peterson, Dowden, & Tobin, 1999). Further, young children are less likely to respond to leading questions with "I don't know" compared with simply picking an answer choice, even to nonsensical questions (Hughes & Grieve, 1980). Leading questions are particularly problematic because the interviewer presupposes certain events occurred (e.g., "He took your clothes off, didn't he?"). However, without knowing exactly what happened, which is almost always the case in forensic interviews, an interviewer's leading question may actually be *misleading*.

The suggestiveness of an interview goes beyond simply indexing the number of leading questions. Rather, one must consider how the concept of *interviewer bias* plays out in the interview. Interviewer bias characterizes those interviewers who hold *a priori* beliefs about what has occurred and mold the interview to maximize disclosures that are consistent with those beliefs. Interviewer bias may be communicated through other suggestive techniques including providing positive and negative reinforcement (e.g., praising the child for providing disclosures or withholding benefits such as trips to the restroom for not disclosing), using peer or parental pressure (e.g., telling the child that his or her classmates or parents have already disclosed), creating a negative or accusatory emotional tone (e.g., urging the child to help keep the defendant in jail), inducing stereotypes about the accused (e.g., referring to the accused as a "bad person"), and repeating questions or interviews until the child provides the desired answer.

Research indicates that combining suggestive techniques tends to result in heightened levels of suggestibility. For example, Leichtman and Ceci (1995) showed that when children had been exposed to stereotypes about a classroom visitor they were more likely to incorporate an interviewer's misleading suggestion than children who were not exposed to stereotypes. In another set of studies, Garven and colleagues (Garven, Wood, Malpass, & Shaw, 1998; Garven, Wood, & Malpass, 2000) examined how the techniques that were used by investigators in the now infamous McMartin Preschool Case (*State of Calif. v. Buckey*, 1990) can taint children's testimony beyond that of misleading questions alone. In one study (Garven et al., 2000), the researchers asked kindergarten children to recall details from when a visitor named Paco came to their classroom and read a story, gave out treats, and wore a funny hat. Half of the children were given interviews that included misleading questions about plausible events (e.g., "Did Paco break a toy?") and bizarre events (e.g., "Did Paco take you to a farm in a helicopter?"). In this group children assented to 13% of the plausible questions and 5% of the fantastic questions. A second group of children were also questioned but these children were given negative feedback to their "no" responses and positive feedback to their "yes" responses. This latter group of children falsely assented to the plausible items 35% of the time and the bizarre items 52% of the time. Furthermore, these group differences remained when children were interviewed neutrally 2 weeks later. London, Bruck, and Melnyk (2009) found suggestive questions negatively affected children's recognition reports during an unbiased interviewing following a delay of 15 months. Thus, it appears that interviewer bias in earlier interviews can taint later interviews even if these later interviews are conducted in an unbiased manner.

However, we would be remiss if we implied that a combination of highly suggestive techniques is necessary in order to taint children's reports. Children can incorporate misleading information into their accounts even after a single suggestive interview (Ceci et al., 2007a; London et al., 2009). Further, other milder forms of suggestions have been shown to influence the accuracy of children's reports. In a recent set of studies, Principe and colleagues have shown how rumors spread among peers may produce false reports (Principe & Ceci, 2002; Principe, Guiliano, & Root, 2008; Principe, Kanaya, Ceci, & Singh, 2006). In one study (Principe et al., 2008), 3- to 6-year-old children watched a magic show that included two failed tricks. Some of the children saw clues to provide them with hints about why these two tricks failed. When interviewed later about the events, both the children who were exposed to the clues *and* their classmates reported inaccurate details consistent with the clues, whereas control children who were not exposed to clues, either directly or through their classmates, rarely reported such details. Not only did children report false details, but many maintained they had *seen* the false events themselves. These results suggest that children need only to be exposed to conversations with peers with false beliefs developed through the children's own causal inferences in order to distort the accuracy of their reports.

Another interesting aspect of Principe et al.'s (2008) study was that older children were more likely to report false details as a result of their own inferences than were younger children. In most typical suggestibility studies there are reliable age differences, with younger children being more suggestible than older children and adults (Ceci & Bruck, 1993). In fact, age appears to be the single best predictor of suggestibility (Geddie, Fradin, & Beer, 2000). However, this is not to say that only young children are suggestible. There is a great deal of evidence that older children and adults can fall prey to suggestive techniques (Ceci et al., 2007a; Finnillä, Mahlberga, Santtilaa, & Niemib, 2003; London et al., 2009). Further, as the Principe et al. (2008) study shows, there are situations when older children may actually be *more* suggestible than younger children. In particular, in some cases older children's more advanced cognitive capabilities actually lead to increased incorporation of false information.

In the case of the Principe et al. (2008) study, older children were likely providing more false details as a result of their own inferences because older children are more capable of developing causal inferences compared to younger children. Children's underlying knowledge representations may also play a role in influencing reverse age trends in suggestibility. For example, in one recent study (Ceci, Papierno, & Kulkofsky, 2007b), 4-year-olds and 9-year-olds were read a story that included a series of objects. Later children were given misinformation about the objects in the story. They were subsequently asked to recall the objects that were part of the original story. The direction of the age differences in suggestibility was predicted by children's semantic representations of the similarity between the actual and suggested objects. For example, compared with younger children, older children were more likely to erroneously report that there had been an orange tree in the story when there had actually been a lemon tree. This is because older children found oranges and lemons to be more similar than younger children did. Similarly, in DRM studies, where lists of semantically related words are presented, false reports of target semantically related but non-presented words rise with age (e.g., Brainerd, Holliday, & Reyna, 2004). London et al. (in press) found similar levels of suggestibility among 4- to 9-year-olds. They suggest the mode delivering suggestions may also affect age findings in suggestibility studies. In their study, they used a forced confabulation paradigm where children were given false information rather than simply being asked whether the false details occurred (also see Zaragoza, Payment, Kichler, Stines, & Drivdahl, 2001).

One argument that is often made against much of the research on suggestibility is that children are only suggestible about inconsequential, peripheral details of events. However, the effects of suggestive questioning are not limited to irrelevant and peripheral details of unemotional events. Children's erroneous reports as a result of suggestive techniques include central details of negative and painful events, such as doctor's office and emergency room visits (Bruck, Ceci, Francoeur, & Barr, 1995; Bruck, Ceci, & Francoeur, 2000; Burgwyn-Bales, Baker-Ward, Gordon, & Ornstein, 2001) and other forms of bodily touching (Poole & Lindsay, 1995; White, Leichtman, & Ceci, 1997).

Finally, it is important to note that children's false reports that emerge through suggestive techniques may be indistinguishable from true statements. Both Ceci, Loftus, Leichtman, and Bruck (1994) and Leichtman and Ceci (1995) had legal and psychological experts watch videos of children's true and false reports that emerged as a result of suggestive questioning techniques. Experts were asked to attempt to classify the true and false events. In both cases, the professionals were no better than chance at distinguishing true from false memories. Furthermore, Bruck and colleagues (Bruck, Ceci, & Hembrooke, 2002) systematically compared children's true and false narratives. In this study, children were repeatedly and suggestively interviewed about two true and two false events. Children's subsequent narratives were then coded for a number of characteristics including number of spontaneous utterances, contradictory statements, narrative cohesion, and aggressive or improbable details. Bruck et al. (2002) found that false narratives contained more spontaneous details, more temporal markers, more elaborations, and more aggressive details than true narratives. In a similar study, Powell and colleagues (Powell, Jones, & Campbell, 2003) found that, like Bruck et al. (2002), false narratives were similar to true narratives in number of details, structure, and quality. Furthermore, Principe and Ceci (2002) found that false narratives were actually *more* elaborate than children's true narratives, and further Kulkofsky and colleagues (2008) found that increases in narrative quality were associated with *decreases* in accuracy.

Even when experts attempt to apply more systematic methods to distinguish true from false reports elicited through suggestive questions, their decisions are not reliable. For instance, criterion-based content analysis (CBCA) has been touted as one way to distinguish true from false reports in forensic contexts (e.g., Vrij, 2005). In CBCA, experts code the witness's statement for the presence of specific contents that are expected to occur more frequently in true reports. Although there is some limited evidence that CBCA can distinguish truthful statements from intentional lies, it cannot reliably distinguish true statements from false statements that were developed as a result of suggestive questioning techniques (Kulkofsky, in press).

The research on children's suggestibility paints a somewhat grim picture of young children's reliability as witnesses in forensic contexts. Children are vulnerable to leading questions and other suggestive techniques, including some very mild forms of suggestion. Although young children appear to be the most suggestible, older children are also susceptible to suggestive techniques. Further, children may be suggestible about central details of events and events that involve pain or bodily touch. Finally children's reports that emerge through suggestive questioning often appear quite credible.

We should note, though, in this section we have focused primarily on aspects of interviewing contexts that tend to impair the accuracy of children's reports. As noted in the previous section, children can often provide highly accurate accounts of past events. Also, concerns about memory accuracy do not only pertain to children: As reviewed in this volume, adults' autobiographical memory also undergoes memory reconstruction. When interviews are neutral in tone and include few or no suggestive questions children can provide accurate and useful information about past events, including traumatic events (Fivush, 1993; Goodman, Batterman-Faunce, & Kenney, 1992; Peterson, 1996; Peterson & Bell, 1996). Recent best-practices guidelines have been developed to encourage forensic interviewers to avoid the pitfalls of suggestive interviewing techniques while still encouraging children to provide as much information as possible (Sternberg, Lamb, Orbach, & Esplin, 2001b; Orbach et al., 2000; Poole & Lamb, 1998). To the degree to which actual forensic and therapeutic interviews follow these practices, we can have greater confidence in the veracity of children's statements.

DISCLOSURE PATTERNS AMONG SEXUALLY ABUSED CHILDREN

In most cases where child sexual abuse (CSA) is suspected, children's statements are the central evidence by which to evaluate abuse allegations (London, Bruck, Ceci, & Shuman, 2005). As reviewed above, a corpus of studies indicates that open-ended questions, where children provide reports in their own words, produce the most trustworthy reports. However, sometimes there are reasons to suspect abuse has occurred in cases where children have not disclosed abuse. For example, perhaps someone gets convicted for sexually abusing one of his step-children, and investigators are concerned that other children in the family might also have been abused. During an initial forensic interview, the other children in the family do not make abuse allegations. In these cases, the investigator must decide whether and how to continue interviewing the child and at what point they should end the investigation.

Some professionals have expressed the view that children may be highly reticent to disclose sexual abuse and that sexually abused children may only disclose abuse in a lengthy process, if at all. In 1983 Roland Summit published a theoretical view based on his clinical experiences with his adult psychiatric patients, termed *child sexual abuse accommodation syndrome* (CSAAS). He postulated that children who have experienced intra-familial sexual abuse may be reluctant to disclose abuse because of motivational reasons such as being ashamed, scared, or embarrassed. As a result, he argued, abused children may delay abuse disclosure, deny abuse when asked, make partial disclosures, and retract abuse disclosures. He later extended the theory to include children who have experienced extra-familial sexual abuse (Summit, 1992).

Summit's theory (1983, 1992) has exerted a tremendous influence on forensic interview practices with children. The paper was rated as one of the most influential in the field of child maltreatment and continues to be taught internationally in many contemporary training seminars for child abuse professionals (e.g., see www.secasa.com.au; www.ndaa.org). For example, CSAAS is on the topic list for the April 2008 training course held by the Advanced Trial Advocacy for Child Abuse Prosecutors in conjunction with the National District Attorneys Association.

In 1992 Summit published a paper entitled "Abuse of the Child Sexual Abuse Accommodation Syndrome" where he cautioned practitioners that CSAAS was a clinical opinion not a scientific or diagnostic instrument and that his model is being misused by practitioners who use it as such. Unfortunately, some investigators have grasped onto the idea that sexually abused children deny abuse, and that denial in and of itself is diagnostic or indicative of abuse. In some of these cases, children were interviewed with misleading and even coercive methods (see Schreiber et al., 2006, for details on the infamous Kelly Michaels and McMartin investigations). In instances such as the rash of suspected ritualistic satanic abuse cases in Salt Lake City (Sorensen & Snow, 1991),[1] themes emerged whereby the investigators reported refusing to believe children despite their repeated denials of abuse (see London et al., 2005, for details that call into question the validity of Sorensen & Snow's 1991 findings). Such cases are not historical artifacts but continue today, both in terms of newly adjudicated cases as well as cases still undergoing appeal. Many clinicians and forensic interviewers continue to interpret abuse denials or inconsistencies in children's statements as consistent with the stages postulated in the CSAAS. For example, in recent testimony from a director of an advocacy center who has interviewed over 800 children:

Well, it's my understanding from reviewing those five areas that she did keep it a secret for a number of years. That, you know, she was helpless; she didn't fight back, things like that. That she just kind of accommodated to the situation. You know, her disclosure was, you know, different at times, and she did not retract, but, you know, she did minimize when she did her first interview about what had happened to her. So, you know, from my – just view of the information and the research, you know, it seems that she has gone through those stages.

(*State of North Dakota v. Art Tibor*, 2007)

Considering CSAAS frequently is taught to forensic interviewers as evidence supporting the notion of extreme reticence among children undergoing forensic interviews, the tenets postulated by CSAAS have undergone little scientific scrutiny to date. This is perhaps because, when originally submitted for publication, Summit's theory was seen as being quite obvious and as consistent with forensic interview practices and general intuition about abuse disclosure (Summit, 1992).

In several recent papers, London and colleagues (London et al., 2005; London, Bruck, Ceci, & Shuman, 2007; London, Bruck, Wright, & Ceci, 2008) reviewed the literature on disclosure patterns among sexually abused children. The goal of these reviews was to examine the contemporary empirical findings regarding the nature and timing of children's sexual abuse disclosures.[2] London et al. reviewed two main sources of data: adults' retrospective accounts of CSA and whether they disclosed the abuse to anyone, and case records from children undergoing contemporaneous forensic evaluation. Below, we first present a summary of research findings from adults' retrospective reports. Then we discuss conclusions that can be drawn from the research on children undergoing forensic evaluations.

Adults' retrospective accounts of CSA and childhood disclosure: Evidence on delayed disclosure

Data from the retrospective accounts yield two central findings: Many adults report that they never told anyone during childhood about the CSA they experienced, and even fewer reported that the abuse came to the attention of authorities. Across 13 retrospective abuse disclosure studies reviewed, 21–87% of participants reported they disclosed the sexual abuse during childhood (see London et al., 2008, Table 1, for studies and citations). A childhood disclosure rate of 87% (reported by Mullen, Martin, Anderson, Romans, & Herbison, 1993) was much higher than the other studies and might be accounted for through methodological factors in their study (London et al., 2005). Of the 13 studies reviewed, 11 found that 34–54% of their adult sample who experienced CSA reported that they had ever told anyone about the abuse during childhood.

Fewer studies reported data on adults' retrospective reports of whether the abuse disclosure involved authorities such as police or social workers. Across seven studies to provide data on disclosure to authorities, 5–18% of adults who reportedly experienced CSA indicated the abuse was brought to the attention of authorities, with four of the seven studies reporting rates between 10 and 13% (London et al., 2008). Though the retrospective accounts are subject to problems inherent in any retrospective account, London et al. (2008) concluded extant data support Summit's notion of secrecy among sexually abused children. According to retrospective reports, only about one third to one half of children ever tell anyone and even fewer cases come to the attention of authorities.

Many of the retrospective studies reported very long delays between the abusive episodes and children's disclosure, sometimes of several years. Though there are limited data at present, adults' retrospective reports suggest that some children disclose relatively close in time to the abuse (e.g., within the first 6 months), while others wait many years or never tell anyone during childhood (London et al., 2008).

The adult retrospective literature yields few individual difference variables (e.g., severity of abuse, presence of threats, intra-familial vs. extra-familial perpetrators, race and gender of child) that predicted whether and when children disclosed the abuse. We suspect such variables do exist (and some have been identified in the literature examining contemporaneous abuse investigations, see London et al., 2005). Likely there are multiple reasons why such findings have not emerged in the retrospective literature. First, only some of the retrospective studies reported relevant data. Second, samples sometimes were not adequately diverse to allow individual difference analyses. Third, individual difference variables may not be detected if adults have difficulties precisely pin-pointing the time at which the disclosure was made. Finally, multivariate methods may be necessary to reveal abuse, child, and perpetrator characteristics that predict CSA disclosure (e.g., see Goodman-Brown, Edelstein, Goodman, Jones, & Gordon, 2003).

While the retrospective accounts indicate a minority of children disclose abuse to authorities, the retrospective accounts do not yield information about the disclosure patterns among the minority of children to undergo forensic interviews. Among adults who retrospectively reported disclosing CSA during childhood, most reported telling a non-offending parent or a friend. Considering that only 10–15% of CSA cases appear to reach authorities, cases that come before forensic interviewers may have different features and characteristics from cases where children disclosed only to friends or family. In the next section, we discuss research findings on children undergoing contemporaneous abuse assessments.

Studies of children undergoing forensic evaluation for suspected abuse: Evidence on abuse denials and recantations

Studies of children undergoing assessment for suspected CSA provide the second source of data on disclosure patterns of abused children. These studies generally examined archival records of children undergoing assessment by police, social workers, physicians, or abuse assessment teams. Such samples allow an exploration of the extent to which children make denials and recantations during forensic assessment.

Unlike the retrospective studies reviewed above, London and colleagues (2005, 2007, 2008) reported a wide range of disclosure rates during forensic or medical interviews across 21 different studies. The reported disclosure rates ranged from a low of about 25% (Gonzales, Waterman, Kelly, McCord, & Oliveri, 1993; Sorensen & Snow, 1991)[3] to a high of 96% (Bradley & Wood, 1996). Methodological features, particularly sample choices and interview methods, appear to play a primary role in accounting for these discrepant rates. Because of its importance, in this section, we focus on this issue. Findings on disclosure rates and specific child/perpetrator and abuse context characteristics have been reviewed and discussed elsewhere (most notably see edited volume on abuse disclosure by Pipe, Lamb, Orbach, & Cederborg, 2007b; also see London et al., 2005).

In order to calculate true rates of disclosures and denials during forensic interviews, information is needed that accurately classifies children as abused or non-abused regardless of whether the child makes an allegation during the interview. At the same time, the chosen sample should be representative of all children who come before forensic interviewers. For example, sampling methods that eliminate children from their sample who readily disclose to forensic interviewers would not provide accurate estimates of the overall rates of disclosure among all children who come before interviewers. At the same time, because abuse substantiation is highly reliant on children's disclosures, samples that only include highly probable or prosecuted cases suffer the limitation of excluding possible true cases where the child denies abuse during interview (see Lyon, 2007). Of course, there could also be cases where the child comes to make an abuse allegation despite not having experienced abuse.

Because of these real-world constraints, disclosure rates in founded and unfounded cases to come before forensic interviewers are unknown and likely vary temporally and across communities (according to varying factors like abuse education, mandatory reporting laws, and community thresholds of what signs constitute abuse suspicion). As reviewed in this chapter, the reliability of children's forensic reports is directly contingent upon the questioning methods employed. Hence, the sensitivity and specificity of abuse diagnoses vary according to interview methods. The difficult task for estimating CSA denial and recantation rates is choosing a sample that is both representative of children to come before forensic interviewers but also one that provides some meaningful measure of abuse certainty.

London et al. (2005, 2007, 2008) argued that disclosure rates during forensic interviews vary systematically according to the certainty with which children in the study samples were abused. They divided the child literature into four major groupings that correspond with ascending disclosure rates: Group 1 – cases of dubious validity, Group 2 – select subsamples, Group 3 – all children to come before forensic interviewers, and Group 4 – cases that come before forensic interviewers that are rated as founded or highly probable.

Group 1 studies reported the lowest disclosure rates. These rates came from studies with very dubious or overturned cases and documented poor interview techniques (Gonzales et al., 1993; Sorensen & Snow, 1991). In these studies, the abuse denials may have been true denials rather than evidence of reluctant disclosure, for which the two articles frequently are cited. Many of the children from Gonzales et al.'s sample were from the infamous McMartin case (see Schreiber et al., 2006, for a systematic evaluation of the methods employed in those interviews). Sorensen and Snow's (1991) children were from a rash of neighborhood ritualistic satanic abuse cases, most of which either were not prosecuted or later were thrown out of court. Based on the documented highly suggestive techniques used in these studies, we argue these studies do not provide any information about disclosure patterns among abused children.

Group 2 is composed of studies which reported disclosure rates among select subsamples of children who come before authorities. These studies provide the second tier of disclosure rates with between 43% and 61% of children disclosing abuse when interviewed (for the study citations see London et al., 2008, Table 2). There are two types of cases in this grouping: (1) children undergoing extended evaluation for non-disclosure with high suspicion of abuse, and (2) children who come to the attention of authorities because of strong evidence of abuse (videotaped abuse evidence or sexually transmitted disease [STD] diagnoses who have not made prior disclosures). While these studies yield important information on abuse disclosure among their specific subsamples, caution is warranted in generalizing the results beyond the context under which these interviews occur. The rates are not based on studies of all children who come before forensic interviewers but rather a select subsample.

Also in this second major grouping of studies, some studies have reported disclosure rates in children who present with an STD (e.g., Lawson & Chaffin, 1992). Lyon (2007) reviewed 21 studies that presented data on children presenting to medical settings with gonorrhea. These studies were published between 1965 and 1993 with all but two being from 1982 and earlier. Across these 21 studies, Lyon (2007) reported a mean disclosure rate of 43%. There are a number of problems with generalizing results from these medical studies to all cases who come before forensic interviewers (Lawson & Chaffin, 1992). Some of the studies that are in this grouping purposely excluded a very large number of girls who were examined and readily disclosed and instead focused on a small number of girls with no prior disclosure. For example, in one study, from over 800 girls to undergo STD evaluation, disclosure rates were reported on 28 girls who were diagnosed with gonorrhea but who did not make a disclosure at the initial medical evaluation (as aptly noted by Lawson & Chaffin, 1992). Also, disclosure was a peripheral issue in these pediatric gonorrhea publications reviewed by Lyon (2007), and in some of these reports it was unclear (a) if the medical professional even attempted to ascertain directly from the child the nature of the abuse – especially consider-ing the questioning took place before the burgeoning research on interview-ing children, (b) if the child was pubertal and engaged in sexual activity with a same-aged peer, (c) the rate of false positives on the gonorrhea tests espe-cially those conducted in the 1960s and 1970s, and (d) whether some of the children contacted gonorrhea via fomite transmission (for more details about disclosure in samples with STDs, see London, McGuire, Bruck, & Poole, in preparation). Among cases to come before forensic interviewers, less than 1% of girls are estimated to fall into the category of testing positive for gonor-rhea and not having previously disclosed abuse (London et al., 2008). While Lyon's (2007) review provides compelling evidence that some children in fact do deny abuse in the face of incontrovertible evidence of abuse, we argue these rates are not representative of all children who come before forensic interviewers. That is, it would be faulty reasoning for forensic interviewers to expect that fewer than half of children presenting before them who truly were abused would readily disclose abuse, as will become evident in the third grouping of studies.

Group 3 studies reported data among all children to come before forensic interviewers regardless of abuse substantiation. In several newly published and provocative studies by Lamb, Pipe, and colleagues, among *all children* with CSA suspicions to come before highly trained forensic interviewers using the NICHD protocol (in the United States and Israel), 71–83% made disclosures (Hershkowitz, Horowitz, & Lamb, 2005; Pipe, Lamb, Orbach, Stewart, Sternberg, & Esplin, 2007c). These findings reveal that disclosure rates in the 40–60% range do not approach the lowest level of disclosure rates found among all children to come before highly trained forensic interviewers. Importantly, with the 71–83% disclosure rates, no efforts were made to weed out unfounded suspicions.

We argue that the rates reported in studies in Group 3 reflect the lower boundary of disclosure rates that should be expected among large general groups of children interviewed by highly trained forensic interviewers (London et al., 2007). One important caveat to this finding is that most children who come before forensic interviewers had made disclosures prior to the inter-views (and continue to do so during formal interviews), which was the impetus to the investigation. This factor probably contributes to the much higher disclosure rates found in studies where children come before forensic interviewers versus medical professionals in Group 2.

Group 4 represents studies which reported disclosure rates among highly probable cases that came before investigators. In these studies, efforts were taken by abuse assessment teams to rate the certainty of abuse in light of all the case materials available (e.g., children's disclosure, medical evidence, perpetrator confession, eyewitness reports, etc.). The highest rates of disclosure, 85–96%, are found among studies that report disclosure rates among cases classified as highly probable. We argue these rates provide the best estimate of disclosure rates among general samples of abused children who come before forensic interviewers as some effort must be made to classify founded and unfounded cases in order to give meaningful abuse disclosure estimates.

Lyon (2007) points out that these studies provide elevated disclosure rates since abuse substantiation often is dependent upon a disclosure. Hence, in true abuse cases where no disclosure is made, the case might get classified as an improbable abuse case. Using substantiated cases to estimate disclosure rates becomes circular, then, if substantiation is largely driven by abuse disclosure, and then disclosure rates are estimated based on substantiated cases. At the same time, some effort must be made to distinguish true and false cases or else the rates simply reflect disclosure among all children interviewed (as in the studies in Group 3). Clearly, each sampling method has limitations.

Finally, we turn to the issue of abuse recantations. Once children have disclosed abuse, how likely are they to recant the allegations? There is much less data on recantation rates than on disclosure rates. Like abuse disclosure rates, recantation rates depend on sampling methods and abuse substantiation. Two of the highest recantation rates (27% and 22%, respectively) were reported in the Gonzales et al. (1993) and Sorensen and Snow (1991) papers. As discussed above and elsewhere (e.g., London et al., 2005, 2007, 2008; Schreiber et al., 2006), due to serious concerns about the forensic interview methods employed and uncertainty of abuse substantiation in the cases, we argue these rates are not representative of cases that come before forensic interviewers who have been highly trained with contemporary interview protocols. Recantation rates of 5–9% are reported in general samples of highly probable abuse cases. A higher rate was reported by Malloy, Lyon, and Quas (2007), who found a rate of 23% among children with substantiated CSA cases facing dependency hearings. Dependency hearings often involve removing the child from the home for reasons stemming from the CSA. There may be different motivations for recanting in these circumstances than in other situations. While these cases are important, it is also important to differentiate the types of samples used and not generalize from samples that are not representative of the wider population of interest.

Overall, extant data on recantation of CSA disclosures suggest (a) recantations occur in a minority of cases and do not typify abuse disclosure patterns, and (b) recantation may be more common in certain situations (e.g., one with pressure or motivation to make recantation such as having a non-supportive non-abusing caregiver; Elliott & Briere, 1994). When evaluating the minority of cases where abuse recantation occurs, like evaluating disclosure evidence, all of the evidence in the case, including potential motivators for recantation, should be considered.

CONCLUSIONS

Legal researchers and practitioners have made great strides over the past 30 years in devising forensic interviewing protocols that are sensitive to children's developing social and cognitive abilities. In this chapter, we have reviewed the contemporary literature on three main areas related to forensic reports from children: autobiographical memory development, suggestibility, and disclosure of child sexual abuse.

Prior to 1980, children rarely were allowed to give courtroom testimony. Beginning in the late 1980s, a rash of childcare center and satanic ritualistic abuse cases were prosecuted. The pendulum swung in the opposite direction, where laypeople and protective services workers sometimes seemed to blindly accept testimony elicited from highly suggestive interviews from children as young as ages 2 or 3. The scientific evidence shows that neither of these extreme views is supported. Instead, research indicates that children can give accurate reports of past events, even traumatic events following delays. At the same time, factors external (e.g., misleading questions) and internal (e.g., reliance on scripts) to children can taint their memory and produce erroneous reports.

In the first half of this chapter, we reviewed the literature on autobiographical memory and suggestibility. Evidence indicates even preschoolers can provide some information about central salient details of personally experienced events. Many studies have found children's free recall reports to be more accurate than recognition responses, though free recall in young children often is very sparse. The natural tendency of an adult interviewer, then, may be to resort to a series of forced-choice or yes/no questions. However, when there are high stakes attached to obtaining correct information, as in the case of forensic interviews, the use of option-posing questions runs a higher risk of eliciting erroneous information. When given forced choice options, young children tend to choose a response rather than indicating they do not know or do not understand a question.

One concern in evaluating forensic interviews with children is the extent to which the interviewers believed they knew what happened before eliciting children's narratives. When interviewers believe they know what happened in a given event, they tend to employ various suggestive interview techniques that are powerful in shaping children's responses to be in accord with their beliefs. Researchers have shown that a variety of suggestive techniques, beyond simply giving leading questions, can detrimentally affect children's reports. Researchers have found suggestive questioning can taint children's reports not just about peripheral details regarding inconsequential events but also about central details regarding events such as doctor's visits or bodily touching.

Children often do not simply parrot back the misinformation to which they have been exposed. Instead they may provide many elaborations that interfere with fact-finders' ability to distinguish true events from suggestively-induced false reports. Hence, the first interviews with children are crucial. Numerous forensic interview protocols have emerged over the past 15 years to provide guidelines for maximizing accurate reports from children. Videotaping forensic interviews with children can help fact-finders evaluate the extent to which information was elicited from children in ways that produce accurate versus inaccurate reports.

Given the large body of work documenting the detrimental effects of repeated suggestive questioning, the following vignette illustrates one pattern of child sexual abuse disclosure that is particularly concerning. An adult develops a suspicion about abuse. Initially the child says nothing. After exposure to repeated questioning by parents and forensic interviewers who doggedly pursue the child for a certain report, the child eventually comes to make some statements that are consistent with the adults' *a priori* beliefs. Interviewers sometimes contend that such methods are justified because of children's extreme reluctance to disclose abuse. We argue that, for two reasons, such a conclusion is unwise.

First, in the event the adults' suspicions are inaccurate, the suggestive questioning may elicit erroneous information from children. Even if there is strong suspicion of abuse, suggestive misleading questioning strategies have been shown to elicit inaccurate information. Second, among high probability cases to come before forensic interviewers, most children make abuse disclosures during the initial open-ended phases of the interview process. Studies that provide data on general samples of CSA cases considered highly probable that come before forensic interviewers report disclosure rates of about 85%. Among the 15–30% of children who do not make a disclosure, some unknown and likely variable percentage of these children are reluctant disclosers and some are making true denials. Evidence from highly probable cases (e.g., see Cederborg, Lamb, & Laurell, 2007; Dickinson, Del Russo, & D'Urso, 2008; Lawson & Chaffin, 1992; Lyon, 2007; Malloy et al., 2007) indicates some sexually abused children do deny abuse during forensic or medical interviews, and a minority of truly abused children do falsely retract abuse.

While there is some disagreement about the overall rates of denial and recantation due to difficulties inherent in the scientific investigation of this issue, several researchers have opined that, while some children may deny or recant abuse, the term "syndrome" does not well characterize CSA disclosures (London et al., 2007; Lyon, 2007; Pipe et al., 2007a; Summit, 1992). We argue that the notion that sexually abused children typically progress through a series of syndrome-like stages from secrecy to partial disclosures and retractions, or that denials and retractions justify highly suggestive and coercive interview strategies, is not scientifically supported.

There are data supporting the notion that many sexually abused children fail to ever come forward to anyone about the abuse. Studies of adults' retrospective reports of their CSA disclosure patterns indicate that only one-third to one-half of sexually abused children ever tell anyone about the abuse during childhood; stated another way, 50–70% of adults report they never told anyone during childhood that they experienced CSA. There appears to be consensus among researchers at this point that Summit's notion of secrecy among sexually abused children has empirical support (e.g., Dickinson et al., 2008; London et al., 2008; Lyon, 2006).

Although the trend is that high probability abuse cases disclose early in well-conducted interviews, there are certain populations where denial (and recantation) during formal interviews may be more common. Some researchers have begun to elucidate variables that predict non-disclosure and recantation among founded abuse cases (e.g., see Cederborg et al., 2007; Horowitz, 2007; Lawson & Chaffin, 1992; Malloy et al., 2007; Orbach, Shioach, & Lamb, 2007; Pipe, et al., 2007c). Identifying social and cognitive factors that interfere with disclosure is an important first step toward exploring interview methods that will motivate reluctant disclosers to come forward[4] without running a high risk of eliciting false reports from non-abused children.

A major advance in better understanding disclosure patterns among sexually abused children are the studies by Michael Lamb and colleagues who employ the empirically driven NICHD interview protocol (see edited volume by Pipe et al., 2007b, for several examples). Since the accuracy of children's reports (and classification as abused or non-abused) is driven by interview quality, estimates of CSA disclosure rates are most accurate under optimal interview conditions. Lamb and colleagues have recently published data showing the majority of children who make an abuse disclosure during forensic interviews do so at the beginning stages of the interview, during open-ended questions. The answer, then, to overcoming reluctance in disclosure among abused children undergoing forensic interviews does not lie in exposing them to repeated suggestive interviews or suggestive influences from non-professionals such as parents. While these techniques might act to overcome reluctance among abused children, they also run the risk of eliciting false allegations in non-abused children. Instead, techniques must be devised that encourage abused children to disclose without elevating false allegations among non-abused children. Fortunately, there is much exciting data emerging on abuse disclosure that can be used to refine and revise best-practice standards.

Notes

1 On February 19, 2008, Barbara Snow's license to practice as a clinical social worker was placed on a four-year probation due to unprofessional conduct (Falk, 2008).
2 Because forensic interview practices have undergone much transformation in recent years, we have limited our reviews to findings published in 1990 or later.
3 Twenty-five percent of Sorensen and Snow's therapy clients disclosed during initial interviews; eventually, after sometimes months of questionable interview techniques, 96% came to make abuse disclosures. Most of these cases either were overturned or did not go to trial. Similarly, Gonzales et al.'s (1993) sample included children from the infamous McMartin case.
4 Given that the vast majority of CSA cases never reach authorities even when

children do disclose to a friend or family member, top-down sexual abuse prevention efforts and community efforts aimed toward adults to whom children might disclose could have far-reaching implications for child protection.

References

Bahrick, L. E., Parker, J. F., Fivush, R., & Levitt, M. (1998). The effects of stress on young children's memory for a natural disaster. *Journal of Experimental Psychology: Applied, 4*, 308–331.

Bauer, P. J., Wenner, J. A., & Kroupina, M. G. (2002). Making the past present: Later verbal accessibility of early memories. *Journal of Cognition and Development, 3*, 21–47.

Bradley, A. R., & Wood, J. M. (1996). How do children tell? The disclosure process in child sexual abuse. *Child Abuse and Neglect, 20*, 881–891.

Brainerd, C. J., Holliday, R. E., & Reyna, V. F. (2004). Behavioral measurement of remembering phenomenologies: So simple a child can do it. *Child Development, 75*, 505–522.

Bruck, M., Ceci, S. J., & Francoeur, E., (2000). Children's use of anatomically detailed dolls to report genital touching in a medical examination: Developmental and gender comparisons. *Journal of Experimental Psychology: Applied, 6*, 74–83.

Bruck, M., Ceci, S. J., Francoeur, E., & Barr, R. J. (1995). "I hardly cried when I got my shot!": Influencing children's reports about a visit to their pediatrician. *Child Development, 66*, 193–208.

Bruck, M., Ceci, S. J., & Hembrooke, H. (2002). The nature of children's true and false memories. *Developmental Review, 22*, 520–554.

Burgwyn-Bales, E., Baker-Ward, L., Gordon, B. N., & Ornstein, P. A. (2001). Children's memory for emergency medical treatment after one year: The impact of individual difference variables on recall and suggestibility. *Applied Cognitive Psychology, 15*, S25–S48.

Ceci, S. J., & Bruck, M. (1993). Suggestibility of the child witness: A historical review and synthesis. *Psychological Bulletin, 113*, 403–439.

Ceci, S. J., Kulkofsky, S., Klemfuss, J. Z., Sweeney, C. D., & Bruck, M. (2007a). Unwarranted assumptions about children's testimonial accuracy. *Annual Review of Clinical Psychology, 3*, 311–328.

Ceci, S. J., Loftus, E. F., Leichtman, M. D., & Bruck, M. (1994). The possible role of source misattributions in the creation of false beliefs among preschoolers. *International Journal of Clinical and Experimental Hypnosis, 62*, 304–320.

Ceci, S. J., Papierno, P., & Kulkofsky, S. (2007b). Representational constraints on children's suggestibility. *Psychological Science, 18*, 503–509.

Cederborg, A. C., Lamb, M. E., & Laurell, O. (2007). Delay of disclosure, minimization, and denial when the evidence is unambiguous: A multi-victim case. In M. E. Pipe, M. E. Lamb, Y. Orbach, & A. C. Cederborg (Eds.), *Child sexual abuse: Disclosure, delay, and denial* (pp. 159–173). Mahwah, NJ: Lawrence Erlbaum Associates, Inc.

Dickinson, J., Del Russo, J., & D'Urso, A. (2008, March). Children's disclosure of sex abuse: A new approach to answering elusive questions. Paper presented at the annual meeting of the American Psychology – Law Society, Jacksonville, FL.

Elliott, D. M., & Briere, J. (1994). Forensic sexual abuse evaluations of older children: Disclosures and symptomatology. *Behavioral Sciences and the Law, 12*, 261–277.

Falk, A. (February 21, 2008). Controversial therapist put on probation. *Deseret Morning News*. Salt Lake City, UT.

Farrar, M. J., & Goodman, G. S. (1992). Developmental changes in event memory. *Child Development*, *63*, 173–187.

Finnillä, K., Mahlberga, N., Santtilaa, P., Sandnabba, K., & Niemi, P. (2003). Validity of a test of children's suggestibility for predicting responses to two interview situations differing in their degree of suggestiveness. *Journal of Experimental Child Psychology*, *85*, 32–49.

Fivush, R. (1993). Developmental perspectives on autobiographical recall. In G. S. Goodman & B. Bottoms (Eds.), *Child victims and child witnesses: Understanding and improving testimony* (pp. 1–24). New York: Guilford.

Fivush, R., Gray, J. T., & Fromhoff, F. A. (1987). Two year olds talk about the past. *Cognitive Development*, *2*, 393–410.

Fivush, R., Haden, C., & Adam, S. (1995). Structure and coherence of preschoolers' personal narratives over time: Implications for childhood amnesia. *Journal of Experimental Child Psychology*, *60*, 32–56.

Fivush, R., & Schwarzmueller, A. (1999). Children remember childhood: Implications for childhood amnesia. *Applied Cognitive Psychology*, *12*, 455–473.

Garven, S., Wood, J. M., & Malpass, R. S. (2000). Allegations of wrongdoing: The effects of reinforcement on children's mundane and fantastic claims. *Journal of Applied Psychology*, *85*, 38–49.

Garven, S., Wood, J. M., Malpass, R., & Shaw, J. S. (1998). More than suggestion: Consequences of the interviewing techniques from the McMartin preschool case. *Journal of Applied Psychology*, *83*, 347–359.

Geddie, L., Fradin, S., & Beer, J. (1999). Child characteristics which impact accuracy of recall in preschoolers: Is age the best predictor? *Child Abuse and Neglect*, *24*, 223–235.

Gonzalez, L. S., Waterman, J., Kelly, R., McCord, J., & Oliveri, K. (1993). Children's patterns of disclosures and recantations of sexual and ritualistic abuse allegations in psychotherapy. *Child Abuse and Neglect*, *17*, 281–289.

Goodman, G. S., Batterman-Faunce, J. M., & Kenney, R. (1992). Optimizing children's testimony: Research and social policy issues concerning allegations of child sexual abuse. In D. Cicchetti & S. Toth (Eds.), *Child abuse, child development, and social policy* (pp. 65–87). Norwood, NJ: Ablex.

Goodman, G. S., Quas, J. A., Batterman-Faunce, J. M., Riddelsberger, M. M., & Kuhn, J. (1994). Predictors of accurate and inaccurate memories of traumatic events experienced in childhood. *Consciousness and Cognition*, *3*, 269–294.

Goodman-Brown, T. B., Edelstein, R. S., Goodman, G. S., Jones, D. P. H., & Gordon, D. S. (2003). Why children tell: A model of children's disclosure of sexual abuse. *Child Abuse and Neglect*, *27*, 525–540.

Hamond, N. R., & Fivush, R. (1991). Memories of Mickey Mouse: Young children recount their trip to Disney World. *Cognitive Development*, *6*, 433–448.

Hershkowitz, I., Horowitz, D., & Lamb, M. E. (2005). Trends in children's disclosure of abuse in Israel: A national study. *Child Abuse and Neglect*, *29*, 1203–1214.

Horowitz, D. (2007). The silence of abused children in Israel: Policy implications. In M. E. Pipe, M. E. Lamb, Y. Orbach, & A. C. Cederborg (Eds.), *Child sexual abuse: Disclosure, delay, and denial* (pp. 281–290). Mahwah, NJ: Lawrence Erlbaum Associates, Inc.

Hudson, J., & Nelson, K. (1986). Repeated encounters of a similar kind: Effects of familiarity on children's autobiographic memory. *Cognitive Development, 1*, 253–271.

Hughes, M., & Grieve, R. (1980). On asking children bizarre questions. *First Language, 1*, 149–160.

Kulkofsky, S. (in press). Credible but inaccurate: Can criterion-based content analysis (CBCA) distinguish true and false memories? In M. J. Smith (Ed.), *Child sexual abuse: Issues and challenges*. New York: Nova Science Publishers.

Kulkofsky, S., Wang, Q., & Ceci, S. J. (2008). Do better stories make better memories? Narrative quality and memory accuracy in preschool children. *Applied Cognitive Psychology, 22*, 21–38.

Lawson, L., & Chaffin, M. (1992). False negatives in sexual abuse disclosure interviews: Incidence and influence of caretaker's belief in abuse in cases of accidental abuse discovery by diagnosis of STD. *Journal of Interpersonal Violence, 7*, 532–542.

Leichtman, M. D. & Ceci, S. J. (1995). The effects of stereotypes and suggestions on preschoolers' reports. *Developmental Psychology, 31*, 568–578.

Leichtman, M. D., Pillemer, D. B., Wang, Q., Korieshi, A., & Han, J. J. (2000). When Baby Maisy came to school: Mother's interview styles and children's event memories. *Cognitive Development, 15*, 99–114.

London, K., Bruck, M., Ceci, S. J., & Shuman, D. (2005). Children's disclosure of sexual abuse: What does the research tell us about the ways that children tell? *Psychology, Public Policy, and the Law, 11*, 194–226.

London, K., Bruck, M., & Ceci, S. J., & Shuman, D. (2007). Disclosure of child sexual abuse: A review of the contemporary empirical literature. In M. E. Pipe, M. E. Lamb, Y. Orbach, & A. C. Cederborg (Eds.), *Child sexual abuse: Disclosure, delay, and denial* (pp. 11–39). Mahwah, NJ: Lawrence Erlbaum Associates, Inc.

London, K., Bruck, M., & Melnyk, L. (2009). Persistence of facilitation and misinformation effects in event memory following a 10 month delay. *Law and Human Behavior*.

London, K., Bruck, M., Wright, D. B., & Ceci, S. J. (2008). How children report sexual abuse to others: Findings and methodological issues. *Memory, 16*, 29–47.

London, K., McGuire, K., Bruck, M., & Poole, D. A. (in preparation). Disclosure of sexual abuse among samples with medical evidence. Manuscript in preparation.

Lyon, T. D. (2007). False denials: Overcoming methodological biases in abuse disclosure research. In M. E. Pipe, M. E. Lamb, Y. Orbach, & A. C. Cederborg (Eds.), *Child sexual abuse: Disclosure, delay, and denial* (pp. 41–62). Mahwah, NJ: Lawrence Erlbaum Associates, Inc.

Malloy, L. C., Lyon, T. D., & Quas, J. A. (2007). Filial dependency and recantation of child sexual abuse allegations. *Journal of the American Academy of Child and Adolescent Psychiatry, 46*, 162–170.

Mullen, P. E., Martin, J. L., Anderson, J. C., Romans, S. E., & Herbison, G. P. (1993). Child sexual abuse and mental health in adult life. *British Journal of Psychiatry, 163*, 721–732.

Nelson, K. (1993a). Events, narratives, memory: What develops? In C. A. Nelson (Ed.), *Memory affect in development* (pp. 1–24). Hillsdale, NJ: Lawrence Erlbaum Associates, Inc.

Nelson, K. (1993b). The psychological and social origins of autobiographical memory. *Psychological Science, 4*, 7–14.

Nelson, K., & Fivush, R. (2004). The emergence of autobiographical memory: A social cultural developmental theory. *Psychological Review, 111*, 486–511.

Orbach, Y., Hershkowitz, I., Lamb, M. E., Sternberg, K. J., Esplin, P. W., & Horowitz, D. (2000). Assessing the value of structured protocols for forensic interviews of alleged child abuse victims. *Child Abuse and Neglect*, *24*, 733–752.

Orbach, Y., Shiloach, H., & Lamb, M. E. (2007). Reluctant disclosers of child sexual abuse. In M. E. Pipe, M. E. Lamb, Y. Orbach, & A. C. Cederborg (Eds.), *Child sexual abuse: Disclosure, delay, and denial* (pp. 115–134). Mahwah, NJ: Lawrence Erlbaum Associates, Inc.

Ornstein, P. A., Merrit, K. A., Baker-Ward, L., Furtado, E., Gordon, B. N., & Principe, G. F. (1998). Children's knowledge, expectation, and long-term retention. *Applied Cognitive Psychology*, *12*, 387–405.

Peterson, C. (1996). The preschool child witness: Errors in accounts of traumatic injury. *Canadian Journal of Behavioral Science*, *28*, 36–42.

Peterson, C., & Bell, M. (1996). Children's memory for traumatic injury. *Child Development*, *67*, 3045–3070.

Peterson, C., Dowden, C., & Tobin, J. (1999). Interviewing preschoolers: Comparisons of yes/no and wh- questions. *Law and Human Behavior*, *23*, 539–555.

Peterson, C., & Rideout, R. (1998). Memory for medical emergencies experienced by 1- and 2-year-olds. *Developmental Psychology*, *34*, 1059–1072.

Peterson, C., & Whalen, N. (2001). Five years later: Children's memory for medical emergencies. *Applied Cognitive Psychology*, *15*, 7–24.

Pipe, M. E., Lamb, M. E., Orbach, Y., & Cederborg, A. C. (2007a). Seeking resolution in the disclosure wars: An overview. In M. E. Pipe, M. E. Lamb, Y. Orbach, & A. C. Cederborg (Eds.), *Child sexual abuse: Disclosure, delay, and denial* (pp. 1–10). Mahwah, NJ: Lawrence Erlbaum Associates, Inc.

Pipe, M. E., Lamb, M. E., Orbach, Y., & Cederborg, A. C. (Eds.) (2007b), *Child sexual abuse: Disclosure, delay, and denial*. Mahwah, NJ: Lawrence Erlbaum Associates, Inc.

Pipe, M. E., Lamb, M. E., Orbach, Y., Stewart, H. L., Sternberg, K. L., & Esplin, P. W. (2007c). Factors associated with nondisclosure of suspected abuse during forensic interviews. In M. E. Pipe, M. E. Lamb, Y. Orbach, & A. C. Cederborg (Eds.), *Child sexual abuse: Disclosure, delay, and denial* (pp. 77–96). Mahwah, NJ: Lawrence Erlbaum Associates, Inc.

Poole, D. A., & Lamb, M. E. (1998). *Investigative interviews of children: A guide for helping professionals*. Washington, DC: American Psychological Association.

Poole, D. A., & Lindsay, D. S. (1995). Interviewing preschoolers: Effects of non-suggestive techniques, parental coaching, and leading questions on reports of non-experienced events. *Journal of Experimental Child Psychology*, *60*, 129–154.

Powell, M. B., Jones, C. H., & Campbell, C. (2003). A comparison of preschoolers' recall of experienced versus non-experienced events across multiple interviewers. *Applied Cognitive Psychology*, *17*, 935–952.

Principe, G. F., & Ceci, S. J. (2002). "I saw it with my own ears": The influence of peer conversations and suggestive questions on preschoolers' event memory. *Journal of Experimental Child Psychology*, *83*, 1–25.

Principe, G. F., Giuliano, S., & Root, C. (2008). Rumor mongering and remembering: How rumors originating in children's inferences can affect memory. *Journal of Experimental Child Psychology*, *99*, 135–155.

Principe, G. F., Kanaya, T., Ceci, S. J., & Singh, M. (2006). Believing is seeing: How rumors can engender false memories in preschoolers. *Psychological Science*, *17*, 243–248.

Schreiber, N., Bellah, L. D., Martinez, Y., McLaurin, K. A., Strok, R., Garven, S., & Wood, J. M. (2006). Suggestive interviewing in the McMartin Preschool and Kelly Michaels daycare abuse cases: A case study. *Social Influence, 1*, 16–47.

Simcock, G., & Hayne, H. (2002). Breaking the barrier? Children fail to translate their preverbal memories into language. *Psychological Science, 13*, 225–231.

Sorensen, T., & Snow, B. (1991). How children tell: The process of disclosure of child sexual abuse. *Child Welfare, 70*, 3–15.

State of Calif. v. Buckey. 1990. Sup. Ct., Los Angeles County, #A750900.

State of North Dakota v. Art Tibor, ND 146 (N.D. 2007).

Sternberg, K. J., Lamb, M. E., Davies, G. M., & Westcott, H. L. (2001a). The memorandum of good practice: Theory versus application. *Child Abuse and Neglect, 25*, 669–681.

Sternberg, K. J., Lamb, M. E., Orbach, Y., & Esplin, P. W. (2001b). Use of a structured investigative protocol enhances young children's responses to free-recall prompts in the course of forensic interviews. *Journal of Applied Psychology, 86*, 997–1005.

Summit, R. C. (1983). The Child Sexual Abuse Accommodation Syndrome. *Child Abuse and Neglect, 7*, 177–193.

Summit, R. (1992). Abuse of the Child Sexual Abuse Accommodation Syndrome. *Journal of Child Sexual Abuse, 1*, 153–163.

Vrij, A. (2005). Criteria-based content analysis: A qualitative review of the first 37 studies. *Psychology, Public Policy, and Law, 11*, 3–41.

White, T. L., Leichtman, M. D., & Ceci, S. J. (1997). The good, the bad, and the ugly: Accuracy, inaccuracy, and elaboration in preschoolers' reports about a past event. *Applied Cognitive Psychology, 11*, S37–S54.

Zaragoza, M. S., Payment, K., Kichler, J., Stines, L., & Drivdahl, S. (2001). Forced confabulation and false memory in child witnesses. Paper presented at the 2001 biennial meeting of the Society for Research in Child Development, Minneapolis, MN.

6 Change blindness and eyewitness testimony

Cara Laney and Elizabeth F. Loftus

A group of young people participates in a protest that turns violent. A police officer sees a man wearing a blue hooded sweatshirt throw a brick, which ends up injuring a passer-by. The officer follows the man, but the man ducks behind a building, out of sight. A few seconds later, a man wearing a blue hooded sweatshirt emerges from the building. The officer identifies him as the same man who threw the brick and promptly arrests him. The man is put on trial in what prosecutors see as a cut-and-dried case. But the man protests his innocence, saying that he was merely leaving the building and that he didn't even know about the protest, let alone participate in it.

The presumed ability of the officer to see and then correctly identify the brick thrower is central to the prosecution's case, but the processes underlying these acts are far from simple. This chapter will focus on the kind of eyewitness testimony that is involved in a case like this. We focus on two related phenomena that until recently have not been connected to the eyewitness situation: change blindness (where significant changes in the visual world go unnoticed) and inattentional blindness (where entire objects, people, or events go unnoticed). As we point out, both of these have been studied for more than a decade in perceptual and cognitive psychology.

Change blindness has been an important area of study in visual perception and cognitive psychology since the early 1990s. Change blindness is said to occur when a significant change in the visual environment is not noticed. For example, in one early study, a man hears a phone ring from another room (Levin & Simons, 1997). The man stands up and leaves the room, then there is a change in camera angle to outside the room, and the man comes out of the room and answers the phone – except that this second "scene" is played by a different actor. Just 33% of the participants who watched this scenario noticed this change – even though the (apparently) single actor was the obvious focus of attention in the brief video. In typical studies of change blindness, these types of changes can be difficult for participants to detect, even when they are expecting to see a change.

A related phenomenon, inattentional blindness, has been defined as "the failure to see an unexpected object that one may be looking at directly when one's attention is elsewhere" (Koivisto & Revonsuo, 2007, p. 845).

Thus, rather than failing to notice a change in an object in the visual scene, people fail to notice a particular object or person altogether. In the classic study, participants watch as six people, some in black and some in white t-shirts, pass two basketballs as they weave amongst one another (Simons & Chabris, 1999). The participants are instructed to count how many times the white-shirted players pass their ball. Because they are concentrating on the white-shirted people, participants commonly fail to notice that a woman wearing a black gorilla costume walks into the middle of the group, beats her chest, and walks back out again. When not counting white-shirt passes, this event is by far the most attention-grabbing thing that happens during the video.

These studies, and others discussed below, demonstrate that *seeing*, that is, having images captured by our retinas, is very different from *perceiving* (Mack & Rock, 1998). Likewise, visual attention is also separate from visual awareness, and this can leave us largely blind to much of the visual world (Levin & Varakin, 2004). The particular role of attention in perceptual processes has been a major source of debate in perception research for decades (Mack & Rock, 1998; Rensink, 2002), and these debates are relevant to eyewitness testimony issues as well. Research in change blindness and inattentional blindness is particularly relevant.

These lapses in human perception have important implications for eyewitnesses. If people can fail to notice substantial changes in their visual environments, or fail to notice central actors or events at all, then we have yet more evidence that people are poor recorders of events, including crimes. Davies and Hine (2007) put the issues succinctly: "witnesses may confuse an offender seen entering a building with an innocent person seen leaving it later. Alternatively, witnesses could be convinced they had seen one offender at a crime scene when they had actually seen two different offenders successively" (p. 433).

And yet, change blindness and inattentional blindness are only just starting to be explored in an eyewitness testimony context. Just three studies (that we are aware of) have explicitly explored these well-studied cognitive and perceptual phenomena in contexts with obvious forensic relevance. All three of these studies will be discussed in some detail later in this chapter. But first we review the relevant paradigms in more depth.

We argue that the phenomena of change blindness and inattentional blindness should thus be added to the long list of potential sources of error in eyewitnesses (see Davis & Loftus, 2007; Wells & Olson, 2003). Further, we suggest that this research (both the few studies conducted at the intersection of the fields, and the change blindness and inattentional blindness work more generally) again demonstrates that eyewitness testimony has more credibility (particularly with jurors) than it perhaps deserves (e.g., Benton, Ross, Bradshaw, Thomas, & Bradshaw, 2006; Leippe, 1995).

CHANGE BLINDNESS

The phenomenon of change blindness has long been understood (and exploited) by filmmakers. Films contain a wide range of minor (and not so minor) errors that result from re-shoots, non-linear filming, and varying camera angles. These are called "continuity errors," and they are rarely noticed by viewers, particularly when they occur at the periphery of the main action (see Levin & Simons, 2000; Simons & Levin, 1997).

Psychological research into change blindness is a newer phenomenon. In particular, it is a relatively recent twist in a broader area of cognitive and perceptual psychology called "change detection," which has been studied for more than half a century (Rensink, 2002). Defined simply as "the appreciation of change in the world around us" (Rensink, 2002, p. 246), change detection is the study of how humans are able to process visual information about new changes in their visual worlds. These changes include the appearance of new people or objects in one's field of view and significant alterations in these objects or people. Change blindness, as a subfield, addresses changes that should be well within our detection abilities, but that are nonetheless missed.

A variety of methodologies have been used to study change blindness (Simons, 2000b; Simons & Levin, 1997), and we mention three important variants. The most basic methodology employs saccade-contingent changes (McConkie & Currie, 1996; Simons & Levin, 1997). When the human eye moves from one focal point to another in a saccade, new information is excluded from processing during the motion, to give us a sense of stability in the visual world. Some researchers have made use of this very short-term blindness by introducing changes to "stable" images during participants' saccades. Participants are warned that the images they are studying in preparation for a memory test might change as they are looking at them, but even so they miss these changes frequently (e.g., McConkie & Currie, 1996). Some researchers suggest, however, that these changes are in fact noticed, but only implicitly (Fernandez-Duque & Thornton, 2000; Ryan & Cohen, 2004). Other research suggests that a variety of cognitive factors, including centrality, meaningfulness of the images, visual imagery skill, and specific instructions given prior to the task can affect the likelihood of detecting a particular change (Pearson & Schaefer, 2005; Rodway, Gillies, & Schepman, 2006).

Generally it is relatively easy to notice a change if one looks at two photographs sitting side by side, but more difficult to notice differences between the two photographs if they are separated by a brief blank display. In the "flicker paradigm" (e.g., Rensink, O'Regan, & Clark, 1997, 2000) a blank display of a fraction of a second is presented between two matched photographs on a loop. Participants are told to expect a change, and then timed until they notice the change. This can take more than a minute, even when the changes are substantial (Simons, 2000b).

Humphreys, Hodsoll, and Campbell (2005) showed participants pictures of a group of four women, using the flicker paradigm. Two of the women were Indian and two were White. Changes in the Indian faces were detected more quickly by Indian participants, and changes in the White faces were detected more quickly by White participants. Thus this study provided an interesting spin on the cross-race identification effect, wherein people have more difficulty recognizing the faces of strangers of a different race than their own race (Malpass & Kravitz, 1969).

Jones, Jones, Blundell, and Bruce (2002) showed that participants' interest in the material they were viewing allowed them to detect changes in a flicker task more quickly. They showed social users of alcohol and marijuana photographs that were relevant to these categories. Each set of pictures had one change to an alcohol- or marijuana-relevant item, and one change to a substance-irrelevant item. Results showed that substance users (but not non-users) were quicker to notice the substance-relevant item than the substance-irrelevant item.

The saccade-dependent and flicker tasks are intentional tasks, meaning simply that participants are told to expect a change and are tasked with noticing when the change happens and what it is. Other change blindness tasks involve incidental encoding, meaning that participants are not told specifically that there will be a change, and are instead tested on whether they notice the change occurring at all (Simons, 2000b). As a rule, changes are easier to detect when they are expected, a phenomenon termed the change probability effect (Beck, Peterson, & Angelone, 2007b).

The third common methodology employs incidental encoding, and it is the most relevant to eyewitness testimony applications. It involves using film clips or real-life interactions rather than simple computer images or still photographs. These studies are more relevant to eyewitness testimony because they involve real, moving people. They demonstrate that, while changes are easier to miss when they occur at the periphery of one's view and to non-attended objects, they can also be missed when they happen to central, attended objects and people. We note, though, that in general the types of changes that are used in these experiments are relatively unlikely to occur outside of a carefully crafted experimental manipulation (or a film shoot). To borrow an example from the Levin and Simons (1997) study described above, real people do not normally change into different people as they get up to answer the phone.

Levin and Simons (1997) also described a second study in which two women had a conversation, lasting more than 30 seconds, about a surprise party one of them was planning. The video included nine separate changes to the positions and contents of items on the table in front of the women and to one woman's clothing. Ten participants watched the video, and on their first viewing, only one of the participants noticed a single change (and this participant was vague about what, exactly, this change had been).

In another study, Simons and Levin (1998, Experiment 2) went out into the real world to trick unsuspecting participants. They had an experimenter, dressed as a construction worker, approach students on a university campus and ask them for directions. After about 10–15 seconds, in which the participant interacted one-on-one with the experimenter, two confederates, also dressed as construction workers and carrying a door, rudely walked between the participant and the experimenter. As the door passed between the experimenter and participant, one of the two confederates switched places with the experimenter and then, after the door was out of the way, continued the conversation with the participant. Just 4 of the 12 participants in the study noticed that the original experimenter had been switched with another individual in the middle of their face-to-face interaction. Simons and Levin blamed this high level of change blindness on the differences between the "in group" of students and the "out group" of construction workers, thus suggesting that social factors could be important in change blindness. The findings have implications for crime witnesses, who are frequently not members of the same social circles as the perpetrators whose crimes they witness.

Also relevant to eyewitness testimony is the fact that, although change blindness errors are common, people tend to believe that they would be immune to these errors. According to Levin (2002), "in at least some situations visual experience is demonstrably not what people think it is" (p. 111). Levin, Momen, Drivdahl, and Simons (2000) described four different change blindness scenarios (from Levin & Simons, 1997; Simons & Levin, 1998) to undergraduates and showed them pictures of the relevant changes. They then asked participants whether they believed that they would have noticed the changes, had they been participants in these studies. Although 0% of participants had noticed any of the first three changes in the original studies, huge proportions (69.5% to 90.5%) of the new participants claimed that they would have noticed the changes. For the fourth described change, 97.6% of participants claimed they would have noticed it, compared to the 46% of participants who had actually noticed the change in the original study. Levin et al. termed this phenomenon "change blindness blindness" (see also Beck, Levin, & Angelone, 2007a; Levin, Drivdahl, Momen, & Beck, 2002a).

A further elegant study shows the power of the change blindness phenomenon (Levin, Simons, Angelone, & Chabris, 2002b, Experiment 1). Undergraduates were recruited from the lobby of the Harvard Psychology building to participate in a short experiment in exchange for candy. When participants arrived in the lab, they first briefly discussed what the study would involve with an experimenter standing behind a counter. Then they signed a consent form. The experimenter then ducked behind the counter on the pretence of picking up a packet of forms. This experimenter was then replaced by a second (similarly dressed but otherwise different looking) experimenter, who had been kneeling behind the desk. This second experimenter continued the conversation with the participant. Participants then completed a packet of forms assessing what they had noticed since they arrived in the lab. Just 5 of 20 participants detected the change of experimenters. It was later discovered that 6 of the 20 participants had inadvertently been recruited immediately following a meeting in which the Simons and Levin (1998) door study had been described. Of these 6 participants, just 2 noticed the change.

In another study, Levin et al. (2002b, Experiment 3) used a new task, in which passers-by were approached and asked to take a photograph of the (female) experimenter, who was replaced by a different woman as the photograph was composed. The photography task ensured that the participant got a good look at both experimenters, but 28% of participants still missed the change. Two four-photograph lineups, one for each of the two experimenters, were then shown to participants. Those participants who missed the change of experimenters performed at chance levels on both lineups (37% for the pre-change experimenter, 31% for the post-change experimenter), while those who detected the change performed significantly better than chance on both lineups (81% and 73%, respectively).

Relevance to eyewitness testimony

Although Levin et al. used lineups as an outcome measure in their studies, they did not draw connections to the eyewitness testimony literature, or suggest that their results had implications for legal psychology. Instead, their conclusions were linked to previous perceptual studies. Specifically, they concluded that change blindness is not always a result of a failure to compare the original and changed objects or people, but rather that it could instead be a function of "relatively ineffective or inaccessible representations of previously attended objects" (Levin et al., 2002b, p. 289).

But we argue that there are clear legal implications for this study.[1] If, instead of asking for directions or having their photographs taken, the actors in these experiments had committed crimes (perhaps especially minor, less emotionally charged crimes like petty theft or vandalism), the participant-witnesses might well have identified innocent individuals as perpetrators. In some ways, the Levin et al. lineups were conducted in ideal circumstances – immediately following the target event, with no time for forgetting or misinformation. Yet their participants still performed quite badly. If the lineups had been conducted in less ideal settings (like those typically associated with crime events), performance would likely have been even worse.

Eyewitness testimony is a huge field of study, encompassing such varied areas as perception and encoding of specific events and decision-making processes undertaken by jurors. But one of the most fundamental areas of eyewitness testimony is the identification of crime perpetrators. The relevant processes and resulting errors have been studied in myriad ways, by a large number of researchers (see Loftus, 1979; Wells & Olson, 2003).

Unconscious transference

A subfield of the identification literature that may be particularly relevant to change blindness studies like those described by Levin et al. (2002b) is that of a phenomenon termed "unconscious transference" (Brown, Deffenbacher, & Sturgill, 1977; Buckhout, 1974; Gorenstein & Ellsworth, 1980; Loftus, 1976). Unconscious transference has been defined as "the transfer of one person's identity to that of another person from a different setting, time, or context" (Read, Tollestrup, Hammersley, McFadzen, & Christensen, 1990, p. 3).

Some authors have argued that unconscious transference is particularly likely when two individuals are seen in close temporal and spatial proximity, but in such a way that one might assume that the two individuals are in fact a single person (Davis, Loftus, Vanous, & Cucciare, 2008; Levin & Simons, 2000). This has been termed an "illusion of continuity." This illusion occurs because human minds have expectations about how the world works, including expectations that motions are continuous (Levin & Simons, 2000). As a simple example, if we see an object moving toward an obstruction, and then that object disappears behind the obstruction, we expect that object to appear again on the other side of the obstruction after a reasonable delay. That is, we have the illusion of continuity of motion, even when there are gaps in the relevant visual information.

The phenomenon of unconscious transference has been studied for more than three decades, and has gained general acceptance among eyewitness researchers (Kassin, Ellsworth, & Smith, 1989; Kassin, Tubb, Hosch, & Memon, 2001). In two of the earliest studies, Buckhout (1974) and Loftus (1976) found support for the phenomenon, with substantial proportions of participants picking an innocent bystander rather than the perpetrator when both were presented in the same lineup. Loftus (1976) assumed that unconscious transference would be more likely if the culprit and the innocent bystander were seen at approximately the same time, which is of course relevant to studies of change blindness.

More recent research (Dysart, Lindsay, Hammond, & Dupuis, 2001; Geiselman, Haghighi, & Stown, 1996; Read et al., 1990; Ross, Ceci, Dunning, & Toglia, 1994) has suggested that unconscious transference occurs only in a relatively narrow range of circumstances, particularly where "bystanders are seen as familiar, but not so familiar that witnesses recall specific contextual cues that disambiguate them from the assailant" (Ross et al., 1994, p. 919). These conditions are particularly relevant to change blindness situations.

Consider one piece of unconscious transference research by Ross et al. (1994). In their first experiment, participants watched a video about preschool teaching in which a surprise last scene showed a theft from one teacher's wallet. For the experimental group, the culprit looked similar to one of the other teachers in the video, an innocent bystander. For the control group, this innocent bystander did not appear in the video. When both groups were shown a lineup that contained the bystander but not the culprit, the experimental group was about three times as likely to identify the bystander (61% versus 22%). When both the culprit and the bystander were present in the lineup, experimental participants were more likely to identify the culprit (53% compared to 18%), but they were still almost twice as likely to identify the bystander as control participants (18% versus 10%). Ross et al. concluded that their participants were making a *conscious inference* that the culprit and the bystander were the same person, but seen in two different contexts, and that this inference was made during or immediately after the encoding of the event. They also argued that "unconscious transference" was perhaps a misnomer. We note, however, that this sort of inference is much easier to make (and need not be conscious) in cases where there is an illusion of continuity (Levin & Simons, 2000).

Change blindness research is also relevant for another important aspect of eyewitness testimony research: misinformation (Loftus & Palmer, 1974; Loftus, Miller, & Burns, 1978). Because misinformation has not yet (to our knowledge) been studied using a change blindness paradigm, the crossover exists, for the time being, at the level of theoretical debate. In particular, the debates about the perceptual and memory phenomena underlying change blindness (see Simons, 2000b) bear a striking resemblance to the debates in eyewitness testimony over how memory is affected by misleading postevent information (see Saunders & MacLeod, 2002). Though the specific arguments are largely different, in both fields, these debates tackle issues about what happens to old information when new information conflicts with it. Is the old information replaced by the new information or combined with it (Loftus, 1979; Loftus et al., 1978)? Or are both pieces of information retained, but to differing degrees (Reyna & Lloyd, 1997)? Or are both pieces of information retained but then not compared to each other (McCloskey & Zaragoza, 1985; Simons, 2000b)?

INATTENTIONAL BLINDNESS

As previously noted, inattentional blindness is another important phenomenon studied by perceptual and cognitive psychologists (Mack, 2003; Mack & Rock, 1998; Simons, 2000a). It too has been studied using very simple visual arrays in highly controlled laboratory settings (e.g., Sinnett, Costa, & Soto-Faraco, 2006), as well as by exposing participants to more complex and lifelike visual situations. The classic study of the latter group was mentioned earlier. Simons and Chabris (1999) had participants count the number of passes of a basketball between actors, some of whom were wearing white shirts and some of whom were wearing black shirts, and this attention-consuming activity prevented their noticing either a woman with an umbrella or a woman dressed as a gorilla walking right through the middle of the action. Simons and Chabris argued that their results suggested that what we perceive are attended objects and events, rather than necessarily what is happening at the visual center of our view (but see Most, Simons, Scholl, & Chabris, 2000).

Interestingly, one study of inattentional blindness found that not seeing an object is not necessarily a result of not looking at that object. Memmert

(2006) tracked children's eye movements as they watched the gorilla video described above. Surprisingly, those children who failed to notice the gorilla had spent as much time looking at it (though apparently without perceiving it) as had those children who noticed the gorilla (about one second).

In a study using more basic visual stimuli (letters moving around a computer screen), Most et al. (2001) found that whether their participants noticed unexpected objects depended on how similar the new objects were to the ones they were attending, with more similar objects noticed more often. Koivisto and Revonsuo's (2007) findings were similar. They exposed participants to simple word and picture stimuli presented on a computer screen. They found that unexpected objects and particularly words were more likely to be seen when they were semantically related to the objects or words that their participants were consciously paying attention to. They argued that the meaning of visual stimuli thus affects their likelihood of being seen.

Research from the field of inattentional blindness has been applied in a variety of domains, from human–computer interaction (Pew, 2004), to defining legal terms in slip-and-fall cases (Campbell, 2006), to the decreases in driving safety that occur when drivers use cell phones (Strayer, Drews, & Johnston, 2003). Most, Scholl, Clifford, and Simons (2005) argued that inattentional blindness should be studied in parallel with a related phenomenon: attention capture. Attention capture is the study of what causes people to notice unexpected objects or events, that is, the inverse of inattentional blindness. They argue that these two literatures have largely failed to interact, though their research and findings mirror one another, with research from both fields suggesting that attentional goals matter more than other factors in determining whether unexpected events will be noticed.

Relevance to eyewitness testimony

Once again, we suggest another combination of related but non-interacting literatures. Research into inattentional blindness, like that into change blindness, could be combined with research into eyewitness testimony, to produce results that could be useful in the legal world. And yet, thus far the application of inattentional blindness to eyewitness testimony has been very limited.

An exception to this rule is a study conducted by Clifasefi, Takarangi, and Bergman (2006). Adult participants from a community sample were told either that they were drinking alcohol or that they were drinking an alcohol placebo (tonic alone), and this was either true or false (for a total of four conditions). Those participants who were given alcohol were given just enough to reach a blood alcohol level of 0.04 (half the common legal driving limit in the US). Data revealed that they believed what they were told, and that they reported feeling physical and cognitive impairment accordingly. After their drinks, participants were run through a modified version of Simons and Chabris' (1999) "gorilla" procedure.

In this study, just a third of all participants noticed the gorilla amongst the basketball players, but this inattentional blindness was made substantially worse by alcohol. The (only mildly) intoxicated participants noticed the gorilla only 18% of the time, relative to 46% of the time for sober participants. Being told that they had received alcohol was not enough to produce the effect, however, as 30% of those who were told they had drunk alcohol noticed the gorilla, compared to 33% of those told they had drunk only tonic.

Clifasefi et al. argue that their results have implications for the perception and memory of intoxicated witnesses (in addition to practical implications, such as legal alcohol limits for driving). In particular, these witnesses may be less likely to experience weapon focus (Pickel, 1999) because they may be slower to notice the weapon in their visual field. This effect could also explain some otherwise irrational driving behavior. If a small quantity of alcohol can cause drivers to fail to notice significant objects or events in their visual field, it can also be the cause of accidents that would not normally be attributed to alcohol. More broadly, these results support the proposition that even small quantities of alcohol alter witnesses' capabilities in the area of witnessing. This is a concern, because crime is often associated with alcohol consumption (Meissner, Sporer, & Schooler, 2007).

CROSS-PARADIGM RESEARCH

There has been, as of yet, very little research that has specifically combined the change blindness paradigm with eyewitness testimony methodology and applications. This is despite the fact that the two areas are often studying very similar phenomena, as we have argued above. To our knowledge, only three papers (including a total of five studies) have specifically used change blindness paradigms to explore their eyewitness testimony implications. These studies will be described here in somewhat more detail.

Davies and Hine (2007) sought explicitly to combine change blindness and eyewitness testimony paradigms, arguing that the work of these two fields had run in parallel for too long. They had 80 participants from a community sample watch a short video depicting a burglary. For all participants, the identity of the burglar changed halfway through the video. Before watching the video, half of the participants were told that they should expect a memory test after the video (intentional condition), while the other half were instead told that they were watching a safety video (incidental condition). Neither group was told that the identity of the burglar would change. The authors anticipated that the former group would demonstrate greater awareness of change and better memory than the latter group (and that these two factors would be associated). After the video, participants completed a questionnaire about its content, including whether they had noticed anything unusual about the burglar. Finally, participants were asked to pick the burglar from a lineup. The lineup contained both actors from the video, plus four foils.

Overall, 39% of participants noticed the change of actors, but almost all of these participants (26 of 31) were in the intentional condition. The participants who noticed the change did better on the subsequent lineup task, perhaps necessarily. Twenty of the 31 change detectors successfully picked both burglars from the lineup, and 9 more picked one of the burglars. By comparison, of the 49 participants who failed to notice the change, none picked both burglars out of the lineup, and 15 failed to pick out either burglar. The results for the memory test were similar, with change detectors performing significantly better than non-detectors, and those in the intentional condition performing particularly well. Davies and Hine conclude that the link between the eyewitness and change blindness literatures should be explored further, and that they had provided "another demonstration of the relatively poor accuracy eyewitnesses can show for unfamiliar people seen in brief encounters" (p. 433).

We note that everyday life (including much crime witnessing) is more like Davies and Hine's incidental condition than it is like their intentional condition. Crime witnesses are not explicitly warned that they may be tested later, and, like the incidental condition participants in this study (who no doubt quickly figured out that they were observing a burglary), they may not be able to adjust to the situation quickly enough to notice important aspects of the scene or perpetrator. And that which they do not notice, they cannot accurately report on later.

Davis et al. (2008) conducted three additional studies specifically assessing the eyewitness testimony implications of change blindness. They argue that one variety of unconscious transference could be explained as a type of change blindness. Specifically, they suggest that unconscious transference is likely when there is an illusion of continuity between the perpetrator and the innocent bystander.

Participants in all three studies (total $N = 578$) watched a video depicting several shoppers in a grocery store, one of whom committed a theft. Three of the shoppers are important to the studies' hypotheses. The "continuous innocent" was first seen browsing in the liquor section. She then passed behind a large stack of paper products, and, in what appeared to be one fluid motion, the perpetrator (rather than the innocent) emerged from behind the stack. Thus there was an illusion of continuity, suggesting that this innocent bystander and the perpetrator were the same person. The perpetrator then wandered in the liquor section, selected a bottle of wine from the shelf, and stashed it in her jacket. The next scene showed another bystander, the "discontinuous innocent," shopping in the produce section and selecting an orange. That is, there was no illusion of continuity between the perpetrator and this second innocent bystander. All three individuals were shown for the same amount of time, and appropriate counterbalancing measures were taken, such that the perpetrator did not look more similar to either innocent, overall.

In the first and third studies, all participants were asked to try to memorize items from the store shelves as they watched the videos. This was done to encourage shallow processing of the people in the video and thus to increase the likelihood of change blindness. In the second study, half of participants engaged in this distracting task and half did not, but all were asked to report on items from the shelves. At the end of the procedures, all participants were given a six-person perpetrator-absent lineup and asked whether the perpetrator was in the lineup, and if so, in which position. For the first two studies, this lineup contained both the continuous innocent and the discontinuous innocent. For the third study, half of participants saw the continuous innocent and five foils, while the other half saw the discontinuous innocent and five foils. Participants were also asked what role each individual had played in the video, to assess whether they had noticed the change.

Across the three studies, between 60% and 68% of participants failed to notice the change between the continuous innocent and the perpetrator. In the second study, those given the distraction task (memorizing items on the store shelves) were less likely to notice the change (20%) than those not given the task (46%). Across the studies, between 71% and 75% of participants identified someone from the perpetrator-absent lineup. False identifications were thus quite common, but they were particularly likely in those who failed to detect change (75–79%, relative to 65–66% for those who noticed the change). In all three studies, the continuous innocent was disproportionately likely to be falsely identified by those who failed to detect the change. Among those who did notice the change, the discontinuous innocent was particularly likely to be falsely identified. Both of these failures are types of unconscious transference.

Davis et al. conclude that their results suggest that unconscious transference results from shallow processing resulting in increased familiarity but not improved memory, and from the witnesses assuming that the perpetrator and the innocent are the same person because of incomplete representations of the individuals they viewed. They further argued that, as demonstrated in numerous other studies of change blindness, adequate attention is crucial for adequate processing of events and thus accurate memory for those events. Davis et al. argue, with reference to the change blindness literature (Levin et al., 2000; Levin et al., 2002b), against the suggestion made by some judges (see Levin, 2002) that change blindness and inattentional blindness are not issues worthy of expert testimony because jurors are already aware of these issues.

The implications of this set of studies for the wider area of eyewitness testimony are clear. If there is reason to believe that witnesses may not have deeply processed the important information from the events they witnessed, there is reason to question the accuracy of these witnesses' subsequent decisions (e.g., in lineups) and their broader memory for the events. In addition, if there were innocent bystanders present when a particular crime was witnessed, then there is a danger that those bystanders could be falsely identified as perpetrators by eyewitnesses.

One final study used a variation on the unconscious transference theme and included a crime severity manipulation (Nelson et al., 2009). These researchers showed more than 700 undergraduate participants one of four different versions of a video of one student stealing money from another student. The thief stole either $5 or $500, tucked it into a book, and left the room. The next shot shows the thief walking down a hallway and around a corner. The change happens at the corner. For experimental participants, another similar-looking student (an innocent bystander), also carrying a book, replaces the thief. For control participants, the same student continues around the corner and is visible for a few extra seconds.

After watching the video and completing a set of individual difference measures, participants were asked to type out everything that they could remember from the video, and then were asked specifically how many people were in the video and what each person did. After they answered the questions, participants were given a six-person lineup that included both the perpetrator and the innocent bystander. Finally, participants were asked questions designed to probe whether they had noticed the change of actors.

In this study, very few experimental participants (4.5%) noticed the change of actors. We note that this contradicts a hypothesis laid out by Davis et al. that change blindness would be less likely if the crime were presented before the change of actors. The small number of individuals who noticed the change precluded statistical comparison of change detectors and non-detectors, but a variety of other comparisons were possible.

Nelson et al. found that participants who were exposed to a change of actors (experimental participants) were much less likely to correctly identify the perpetrator (36%) than those not exposed to the change (controls; 64%). Part of this difference may be attributable to the longer exposure time of the controls to the perpetrator. But we note that neither of the previously described studies (Davies & Hine, 2007; Davis et al., 2008) had a control condition at all. Within the experimental condition of the Nelson et al. study, participants were as likely to select the innocent bystander from the lineup (35%) as the true perpetrator (36%). This again demonstrates that being an innocent bystander at a crime scene can be risky.

The crime severity manipulation had a small effect on identification accuracy, such that those participants who saw more money stolen were somewhat more likely to correctly identify the perpetrator (51%) than those who saw less money stolen (46%). This difference did not reach statistical significance, however.

None of the studies described here represents a perfect test of the potential implications of change blindness for eyewitness testimony, but each makes a useful contribution. The study by Davies and Hine (2007) demonstrates that the expectation of having to remember a crime event later can improve identification accuracy, but not expecting to be tested can make for sloppy witnessing, including the possibility of identifying two separate perpetrators as a single person. The set of studies by Davis et al. (2008) shows that being an innocent bystander at a crime scene can lead to one being falsely identified as a perpetrator, especially if the bystander can be mistaken for the same person as the perpetrator and witnesses are paying insufficient attention. The Nelson et al. (2009) study provides further evidence that witnesses, including those who already know that a crime has taken place, can be utterly oblivious to a change of identity, and thus end up identifying the wrong person as the culprit.

CONCLUSIONS

Together these studies suggest that the intersection of change blindness (and inattentional blindness) and eyewitness testimony is an important area of study that can yield useful conclusions with important real-world implications. But there is a great need for additional research into this new field. Many questions remain unanswered, including the effects of various characteristics of the perpetrator, witnesses, and crime. The interaction between change blindness and the misinformation effect is another substantial area for study in which no research has yet been done. Likewise, the whole related field of inattentional blindness remains to be studied thoroughly in an eyewitness testimony context.

At this point in time, we can only speculate that there are likely to be complex interactions between various suspect factors and witness factors that should be reflected in instances of eyewitness change blindness. For example, the cross-race identification effect, described above, may make it particularly difficult for witnesses to notice changes between perpetrators and innocent bystanders of a different race from themselves. Likewise, disguises used by perpetrators (see Cutler, Penrod, & Martens, 1987) may make change blindness particularly likely to occur. Characteristics that tend to make individuals poorer witnesses, or events more difficult to witness, may also interact with change blindness to make correct identification less likely. For example, old age (Pozzulo & Lindsay, 1998), insufficient attention (Schacter, 2001), and extreme stress (Deffenbacher, Bornstein, Penrod, & McGorty, 2004) can all make witnesses less reliable, and may all interact with change blindness to produce even poorer identifications.

Note

1 We note that Debbie Davis, University of Nevada, Reno, was an early proponent of the potential eyewitness testimony implications of change blindness research.

References

Beck, M. R., Levin, D. T., & Angelone, B. (2007a). Change blindness blindness: Beliefs about the roles of intention and scene complexity in change detection. *Consciousness and Cognition, 16*, 31–51.

Beck, M. R., Peterson, M. S., & Angelone, B. L. (2007b). The role of encoding, retrieval, and awareness in change detection. *Memory and Cognition, 35*, 610–620.

Benton, T. R., Ross, D. F., Bradshaw, E., Thomas, W. N., & Bradshaw, G. S. (2006). Eyewitness memory is still not common sense: Comparing jurors, judges and law enforcement to eyewitness experts. *Applied Cognitive Psychology, 20*, 115–129.

Brown, E. L., Deffenbacher, K. A., & Sturgill, W. (1977). Memory for faces and the circumstances of encounter. *Journal of Applied Psychology, 62*, 311–318.

Buckhout, R. (1974). Eyewitness testimony. *Scientific American, 231*, 23–31.

Campbell, T. W. (2006). Open and obvious under what conditions? *American Journal of Forensic Psychology, 24*, 23–32.

Clifasefi, S. L., Takarangi, M. K., & Bergman, J. S. (2006). Blind drunk: The effects of alcohol on inattentional blindness. *Applied Cognitive Psychology, 20*, 697–704.

Cutler, B. L., Penrod, S. D., & Martens, T. K. (1987). The reliability of eyewitness identification: The role of system and estimator variables. *Law and Human Behavior, 11*, 233–258.

Davies, G., & Hine, S. (2007). Change blindness and eyewitness testimony. *Journal of Psychology: Interdisciplinary and Applied, 14*, 423–434.

Davis, D., & Loftus, E. F. (2007) Internal and external sources of misinformation in adult witness memory. In M. P. Toglia, J. D. Read, D. F. Ross, & R. C. L. Lindsay (Eds.), *The handbook of eyewitness psychology: Volume I. Memory for events* (pp. 195–237). Mahwah, NJ: Lawrence Erlbaum Associates, Inc.

Davis, D., Loftus, E. F., Vanous, S., & Cucciare, M. (2008). "Unconscious transference" can be an instance of "change blindness." *Applied Cognitive Psychology, 22*, 605–623.

Deffenbacher, K. A., Bornstein, B. H., Penrod, S. D., & McGorty, E. K. (2004). A meta-analytic review of the effects of high stress on eyewitness memory. *Law and Human Behavior, 28*, 687–706.

Dysart, J. E., Lindsay, R. C. L., Hammond, R., & Dupuis, P. (2001). Mug shot exposure prior to lineup identification: Interference, transference, and commitment effects. *Journal of Applied Psychology, 86*, 1280–1284.

Fernandez-Duque, D., & Thornton, I. M. (2000). Change detection without awareness: Do explicit reports underestimate the representation of change in the visual system? *Visual Cognition, 7*, 323–344.

Geiselman, R. E., Haghighi, D., & Stown, R. (1996). Unconscious transference and the characteristics of accurate and inaccurate eyewitnesses. *Psychology, Crime, and Law, 2*, 197–209.

Gorenstein, G. W., & Ellsworth, P. C. (1980). Effect of choosing an incorrect photograph of a later identification by an eyewitness. *Journal of Applied Psychology, 65*, 616–622.

Humphreys, G. W., Hodsoll, J., & Campbell, C. (2005). Attending but not seeing: The "other race" effect in person perception studied through change blindness. *Visual Cognition, 12*, 249–262.

Jones, B. C., Jones, B. T., Blundell, L., & Bruce, G. (2002). Social users of alcohol and cannabis who detect substance-related changes in a change blindness paradigm report higher levels of use than those detecting substance-neutral changes. *Psychopharmacology, 165*, 93–96.

Kassin, S. M., Ellsworth, P. C., & Smith, V. L. (1989). The "general acceptance" of psychological research on eyewitness testimony. *American Psychologist, 44*, 1089–1098.

Kassin, S. M., Tubb, V. A., Hosch, H. M., & Memon, A. (2001). On the "general acceptance" of eyewitness testimony research. *American Psychologist, 56,* 405–416.

Koivisto, M., & Revonsuo, A. (2007). How meaning shapes seeing. *Psychological Science, 18,* 845–849.

Leippe, M. R. (1995). The case for expert testimony about eyewitness memory. *Psychology, Public Policy, and Law, 1,* 909–959.

Levin, D. T. (2002). Change blindness blindness as visual metacognition. *Journal of Consciousness Studies, 9,* 111–130.

Levin, D. T., Drivdahl, S. B., Momen, N., & Beck, M. R. (2002a). False predictions about the detectability of visual changes: The role of beliefs about attention, memory, and the continuity of attended objects in causing change blindness blindness. *Concsiousness and Cognition, 11,* 507–527.

Levin, D. T., Momen, N., Drivdahl, S. B., & Simons, D. J. (2000). Change blindness blindness: The metacognitive error of overestimating change-detection ability. *Visual Cognition, 7,* 397–412.

Levin, D. T., & Simons, D. J. (1997). Failure to detect changes to attended objects in motion pictures. *Psychonomic Bulletin and Review, 4,* 501–506.

Levin, D. T., & Simons, D. J. (2000). Perceiving stability in a changing world: Combining shots and integrating views in motion pictures and the real world. *Media Psychology, 2,* 357–380.

Levin, D. T., Simons, D. J., Angelone, B. L., & Chabris, C. F. (2002b). Memory for centrally attended changing objects in an incidental real-world change detection paradigm. *British Journal of Psychology, 93,* 289–302.

Levin, D. T., & Varakin, D. A. (2004). No pause for a brief disruption: Failures of visual awareness during ongoing events. *Consciousness and Cognition, 13,* 363–372.

Loftus, E. F. (1976). Unconscious transference. *Law and Psychology Review, 2,* 93–98.

Loftus, E. F. (1979). *Eyewitness testimony.* Cambridge, MA: Harvard University Press.

Loftus, E. F., Miller, D. G., & Burns, H. J. (1978). Semantic integration of verbal information into a visual memory. *Journal of Experimental Psychology: Human Learning and Memory, 4,* 19–31.

Loftus, E. F., & Palmer, J. C. (1974). Reconstruction of automobile destruction: An example of interaction between language and memory. *Journal of Verbal Learning and Verbal Behavior, 13,* 585–589.

McCloskey, M., & Zaragoza, M. (1985). Misleading postevent information and memory for events: Arguments and evidence against memory impairment hypotheses. *Journal of Experimental Psychology: General, 114,* 1–16.

McConkie, G. W., & Currie, C. B. (1996). Visual stability across saccades while viewing complex pictures. *Journal of Experimental Psychology: Human Perception and Performance, 22,* 563–581.

Mack, A. (2003). Inattentional blindness: Looking without seeing. *Current Directions in Psychological Science, 12,* 180–184.

Mack, A., & Rock, I. (1998). *Inattentional blindness.* Cambridge, MA: MIT Press.

Malpass, R. S., & Kravitz, J. (1969). Recognition for faces of own and other race. *Journal of Personality and Social Psychology, 13,* 330–334.

Meissner, C. A., Sporer, S. L., & Schooler, J. W. (2007). Person descriptions as eyewitness evidence. In M. P. Toglia, J. D. Read, D. F. Ross, & R. C. L. Lindsay (Eds.), *The handbook of eyewitness psychology: Volume II. Memory for people* (pp. 3–34). Hove: Lawrence Erlbaum Associates Ltd.

Memmert, D. (2006). The effects of eye movements, age, and expertise on inattentional blindness. *Consciousness and Cognition, 15,* 620–627.

Most, S. B., Scholl, B. J., Clifford, E. R., & Simons, D. J. (2005). What you see is what you set: Sustained inattentional blindness and the capture of awareness. *Psychological Review, 112,* 217–242.

Most, S. B., Simons, D. J., Scholl, B. J., & Chabris, C. F. (2000). Sustained inattentional blindness: The role of location in the detection of unexpected dynamic events. *Psyche, 6.* http://psyche.cs.monash.edu.au/v6/psyche-6-14-most.html

Most, S. B., Simons, D. J., Scholl, B. J., Jimenez, R., Clifford, E., & Chabris, C. F. (2001). How not to be seen: The contribution of similarity and selective ignoring to sustained inattentional blindness. *Psychological Science, 12,* 9–17.

Nelson, K. J., Laney, C., Le, A. J., Bowman Fowler, N., Loftus, E. F., Knowles, E. D., & Davis, D. (2009). Change blindness can cause mistaken eyewitness identification. Manuscript unpublished.

Pearson, P. M., & Schaefer, E. G. (2005). Toupee or not toupee? The role of instructional set, centrality, and relevance in change blindness. *Visual Cognition, 12,* 1528–1543.

Pew, R. W. (2004). Introduction to this special section on change blindness. *Human–Computer Interaction, 19,* 387–388.

Pickel, K. L. (1999). The influence of context on the "weapon focus" effect. *Law and Human Behavior, 23,* 299–311.

Pozzulo, J. D., & Lindsay, R. C. L. (1998). Identification accuracy of children versus adults: A meta-analysis. *Law and Human Behavior, 22,* 549–570.

Read, J. D., Tollestrup, P., Hammersley, R., McFadzen, E., & Christensen, A. (1990). The unconscious transference effect: Are innocent bystanders ever misidentified? *Applied Cognitive Psychology, 4,* 3–31.

Rensink, R. A. (2002). Change detection. *Annual Review of Psychology, 53,* 245–277.

Rensink, R. A., O'Regan, J. K., & Clark, J. J. (1997). To see or not to see: The need for attention to perceive changes in scenes. *Psychological Science, 8,* 368–373.

Rensink, R. A., O'Regan, J. K., & Clark, J. J. (2000). On the failure to detect changes in scenes across brief interruptions. *Visual Cognition, 7,* 127–145.

Reyna, V. F., & Lloyd, F. (1997). Theories of false memories in children and adults. *Learning and Individual Differences, 9,* 95–123.

Rodway, P., Gillies, K., & Schepman, A. (2006). Vivid imagers are better at detecting salient changes. *Journal of Individual Differences, 27,* 218–228.

Ross, D. F., Ceci, S. J., Dunning, D., & Toglia, M. P. (1994). Unconscious transference and mistaken identity: When a witness misidentifies a familiar but innocent person. *Journal of Applied Psychology, 79,* 918–930.

Ryan, J. D., & Cohen, N. J. (2004). The nature of change detection and online representations of scenes. *Journal of Experimental Psychology: Human Perception and Performance, 30,* 988–1015.

Saunders, J., & MacLeod, M. D. (2002). New evidence on the suggestibility of memory: The role of retrieval-induced forgetting in misinformation effects. *Journal of Experimental Psychology: Applied, 8,* 127–142.

Schacter, D. L. (2001). *The seven sins of memory: How the mind forgets and remembers.* New York: Houghton Mifflin.

Simons, D. J. (2000a). Attentional capture and inattentional blindness. *Trends in Cognitive Sciences, 4,* 147–155.

Simons, D. J. (2000b). Current approaches to change blindness. *Visual Cognition, 7,* 1–15.

Simons, D. J., & Chabris, C. F. (1999). Gorillas in our midst: Sustained inattentional blindness for dynamic events. *Perception, 28,* 1059–1074.

Simons, D. J., & Levin, D. R. (1997). Change blindness. *Trends in Cognitive Sciences, 1,* 261–267.

Simons, D. J., & Levin, D. R. (1998). Failure to detect changes to people during a real-world interaction. *Psychonomic Bulletin and Review, 5,* 644–649.

Sinnett, S., Costa, A., & Soto-Faraco, S. (2006). Manipulating inattentional blindness within and across sensory modalities. *Quarterly Journal of Experimental Psychology, 59,* 1425–1442.

Strayer, D. L., Drews, F. A., & Johnston, W. (2003). Cell phone-induced failures of visual attention during simulated driving. *Journal of Experimental Psychology: Applied, 9,* 23–32.

Wells, G. L. & Olson, E. (2003). Eyewitness testimony. *Annual Review of Psychology, 54,* 277–295.

Applications to neuroscience

It is like a tale of gothic fiction. Electrical impulses fluctuate across a web of biological matter. As the pulsation increases the creature awakes, and nowadays rather than terrorize the villagers he turns on an MP3 player and starts text messaging. Modern neuroscience has advanced beyond those studies which may have inspired Shelley. Studies of brain-damaged people, like HM (Corkin, 2002), have helped to identify locations necessary for specific cognitive functions. Modern versions of phrenology have mapped brain areas to functions, and cognitive theories have specified how these different areas may interact (Fodor, 1983). Biologically inspired models, like some forms of connectionism, have found success in predicting many behaviors (McClelland, Rumelhart, & the PDP Research Group, 1986). Due to advances in technology we are even beginning to understand how systematic patterns in these pulses relate to cognition (Anderson, 2007). George Bush Senior declared that the 1990s were the Decade of the Brain, emphasizing how many technologies and theories are coming together and helping to inform some of the big questions in human inquiry.

Memory is one of those big questions. Most of the readers of this book are not interested in neuroscience per se, but rather applied memory research. All memory researchers realize that memory phenomena occur with (and are causally related to) brain activity, but we often step back from biological models and think in terms of boxes, arrows, and mental symbols being manipulated. In this section of the book the authors step toward the biological models and show how this knowledge can be important for applied memory.

Wang's chapter explores a frightening aspect of some surgeries. Sometimes when people are under anesthesia they still experience excruciating pain. There are also examples where people have implicit memory for events that occurred, but lack the recollective experience. These findings are important for cognitive psychologists interested in the implicit/explicit distinction in memory and the biological bases for this disorder. Importantly from an applied perspective, Wang charts the history of this research. Because of the early research, the anesthetic methods have been changed and nowadays it is much less likely that a person under anesthesia will experience pain. A theme of this and the next two chapters is how having a model of how the brain may work adds further understanding to our cognitive models and can also help with applied concerns.

In the section's second chapter, Christman and Propper underline the fact that the brain is not a single unitary object, but two "brains" connected in a few places, with the main channel of sharing information being the corpus callosum. They have taken a simple behavioral measure, the Edinburgh Handedness Scale, that previously had been used to differentiate right- and left-handed people, and twisted it around to measure extreme versus mixed-handedness. They argue that mixed-handed people have better callosally mediated interhemispheric communication and in their chapter discuss a series of studies showing how this relates to different types of memory including topics of applied interest like false memories. Further, they show a method (involving the induction of alternating leftward–rightward eye movements) that appears to grease the gears, allowing for efficient interhemispheric communication, and illustrate this with a further series of studies. This method is an important component of a popular therapy for patients with post-traumatic stress disorder, but as yet lacks a convincing explanation for why it may work. Their twist of a short behavioral measure, coupled with interest in neuropsychology, produced one of the most exciting series of studies of memory in recent years and one with potentially great applied importance.

In the section's final chapter, Moulin and Chauvel take century-old notions of déjà vu from James (1890) and others and show how this has been incorporated into popular culture. They then look at the concept using methods from neuropsychology and analog studies in experimental psychology. Déjà vu is one of those exciting topics that can seem more in the realm of fiction than what scientists should study. In fact, Moulin and Chauvel talk about how some of the emails they receive state that they should keep their scientific methods away from this exciting phenomenon. As scientists, though, they see an exciting phenomenon and know that scientific exploration is only likely to increase the excitement (at least to those more trusting of science than mysticism). Moulin and Chauvel show how déjà vu can be seen as a memory phenomenon and one which offers unique insight into normal brain/mind function. Unfortunately some people experience déjà vu often and these episodes can be extremely disturbing. From this perspective, it is a phenomenon that should not be left to the mystics (they have had millennia to do something to help these people), and it is time for applied memory researchers to explore this with all of our methodological tools.

References

Anderson, J. R. (2007). *How can the human mind occur in the physical universe?* Oxford, UK: Oxford University Press.

Corkin, S. (2002). What's new with the amnesiac patient H.M.? *Nature Reviews Neuroscience, 3*, 153–160.

Fodor, J. (1983) *The modularity of mind.* Cambridge, MA: MIT Press.
James, W. (1890). *The principles of psychology.* Cambridge, MA: Harvard University Press.
McClelland, J. L., Rumelhart, D. E., & the PDP Research Group (1986). *Parallel distributed processing: Explorations in the microstructure of cognition. Vol. 2: Psychological and biological models.* Cambridge, MA: MIT Press.

7 Implicit memory, anesthesia and sedation

Michael Wang

The recent history of anesthesia and implicit memory begins with a young South African trainee anesthetist called Bernie Levinson who was working in London in the late 1950s. He was shocked at the pejorative remarks made by surgical staff about the patients lying apparently unconscious on the operating theater table. Levinson was convinced that these remarks must be processed in the anesthetized brain at some level and that they must have had a detrimental effect. He then set about attempting to prove this through an experiment which, these days, would not get past a hospital ethics committee. Using ten dental surgery patients, he role-played a fictitious anesthetic crisis. After administering the induction anesthetic and allowing the surgeon to begin, he shouted "Stop the operation, I don't like the patient's color. His/her lips are turning too blue. I'm going to give a little oxygen." He then waited one minute and then said to the surgeon "OK, everything is fine now." One month later he interviewed the patients and hypnotized them, and gave instructions designed to "regress" them back to the time of the operation.

Four of the patients repeated verbatim the words Levinson had used to indicate the manufactured anesthetic crisis and a further four became distressed at the appropriate point in the re-lived operation. While this experiment had no control group, was not blinded, and Levinson himself both delivered the "crisis" information and conducted the hypnotic regression follow-up, the brief report of the experiment in the *British Journal of Anaesthesia* (Levinson, 1965) had profound and far-reaching effects, not to mention excitement. Cognitive psychologists and anesthetists alike were impressed with these findings and this prompted worldwide interest in investigating implicit memory in anesthesia.

Throughout the 1970s and 1980s anesthetists and psychologists tried to implant positive suggestions about the course of recovery in the hope that this might somehow unconsciously influence somatic processes. A couple of studies tried to use intra-operative suggestion to stop patients from smoking post-operatively. Cognitive psychologists began to employ implicit memory paradigms borrowed from memory research into dense amnestic syndromes, in which specially selected words were presented to patients during surgery under general anesthesia to demonstrate *priming effects* – although patients have no post-operative explicit recall of these words, enhanced retrieval can be demonstrated through implicit memory probes (see below).

Initially, results seemed extremely promising with many significant findings under rigorous, controlled, double-blinded conditions. By the 1990s, however, many attempts to replicate such phenomena met with failure – rather reminiscent of the earlier sleep learning studies of the 1970s (Figure 7.1). Psychologists were compelled to use increasingly sensitive tests of implicit memory to demonstrate what now appeared to be an ephemeral phenomenon, despite the outcomes of the earlier studies. What could have happened? Why had what had seemed such robust and remarkable implicit memory phenomena apparently evaporated? In fact, what had changed was not so much the methodology or implicit memory concept, but rather, the nature of general anesthesia. In order to understand this, we need to examine what constitutes general anesthesia, how it is administered and how it has changed.

The nature of anesthesia

Psychologists had assumed that the state of anesthesia represented unitary and reliable unconsciousness (Figure 7.2); however, as we shall see, this turned out to be naïve and quite simply wrong.

General anesthesia typically involves two distinct, successive phases and three independent components. In the first phase, known as induction, the patient is given a relatively short-acting anesthetic (10 to 20 minutes). Typically the patient is intubated: a tube is introduced through the mouth past the larynx and into the trachea. This is necessary especially when muscle relaxants are to be used (see below) and the patient consequently needs to be mechanically ventilated because the diaphragm and intercostal muscles will be paralyzed by the drug. A short-acting muscle relaxant lasting about

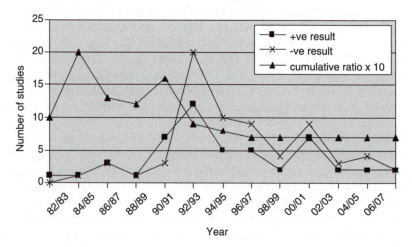

Figure 7.1 The outcome of implicit memory studies over time.

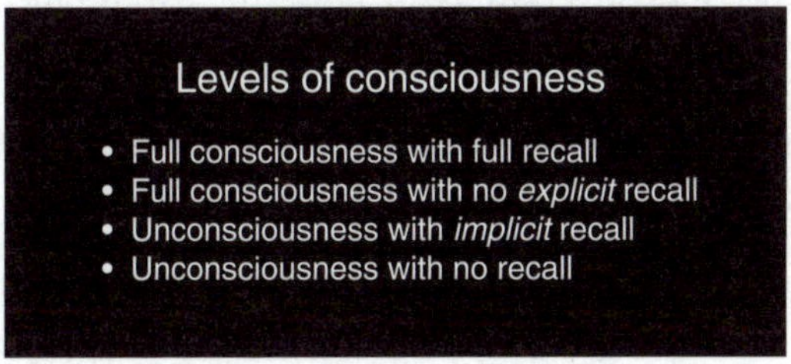

Levels of consciousness

- Full consciousness with full recall
- Full consciousness with no *explicit* recall
- Unconsciousness with *implicit* recall
- Unconsciousness with no recall

Figure 7.2 Assumed model of anesthetic cognitive states.

10 minutes is often administered at this point to aid the process of intubation. The patient may also be prepared for surgery at this stage by use of topical sterilization of the skin where the initial incision will be made and the placing of protective drapes. In the second stage, known as the maintenance phase, another anesthetic is introduced which will be longer acting and will be the mainstay for keeping the patient unconscious during the operation itself. With some anesthetic techniques, the same anesthetic drugs will be administered continuously for both induction and maintenance phases, e.g., using halothane gas, or propofol (liquid) in a total intravenous anesthesia technique (TIVA) using a syringe pump.

Up until the 1990s, it was very common in Europe and the UK for anesthetic maintenance phase techniques involving nitrous oxide ("laughing gas") plus oxygen along with an opioid (morphine-related) drug to be employed. During the late 1980s and early 1990s it was increasingly apparent that this technique did not ensure surgical oblivion for the patient to the extent it should. This coincided with the advent and widespread use of what are known as volatile agents: liquids akin to ether that could be vaporized and in gaseous phase, breathed in and absorbed into the bloodstream through the lining of the lung. By the mid 1990s, only a minority of anesthetists were making regular use of the old nitrous oxide/oxygen/opioid techniques and most had adopted volatile anesthetics for the maintenance phase. Some were also beginning to use total intravenous anesthesia in which drugs that hitherto might have been used just for the induction phase are pumped continuously into the bloodstream using sophisticated microchip computer-controlled infusion pumps which maintain set anesthetic concentrations in the blood. These historical changes in anesthetic practice are crucial in understanding what has transpired with regard to the history of implicit memory studies.

The three independent components of a typical general anesthetic are:

- a substance designed to induce hypnosis or loss of consciousness;
- an analgesic to pre-empt pain and the physiological stress reaction; and
- a muscle relaxant.

As stated earlier, muscle relaxants are powerful, paralyzing drugs which are necessary to facilitate surgery. Delicate surgical maneuvers could be easily compromised by bodily movement by the patient; also, if the surgeon needs to cut through muscle (as, for example, in abdominal surgery), taut, tense muscles will cause tearing, impairing good wound healing. Both of these problems are solved by muscle relaxants. Muscle relaxants also facilitate surgical access through the abdomen. However, because the three anesthetic components are independent, it is perfectly possible for the patient to receive inadequate doses of hypnotic and analgesic, but adequate doses of muscle relaxant, creating the horrific circumstance of anesthetic awareness in which the patient is conscious and in pain, but unable to move or indicate their predicament.

ASSESSING CONSCIOUSNESS DURING OPERATIONS

The isolated forearm technique

During the late 1980s Dr Ian Russell and the author began using the isolated forearm technique (IFT) as an aid to the investigation of cognitive and memory processes during general anesthesia.

Tunstall (1977) had first described the basic technique in the context of cesarean section. Russell (1989) subsequently modified the technique to allow for its general use and for extended periods of surgery and anesthesia. The concept is simple: a pneumatic tourniquet is placed on the forearm and inflated just before administration of the muscle relaxant. This preserves the forearm and hand from muscle paralysis and allows the patient to move her hand in response to command if her level of consciousness is sufficient to allow for this. A Walkman tape or mini disc player can then be used to present instructions to move the unparalyzed hand if the patient is able to process the information (Figure 7.3). It has been found to be important to include the patient's first or familiar name at the beginning of the command to draw the patient's attention and to ensure that there is no confusion regarding to whom the instructions are intended.

When Russell and Wang first started to use this technique, they were surprised to discover that as many as half of the patients on a typical operating list using a nitrous oxide/oxygen/opioid technique would respond sensibly to command (verified by further spoken commands). Interestingly, however, hardly any of these patients had post-operative recall. This has led to the erroneous conclusion by many anesthetists that the IFT "does not work." Cognitive psychologists, with a more sophisticated understanding of the nature of memory processes, will recognize that what is happening is that the encoding phase of memory is being compromised by anesthetic drugs (Richardson, 1989). So patients are certainly in a sufficiently high state of consciousness to assimilate, comprehend, and respond to motor command, but such conscious experience is not being registered in accessible explicit

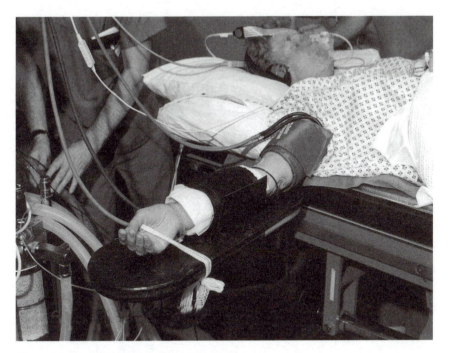

Figure 7.3 The isolated forearm technique.

long-term memory. Tunstall labeled this state as "wakefulness" in contra-distinction to "awareness" in which there is full explicit recall of intra-operative events. Russell and Wang's identification of the frequency of wakefulness with nitrous oxide/oxygen/opioid techniques caused them to suspect that many of the early positive implicit memory results in anesthetic studies were due to patients who had in fact been wakeful during stimulus presentation, but whose explicit recall had been obliterated by anesthetic drugs (albeit at sub-anesthetic dose).

No attempt had been made in these early studies to assess hypnotic depth: researchers had rather made the assumption that patients were truly uncon-scious. Subsequent experience using the IFT with the more modern volatile agents demonstrated that these states of wakefulness were now much less common, and this suggested to Wang and Russell the reason for the failure to replicate in later studies. Russell and Wang went on to demonstrate in a series of studies that if word stimuli are presented to patients while being moni-tored with the IFT and in the absence of IFT responses, no implicit priming is found, even if a series of implicit memory probes for the same word stimuli are used, magnifying the likelihood of type 1 error. Wang has developed a classification of progressive states of anesthetic awareness based on the identification of intra-operative state (response to command) and subsequent post-operative memory conditions (Table 7.1).

Table 7.1 A classification of anesthetic awareness states based on intra-operative, immediate, and late post-operative conditions

Grade	Intra-operative state	Immediate post-operative state	Late post-operative state (1 week +)	Descriptor
0	Unconscious	No signs	No recall	No recall	Adequate anesthesia
1	Conscious	Signs/+IFT	No recall	No recall or sequelae	Intra-operative *wakefulness* with obliterated explicit and implicit memory
2	Conscious; Word stimuli presented	Signs/+IFT	No recall	No explicit recall, but implicit memory for word stimuli but no sequelae	Intra-operative *wakefulness* with subsequent *implicit memory*
3	Conscious	Signs/+IFT	No recall	PTSD/nightmares/etc. No explicit recall	Intra-operative *wakefulness* with *implicit emotional memory*
4	Conscious	Signs/+IFT	Explicit recall with or without pain	Explicit recall but no sequelae	*Awareness* but resilient patient
5	Conscious	Signs/+IFT	Explicit recall with distress and/or pain	Explicit recall and PTSD/ nightmares	*Awareness* with sequelae

Use of electroencephalographic (EEG) procedures

Much work has taken place over the past three decades with the aim of producing a clinically useful and commercially viable consciousness monitor to assist clinical anesthetists in their task of maintaining oblivion without overdosing the patient. The most successful of these are based on processed EEG (the Bispectral Index or BIS, and the Narcotrend monitors) and evoked response EEG (e.g., the A-line monitor). The BIS monitor, which uses EEG spectral frequency analysis combined with electromyography (EMG) in a complex algorithm to produce an index that is statistically correlated with level of consciousness, is becoming increasingly common in North American operating theaters, but is yet to play a significant role in clinical practice in Europe and other continents. Despite the level of investment and effort, these monitors (along with the isolated forearm technique) remain controversial, with contradictory study reports concerning specificity and reliability (Avidan et al., 2008; Messner, Beese, Romstöck, Dinkel, & Tschaikowsky, 2003; Russell, 2006). Nevertheless, there is a consensus within the anesthetic awareness research community that the IFT (i.e., response to command) remains the "gold standard" test of intra-operative consciousness against which other monitors must be validated (Jessop & Jones, 1991). These various monitors will be discussed later in the context of determination of intra-operative state at the time of stimulus presentation in implicit memory studies.

Use of implicit memory paradigms

A distinction is made between two types of memory processes: *explicit* and *implicit* memory. Briefly, *explicit recall* of an event or stimulus is said to be present when the subject provides evidence of memory of both the *content* and *context* of the learning episode. So, for example, in the specific situation of intra-operative learning, the patient having post-operative memory that they heard the word "gooseberry" (content) spoken by a man's voice at some point in the operation (context) would be classed as explicit recall. *Implicit recall* is said to be present when, although there is no recollection of a learning episode or its context, changes in response or task performance showing that learning has taken place can be demonstrated. A mundane example of implicit recall is that of riding a bicycle without any specific recollection of the period when the skill of bike-riding was first acquired.

This is the case when the patient, despite having no post-operative recall of any intra-operative events or stimuli, nevertheless responds to "gooseberry" (rather than the more common responses of "apple" or "orange") following the instruction to think of the first fruit that comes into their mind (the word "gooseberry" having been presented intra-operatively). The assumption in all intra-operative learning studies is that *explicit* recall indicates absence of, or inadequate, general anesthesia: studies invariably attempt to demonstrate evidence of *implicit* learning in the context of assumed adequate general anesthesia.

A range of implicit memory tasks have been employed in the context of general anesthesia. The "gooseberry" example given above is known as *category association*, where one or two slightly unusual examples of a category of words (in this case fruit) are presented intra-operatively. The investigator would normally have first established the natural frequency or base rate of fruit-names in the local population for comparison, in order to select the most appropriate word(s) for presentation.

Word stem completion involves presenting a two-syllable word such as "carton" intra-operatively, and then asking the patient to complete the word stem "car . . ." following the operation. Again, the natural frequency of responses to this task in the general population needs to be ascertained beforehand, but in this case, the response of "carpet" is common, whereas the response of "carton" would be unusual. *Word association* simply involves presenting unusual word-pair combinations such as "sharp–apple" intra-operatively, and then asking for the first word that comes to mind in response to "sharp" post-operatively. *Unfamiliar knowledge* tasks involve the intra-operative presentation of uncommonly known or trivial facts such as the blood pressure of an octopus. Patients are then asked to guess the answers to these questions at post-operative interview.

A comprehensive analysis conducted by the author of studies of implicit verbal learning showed that, while 15 studies demonstrated intra-operative learning, 30 others found no such evidence. In their meta-analysis, Merikle and Daneman (1996) show how, when considering both explicit and implicit memory for intra-operative information combined, significant evidence of recall is obtained if the post-operative test takes place *less than 12 hours after intra-operative presentation*. Their analysis shows there is no evidence of persistence of memory, either implicit or explicit, beyond 36 hours. Furthermore, when examining implicit versus explicit recall separately, Merikle and Daneman found rather similar effect sizes for each, undermining the notion that implicit memory effects are more potent and persistent than those for explicit memory.

POSITIVE SUGGESTION STUDIES

Meanwhile, several authors had begun experimenting with the corollary of the Levinson study: if negative intra-operative information can be assimilated and perhaps produce negative post-operative effects, could positive intra-operative information produce positive post-operative effects? Like the Levinson study, the earliest reports were of uncontrolled case series. Pearson (1961) described the first double-blind controlled study in which intra-operative suggestions for relaxation and post-operative coping were given. The outcome variables included the surgeon's ratings of recovery, dose of narcotic required, and days to discharge. A statistically significant difference between the groups on days to discharge was obtained.

In the typical design of these studies (Figure 7.4), two audiotapes for intra-operative presentation are prepared: one contains positive suggestions such as "the operation is going extremely well, you are doing fine, you are going to recover unusually quickly, etc."; the other contains a story which bears no relationship to the operative situation, or alternatively, white masking noise. The tapes are coded so that theater staff and the investigators cannot tell which is which. A randomization code is then used to allocate a tape to each successive patient entered into the trial. Relevant post-operative outcome variables are carefully monitored by recovery ward staff who again do not know which tape the patient has received. Patients are checked for any evidence of conscious knowledge of the taped material. In this way double-blinding is assured.

A comprehensive analysis was conducted by the author of the results from some 29 double-blind controlled trials published thus far, in terms of those obtaining a statistically significant difference between experimental and control groups versus those that found no such difference. A great variety of outcome variables have been monitored in these studies, e.g., post-operative narcotic dose, days till discharge, ratings of pain, post-operative pyrexia and other complications. One immediate methodological difficulty is that the use of a large number of outcome variables in the same study increases the

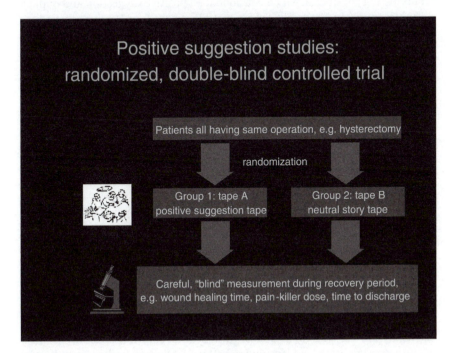

Figure 7.4 The design of therapeutic suggestion studies.

probability of obtaining a significant result, and statistical adjustment to take account of this problem is rarely employed.

In terms of outcome, the author's analysis suggests that the ratio of studies obtaining a significant difference compared with those which did not is about 2:1. A particular feature of this literature is the invariable failure to replicate an originally significant study, even when it involves the same author(s). Millar (1993) has eloquently identified the numerous and often critical methodological difficulties associated with these studies. One salutary example concerns the first study of this type to be conducted in the United Kingdom. Evans and Richardson (1968) appeared to demonstrate a significant difference between experimental and control groups in terms of time to discharge. A subsequent attempt to replicate Evans and Richardson's findings not only failed to show a significant difference between the groups, but demonstrated that Evans and Richardson's control group had been kept in hospital following surgery for an unusually lengthy period, and thus it was the abnormality of the control group that accounted for the difference in the original report (Lui, Standen, & Aitkenhead, 1992; Millar, 1993).

A further difficulty is that for those few, methodologically sound studies obtaining statistically significant results, it is usually the case that extremely small actual differences in variables give rise to statistical significance: there may be little or no *clinical significance* attaching to such differences.

Merikle and Daneman (1996) conducted a meta-analysis of memory for events during anesthesia, which considered all positive suggestion and implicit verbal learning studies published up to 1995. Forty-four studies satisfied the inclusion criteria, involving a cumulative total of 2179 patients. Merikle and Daneman calculated effect sizes for individual outcome variables, and demonstrated that only amount of morphine delivered by patient-controlled analgesia (PCA) reached unequivocal significance. Duration of hospital stay in the total of 5 studies up to 1989 was associated with a highly significant effect size ($p < .003$), but no effect was associated with the 9 studies published between 1989 and 1995 ($p < .488$). The authors deliberately omitted studies involving cardiac surgery from the main meta-analysis, arguing that the nature of the anesthetic and surgery was quite different from that associated with the bulk of the studies. However, they did perform a separate analysis on these cardiac studies, and found a considerably larger effect size for duration of hospital stay than that for the other studies, leading them to conclude that cardiac patients may be more likely to benefit from intra-operative positive suggestion.

The recent literature is characterized by a preponderance of non-significant results (e.g., Lui et al., 1992; Russell & Wang, 1997) and it may be no coincidence that this period has also been associated with the more widespread use of volatile agents and better intra-operative monitoring in general anesthesia, as discussed above. Various studies have demonstrated that the use of volatile agents even at sub-anesthetic concentrations (0.2–0.4 MAC[1]) abolishes intra-operative assimilation and learning, whether implicit or explicit, in volunteer studies not involving surgical stimulation. This is certainly not the case for similar MACs of nitrous oxide (N_2O) and indeed, nitrous oxide administered in combination with a volatile agent such as isoflurane tends to compromise this effect.

Impact of suggestion on post-operative behavior

Smoking cessation

Most studies investigate the effects of intra-operative suggestion on aspects of post-operative recovery. Some studies have attempted to modify post-operative behavior. Hughes, Sanders, Dunne, Tarpey, & Vickers (1994) presented intra-operative suggestions to reduce or stop smoking post-operatively, in a double-blind randomized controlled study. They found a significant difference between the groups at 1-month follow-up in the expected direction, but this difference had disappeared by the 6-month point (Sanders, personal communication). An attempt to replicate the finding using a more substantial sample failed to demonstrate a significant effect (Myles et al., 1996).

Ideomotor studies

A number of studies have sought to demonstrate that intra-operative suggestions to touch a particular part of the body, such as the ear or nose, have resulted in a significant increase in such behavior during post-operative interview, as compared with a control group which did not receive such suggestions.

In one of the first of this type of study, Bennett, Davis, and Giannini (1985) presented surgical patients with intra-operative suggestions to touch their ear at post-operative interview, in a randomized, double-blind design involving 33 subjects. Bennett et al. reported that patients in the experimental group did indeed touch their ears more frequently, despite having no conscious knowledge of the intra-operative suggestion. The study was subsequently criticized by Millar (1993) on the grounds of there having been no pre-operative baseline assessment of ear-touching frequency, and the small size of the experimental group.

There is a clear preponderance of negative results in such studies. Of the 13 studies subsequently published, only three yielded significant results. None of the eight studies since 1991 have found evidence of ideomotor learning.

Enhanced reading speed and lexical decision-making

Münte and her colleagues in Hanover have conducted a series of studies in which they demonstrate significantly faster reading following previous, intra-operative exposure to the material despite absence of explicit recall, in comparison with controls who received no such priming (Münte et al., 1999, 2000, 2003). The Hanover group have also employed a linked Lexical Decision Task in which patients were asked to distinguish between low frequency nouns and neologisms. Some of the low frequency nouns had been presented during surgery (Münte et al., 2002). Speed of decision measured from time to press a "yes" or "no" button was found to be associated with intra-operative priming.

Intra-operative music

A further group of studies have investigated the effects of the intra-operative presentation of music. Some of these studies have attempted to demonstrate post-operative therapeutic effects, whilst others have tested patients to see if they have any form of implicit memory for the particular music presented. Once again there is a preponderance of negative results: of seven published studies, only one (Nilsson, Rawal, Unestahl, Zetterberg, & Unosson, 2001) obtained evidence of an effect of intra-operative music on post-operative outcome.

Use of the process dissociation procedure (PDP)

Jacoby (1991) first proposed the use of process dissociation to evaluate the relative contribution of explicit and implicit components in word recall. This has subsequently been applied to cognitive research in anesthesia. Typically, a word is presented during anesthesia. After the patient has recovered, she is asked to retrieve the word in two different ways with help of a word stem cue: in the first, the patient says what she thinks she may have heard during the operation, or whatever first comes into her head; and then in the second, she is asked to generate a word that is different from what first came to mind that completes the stem meaningfully. This second task requires exclusion of any conscious or explicit influences on recall. Thus the first retrieval task makes use of both explicit and implicit retrieval processes; but in the second task, explicit and implicit processes are working in opposite directions and the relative contribution of each can be estimated using an equation which takes account of base rates and the response rate to the first task.

Several studies have applied the PDP approach to anesthesia. In particular, the Rotterdam group of Kerssens, Lubke, and Bonke (Kerssens, Klein, van der Woerd, & Bonke, 2001; Lubke, Kerssens, Gershon, & Sebel, 2000) have conducted a number of studies of this kind. Generally these more recent studies have taken note of the importance of attempting to determine hypnotic depth at the time of intra-operative stimulus presentation in order to address the following question.

Is implicit priming possible during adequate or deep general anesthesia?

A series of recent studies have attempted to determine the relationship between depth of anesthesia on the one hand and explicit and implicit memory function on the other (Dobrunz, Jaeger, & Vetter, 2007; Lubke, Kerssens, Phaf, & Sebel, 1999; Münte et al., 2003). At what point, during progressive deepening of anesthesia, is explicit and then implicit memory compromised?

Most studies fail to find evidence of any form of memory for stimuli presented during what has been termed "deep" anesthesia (equated with BIS readings of 40 and below). Several studies have demonstrated evidence of implicit memory (usually in the absence of explicit memory) in what are termed "moderate to light" states of anesthesia (equated with BIS readings of 40 to 60 for moderate, and 60 to 80 for light). Given the depth is generally defined in terms of the output from a BIS or other processed EEG monitor, what does this mean in terms of consciousness? Does a BIS of 40 to 60 actually correspond with adequate anesthesia (or reliable oblivion for the patient)? The studies mentioned above raise serious doubts as to whether this is the case (Avidan et al., 2008; Messner et al., 2003; Russell, 2006). This implies that it is probable that a significant number of participants in these experiments titrating anesthetic depth against memory function and classed as "moderately anesthetized" will have been capable of response to command, but with obliterated explicit recall (Muncaster, Sleigh, & Williams, 2003). It is problematic to describe this condition as "adequate anesthesia" or indeed "moderate" in terms of depth.

The role of surgical corticosteroid release in implicit memory: the Andrade hypothesis

Andrade has published extensively in this area and has suggested that one explanation for the variability in the outcome of implicit memory studies is the key but hitherto unnoticed variable of surgical stress, provoking release of stress hormones (Andrade, Englert, Harper, & Edwards, 2001). She argues that corticosteroids have already been shown to influence memory mechanisms by promoting encoding in the hypothalamus. Implicit memory studies in anesthesia rarely control for, or record the extent of, surgical and physiological stress provoked by the surgical procedure: certainly there have not been any studies that have monitored blood corticosteroid levels at the time of intra-operative stimulus presentation.

Evidence for the hypothesis comes primarily from studies (Deeprose, Andrade, Varma, & Edwards, 2004; Deeprose, Andrade, Harrison, & Edwards, 2005) in which absence of intra-operative consciousness is inferred from monitoring of the Bispectral Index (BIS – see above). The relationship between the index and actual consciousness in the patient is probabilistic and not definitive, and a number of studies have demonstrated that the index can be misleading and unreliable (Avidan et al., 2008; Messner et al., 2003). Deeprose and Andrade's studies, like a previous study by Lubke and colleagues (1999) which appeared to indicate implicit priming in definitively unconscious patients, are entirely dependent on the specificity and reliability of the BIS to determine unconsciousness. Thus all three studies are compromised because of their dependence on this Achilles heel. With both of the Deeprose and Andrade studies, it is difficult to disentangle the hormonal effects of surgical stress from increased risk of consciousness. Thus in the first study (Deeprose et al., 2004), priming stimuli were presented prior to the initial surgical incision in one group, and in another, the stimuli were presented at the time of incision. The problem here is that, even though significantly more anesthetic was administered at the time of incision, it is well known that the surgical incision invariably stimulates the central nervous system and causes lightening of anesthetic state with increased risk of consciousness (as well as provoking cortisol release). Deeprose et al. (2004) sought to pre-empt such criticism by the use of the BIS to demonstrate comparable anesthetic depth: unfortunately, given the lack of specificity of the BIS, the study's assertions are compromised.

Similarly, in the second study (Deeprose et al., 2005) two groups were compared, one which received an opioid analgesic (fentanyl) in addition to the hypnotic (propofol) at anesthetic induction, and one which did not. It was reasoned that the group receiving pre-emptive analgesic would have an attenuated stress response to the surgery, while the other group would not, making the latter more amenable to priming due to the increased levels of corticosteroids. Again, the problem here is that an opioid in combination with a hypnotic is likely to enhance the hypnotic action and there is less chance of lightening of anesthesia and therefore consciousness. As in the previous study, Deeprose et al. (2005) rely on the BIS to pre-empt this criticism, and although they obtained similar mean BIS scores for the two groups, this cannot guarantee that some of the non-fentanyl group were not wakeful at the time of stimulus presentation. However, Andrade (personal communication) points out that these groups did not receive paralyzing muscle relaxants, yet none attempted to get off the operating theater table or move significantly at time of incision.

Finally, the hypothesis does not explain the historical profile of an initial proliferation of positive implicit memory study findings during the 1980s followed by a series of negative findings and failures to replicate during the subsequent two decades.

Robinson Crusoe and implicit emotional memory

Meanwhile, in Munich, Schwender, Kaiser, Klasing, Peter, and Pöppel (1993) conducted a ground-breaking study in which a synopsis of the Robinson Crusoe story was presented, intra-operatively, to surgical patients. The story was carefully chosen for the emotional parallels between Crusoe's predicament and that of the (possibly wakeful) surgical patient – isolated, alone, powerless, and in danger. Post-operatively, in recovery, each patient was asked to freely associate to the word "Friday". Many patients talked about the weekend, not having to go to work, leisure activity, etc. However, a significant minority of patients began to talk about desert islands and in some cases the

Robinson Crusoe story itself. Note that none of these patients had explicit recall for the intra-operative presentation or events. Indeed, many of those showing the priming effect, when told that the reason why they had responded in the way they did was because they had been presented with the story intra-operatively, strongly denied that this could be the case. Schwender et al. also demonstrated that those patients who had exhibited the desert island association displayed EEG evoked potential evidence that they had not been properly anesthetized at the point of presentation and that they were probably in a high state of consciousness.

This study and its results begin to open up the possibility of *implicit emotional memory* effects which might be more potent than simple word priming. In a keynote speech at the 4th International Symposium on Memory and Awareness in Anesthesia in Rotterdam in 1995, Bernie Levinson (now a psychiatrist) helpfully provided an illustrative parody of the typical implicit memory study:

> I am walking across a suspension bridge. It is only ropes and a few slates of wood. Thousands of feet below me is a raging, rock-strewn river. Falling means appalling mutilation and possibly death. The bridge quivers and sways with each step. I am holding the ropes as tightly as I can. My whole being is focused on getting to the other side. Behind me, someone is saying – orange – pigeon – what is the blood pressure of an octopus . . .?
>
> (Levinson, 1993, p. 499)

Levinson highlights here the irrelevance of the word-priming stimuli, so often used in cognitive priming studies, to the patient's predicament – in contrast to the emotional congruence of the Robinson Crusoe synopsis chosen by Schwender and colleagues.

Can implicit emotional memories create post-operative disturbance?

If it is the case that, as Wang and Russell's data suggest, episodes of intra-operative consciousness with compromised encoding are more common than full awareness with post-operative explicit recall, and if this is a condition in which emotional priming may take place, might this have post-operative effects? Wang (2000) reviewed a series of intriguing studies in which surgical patients experienced psychological problems (anxiety states including panic disorder and phobias, recurrent nightmares) following operations for which they had no explicit recall. In some of these cases, anesthetic records were obtained and these provided circumstantial evidence of inadequate anesthesia.

Wang, Russell, and Logan (2004a) conducted a prospective, double-blind follow-up of a consecutive series of hysterectomy patients who had no explicit recall, investigating post-operative mental state. Patients' intra-operative state was carefully monitored using a variety of measures including the IFT and hemodynamic and autonomic indicators (heart rate, blood pressure, etc.). Two of the authors categorized patients into those who were judged as only lightly anesthetized versus those who were deeply anesthetized. The second author (Logan) interviewed patients at 1- and 3-month follow-up, with no knowledge of the categorization of individuals. The General Health Questionnaire was used to investigate mental state psychometrically. The results provided evidence that light anesthesia was associated with higher levels of anxiety and depression at 1 and 3 months in comparison with the more deeply anesthetized patients. The implication here is that some of the "light" group may have become sufficiently conscious intra-operatively to become distressed, and despite the absence of explicit post-operative memory, this was enough to give rise to implicit emotional priming and associated psychopathology.

Wang, Russell, and Nicholson (2004b) took advantage of a "natural experiment" circumstance to investigate implicit emotional priming effects in a quasi-experimental study. In 1989, Desidero and colleagues had presented a new "anesthetic" technique at the first International Symposium on Memory and Awareness in Glasgow (Desidero, Thorne, & Shah, 1989). Russell then tried out the new technique involving a pumped intravenous infusion of a benzodiazepine and an opiate, only, unlike Desidero, he used the IFT to monitor levels of consciousness intra-operatively. Russell had to abandon his trial after 32 cases, on ethical grounds, since of this group, 20 patients indicated not only intra-operative consciousness, but worryingly, also pain (Russell, 1993). Nevertheless, none of these patients had post-operative recall of their consciousness or pain. Ten years after this trial, Wang et al. (2004b) conducted an extensive retrospective follow-up of these patients, reasoning that, if intra-operative implicit emotional priming was a significant phenomenon, it should be apparent in the group who had experienced intra-operative pain and distress, but without post-operative explicit recall. The smaller number of patients in Russell's original trial who provided no indication of consciousness on the IFT could act as a control group. Unfortunately, the numbers were too small to conduct formal statistical analysis, but three of the patients were found to have suffered *de novo* psychiatric difficulties (including anxiety disorders) during the follow-up period and, of these, two were from the group who had indicated pain. The third had simply indicated consciousness without pain. While clearly not a definitive study, the results provide support for the implicit emotional memory hypothesis: that a dissociated memory state with preserved implicit memory of emotional distress in the absence of explicit recall may cause psychological disturbances. Such disturbances may be insidious and difficult to treat because the patient has no understanding of their origin.

Implicit emotional memory in anesthesia and sedation

To investigate the implicit emotional memory hypothesis in a more prospective and experimental fashion, Woodruff and Wang (2004) used the common clinical circumstance of conscious sedation during endoscopic investigation as another model in which intravenous benzodiazepine tends to obliterate explicit memory while preserving implicit memory. Thus many endoscopy patients erroneously believe they have had a general anesthetic since they have a "blank" in their memory for the period of the examination. Woodruff and Wang presented three words to colonoscopy patients whilst monitoring skin conductance responses, before and after the period of conscious sedation. Patients had been randomly allocated to one of three groups: each of these heard one only of the three words presented repeatedly during the sedated colonoscopy. The rationale was that, given that colonoscopy is generally an unpleasant and sometimes distressing experience, such emotions might, by a process of classical conditioning, become associated with the presented word despite the absence of explicit memory. This would then lead to enhancement of the skin conductance response in the follow-up presentation coinciding with the word presented, in contrast with the other two words.

The expected effect was indeed found, but only in the one-week follow-up which comprised a small subset of the total cohort. The initial post-sedation assessment was found to be contaminated by the effects of remaining benzodiazepine, masking any differential effects. Given the small number of participants involved in the late follow-up group, interpretation of results needs to be made with caution. Nevertheless, the study provides some prospective evidence of emotional priming. Clearly these findings need to be replicated in a much larger study.

CONCLUSION

Numerous studies have been conducted to investigate implicit memory in the context of surgery under general anesthesia. There has been a general trend of a preponderance of significant findings during the 1970s and 1980s but by the mid 1990s the trend was reversed such that many studies failed to demonstrate implicit priming effects, with even authors themselves being unable to replicate their earlier studies. It is likely that the reason for this pattern is the introduction of volatile anesthetic agents which more reliably induce anesthetic oblivion than previous anesthetic regimens, along with the introduction of more rigorous anesthetic delivery monitoring such as end-tidal drug measurement. This highlights the most favorable conditions in which priming can take place, where there is a high state of consciousness but in the presence of drugs which impair or disrupt explicit encoding. Whilst it may be of academic and experimental interest to the cognitive psychologist that such implicit memory effects can occur, there may also be important clinical implications relevant to models of the genesis of psychopathology such as post-traumatic stress disorder, other anxiety states, and sleep disorders. In sum, it may be possible to experience distress and psychological trauma in these circumstances of impaired explicit encoding, and subsequently be left with psychological disturbances, the origins for which the sufferer has no explicit recall.[2]

Notes

1 MAC = minimum alveolar concentration. This is the concentration of gaseous anesthetic agent in the lung sufficient to prevent movement in response to initial incision in 50% of patients.
2 A full list of the studies included in the literature analyses cited, together with the measures employed and outcomes, is obtainable on application to the author (mw125@le.ac.uk).

References

Andrade, J., Englert, L., Harper, C., Edwards, N. D. (2001). Comparing the effects of stimulation and propofol infusion rate on implicit and explicit memory formation. *British Journal of Anaesthesia, 86*, 189–195.

Avidan, M., Zhang, L., Burnside, B., Finkel, K., Searleman, A., Selvidge, J., et al. (2008). Anesthesia awareness and the Bispectral Index. *New England Journal of Medicine, 358*, 1097–1108.

Bennett, H. L., Davis, H. S., & Giannini, J. A. (1985). Non-verbal response to intraoperative conversation. *British Journal of Anaesthesia, 57*, 174–179.

Deeprose, C., Andrade, J., Harrison, D., & Edwards, N. (2005). Unconscious auditory priming during surgery with propofol and nitrous oxide anaesthesia: A replication. *British Journal of Anaesthesia, 94*, 57–62.

Deeprose, C., Andrade, J., Varma, S., & Edwards, N. (2004). Unconscious learning during surgery with propofol anaesthesia. *British Journal of Anaesthesia, 92*, 171–177.

Desidero, D., Thorne A., & Shah, N. (1990). Alfentanyl-Midazolam anaesthesia: Protection against awareness. In B. Bonke, W. Fitch, & K. Millar (Eds.), *Memory and awareness in anaesthesia* (pp. 185–188). Amsterdam: Swets & Zeitlinger.

Dobrunz, U. E., Jaeger. K., & Vetter, G. (2007). Memory priming during light anaesthesia with desflurane and remifentanil anaesthesia. *British Journal of Anaesthesia, 98*, 491–496.

Evans, C., & Richardson, P. H. (1988). Improved recovery and reduced postoperative stay after therapeutic suggestions during general anaesthesia. *Lancet, 2*, 491–492.

Hughes, J. A., Sanders, L. D., Dunne, J. A., Tarpey, J., & Vickers, M. D. (1994). Reducing smoking: The effect of suggestion during general anaesthesia on postoperative smoking habits. *Anaesthesia, 49*, 126–128.

Jacoby, L. L. (1991). A process dissociation framework: Separating automatic from intentional uses of memory. *Journal of Memory and Language, 30*, 513–541.

Jessop, J., & Jones, J. G. (1991). Editorial: Conscious awareness during general anaesthesia – what are we attempting to monitor? *British Journal of Anaesthesia, 66*, 635–637.

Kerssens, C., Klein, J., van der Woerd, A., & Bonke, B. (2001). Auditory information processing during adequate propofol anesthesia monitored by electroencephalogram bispectral index. *Anesthesia and Analgesia, 92*, 1210–1214.

Levinson, B. (1965). States of awareness under general anaesthesia. *British Journal of Anaesthesia, 37*, 544–546.

Levinson, B. (1993). Quo vadis. In P. S. Sebel, B. Bonke, & E. Winograd (Eds.), *Memory and awareness in anaesthesia* (pp. 64–73). Englewood Cliffs, NJ: Prentice Hall.

Lubke, G. H., Kerssens, C., Gershon, R. Y., & Sebel, P. S. (2000). Memory formation during general anesthesia for emergency cesarean sections. *Anesthesiology, 92*, 1029–1034.

Lubke, G. H., Kerssens, C., Phaf, H., & Sebel, P. S. (1999). Dependence of explicit and implicit memory on hypnotic state in trauma patients. *Anesthesiology, 90*, 670–680.

Lui, W. H. D., Standen, P. J., & Aitkenhead, A. R. (1992). Therapeutic suggestions during general anaesthesia in patients undergoing hysterectomy. *British Journal of Anaesthesia, 68*, 277–281.

Merikle, P. M., & Daneman, M. (1996). Memory for events during anaesthesia: A meta-analysis. In B. Bonke, J. G. Bovill, & N. Moerman (Eds.), *Memory and awareness in anaesthesia* (pp. 108–121). Assen: Van Gorcum & Comp.

Messner, M., Beese, U., Romstöck, J., Dinkel, M., & Tschaikowsky, K. (2003). The Bispectral Index declines during neuromuscular block in fully awake persons. *Anesthesia and Analgesia, 97*, 488–491.

Millar, K. (1993). The neglected factor of individual variation in studies of memory during general anaesthesia. In P. S. Sebel, B. Bonke, & E. Winograd (Eds.), *Memory and awareness in anaesthesia* (pp. 31–47). Englewood Cliffs, NJ: Prentice Hall.

Muncaster, A. R. G., Sleigh, J. W., & Williams, M. (2003). Changes in consciousness, conceptual memory, and quantitative electroencephalographical measures during recovery from sevoflurane- and remifentanil-based anesthesia. *Anesthesia and Analgesia, 97*, 1206–1206.

Münte, S., Kobbe, I., Demertzis, A., Lullwitz, E., Münte, T. F., Piepenbrock, S., & Leuwer, M. (1999). Increased reading speed for stories presented during general anesthesia. *Anesthesiology, 90*, 662–669.

Münte, S., Lullwitz, E., Leuwer, M., Mitzlaff, B., Münte, T. F., Hussein, S., & Piepenbrock, S. A. (2000). No implicit memory for stories played during isoflurane/alfentanil/nitrous oxide anesthesia: A reading speed measurement. *Anesthesia and Analgesia, 90*, 33–38.

Münte, S., Münte, T. F., Grotkamp, J., Haeseler, G., Raymondos, K., Piepenbrock, S., & Kraus G. (2003). Implicit memory varies as a function of hypnotic electroencephalogram stage in surgical patients. *Anesthesia and Analgesia, 97*, 132–138.

Münte, S., Schmidt, M., Meyer, M., Nager, W., Lullwitz, E., Münte, T. F., & Piepenbrock, S. (2002). Implicit memory for words played during isoflurane- or propofol-based anesthesia: the lexical decision task. *Anesthesiology, 96*, 588–594.

Myles, P. S., Hendrata, M., Layher, Y., Williams, N. J., Hall, J. L., Moloney, J. T., & Powell, J. (1996). Double-blind, randomized trial of cessation of smoking after audiotape suggestion during anaesthesia. *British Journal of Anaesthesia, 76*, 694–698.

Nilsson, U., Rawal, N., Unestahl, L. E., Zetterberg, C., & Unosson, M. (2001). Improved recovery after music and therapeutic suggestions during general anaesthesia: A double-blind randomised controlled trial. *Acta Anaesthesiologica Scandinavica, 45*, 812–817.

Pearson, R. P. (1961). Response to suggestions given under general anesthesia. *American Journal of Clinical Hypnosis, 4,* 106–114.

Richardson, J. T. E. (1989). Human memory, psychology, pathology and pharmacology. In J. G. Jones (Ed.), *Baillière's clinical anaesthesia, Vol. 3, No. 3: Depth of anaesthesia* (pp. 451–472). London: Baillière Tindall.

Russell, I. F. (1989). Conscious awareness during general anaesthesia: Relevance of autonomic signs and isolated arm movements as guides to depth of anaesthesia. In J. G. Jones (Ed.), *Baillière's clinical anaesthesia, Vol. 3, No. 3: Depth of anaesthesia* (pp. 511–532). London: Baillière Tindall.

Russell, I. F. (1993), Midazolam-alfentanyl: An anaesthetic? An investigation using the isolated forearm technique. *British Journal of Anaesthesia, 70,* 42–46.

Russell, I. F. (2006). The Narcotrend "depth of anaesthesia" monitor cannot reliably detect consciousness during general anaesthesia: An investigation using the isolated forearm technique. *British Journal of Anaesthesia, 96,* 346–352.

Russell, I. F., & Wang, M. (1997). Absence of memory for intra-operative information during surgery under adequate general anaesthesia. *British Journal of Anaesthesia, 78,* 3–9.

Schwender, D., Kaiser, A., Klasing, S., Peter, K., & Pöppel, E. (1993). Explicit and implicit memory and mid-latency auditory evoked potentials during cardiac surgery. In P. S. Sebel, B. Bonke, & E. Winograd (Eds.), *Memory and awareness in anaesthesia* (pp. 85–98). Englewood Cliffs, NJ: Prentice Hall.

Tunstall, M. E. (1977). Detecting wakefulness during general anaesthesia for caesarean section. *British Medical Journal, 1,* 1321.

Wang, M. (2000). The psychological consequences of awareness during surgery. In C. Jordan, D. J. A. Vaughan, & D. E. F. Newton (Eds.), *Memory and awareness in anaesthesia IV* (pp. 315–324). London: Imperial College Press.

Wang, M., Russell, I. F., & Logan, C. (2004a). Light anaesthesia without explicit recall during hysterectomy is associated with increased post-operative anxiety over a 3-month follow-up period. *British Journal of Anaesthesia, 93,* 492–493.

Wang, M., Russell, I. F., & Nicholson, J. (2004b). A 10-year retrospective follow-up of alfentanil–midazolam patients who indicated intra-operative pain without explicit recall. *British Journal of Anaesthesia, 93,* 493.

Woodruff, G., & Wang, M. (2004). An investigation of implicit emotional memory and midazolam amnesia following colonoscopy. *British Journal of Anaesthesia, 93,* 488.

8 Episodic memory and interhemispheric interaction

Handedness and eye movements

Stephen D. Christman and
Ruth E. Propper

An important advance in our understanding of the neural bases of human memory was provided by Tulving and colleagues who proposed the hemispheric encoding/retrieval asymmetry (HERA) model of episodic memory (Tulving, Kapur, Craik, Moscovitch, & Houle, 1994). The HERA model argues that the left versus right cerebral hemispheres are specialized for the encoding versus retrieval, respectively, of episodic memories (in contrast, both the encoding and retrieval of semantic memories are handled by the left hemisphere only). Subsequent brain imaging studies have provided further support for the HERA model (e.g., Habib, Nyberg, & Tulving, 2003).

While most work on the HERA model has focused on the questions of which specific left hemisphere regions are involved in encoding and which right hemisphere regions are involved in retrieval, Christman, Propper, and colleagues have focused on the implications of the HERA model for interhemispheric interaction. Specifically, the fact that episodic encoding and retrieval processes take place in different hemispheres implies an important role of the corpus callosum, the primary tract of axons connecting the left and right hemispheres. Over the past seven years, Christman and Propper have published a series of papers demonstrating an interhemispheric basis for the retrieval of episodic memories.

This research has focused on two factors that influence interhemispheric interaction. One is degree of handedness, a trait-like variable for which consistent right-handedness is associated with decreased interhemispheric interaction and poorer episodic retrieval. The second involves the effects of bilateral eye movements that induce state-like changes in which eye movements lead to increased interhemispheric interaction and enhanced episodic retrieval. In this chapter, we review the conceptual and empirical bases for these effects, and discuss their implications for applied contexts such as eyewitness testimony.

DEGREE OF HANDEDNESS

Behavioral and neural foundations

Research on memory has long recognized the importance of individual differences. Specifically, two dimensions of individual difference have received considerable attention: age and sex. For example, young children (e.g., Roberts & Blades, 2000) and older adults (e.g., Roediger & Geraci, 2007) have difficulties with source monitoring (i.e., attributing the origin of a memory to the correct source). Similarly, females have better object location memory (e.g., Voyer, Postma, Brake, & Imperato-McGinley, 2007), verbal episodic memory (e.g., Lewin, Wolgers, & Herlitz, 2001), and face recognition abilities (e.g., Rehnman & Herlitz, 2007) than males.

In this chapter, we argue that handedness represents another important dimension of individual difference in memory abilities that has heretofore been neglected. The basis of this neglect stems from two sources. First, until Tulving and colleagues proposed their HERA model, there was no neurally based theoretical framework within which to interpret potential handedness differences. Second, the vast majority of research on handedness involves comparisons of left- versus right-handed individuals. However, a growing body of evidence suggests that *degree* of handedness (i.e., consistent/strong versus inconsistent/mixed) is as important as or more important than *direction* of handedness (i.e., left versus right).

Schacter (1994) warned that studies that do not distinguish between degree and direction of handedness lose statistical power by combining consistent and inconsistent right-handers. In support of this position, studies that *do* distinguish between degree and direction of handedness routinely find that consistent left-handers resemble consistent right-handers, with the inconsistent-handedness group standing out from the other two.

Christman and Propper and colleagues have hypothesized that a key difference between consistent and inconsistent handedness groups involves interhemispheric interaction, with consistent handedness being associated with decreased interaction between the left and right cerebral hemispheres relative to inconsistent handedness. This hypothesis is based on both neural and behavioral findings.

From a neural perspective, there is evidence that consistent handedness is associated with a smaller corpus callosum (Figure 8.1). For example, Witelson and Goldsmith (1991) examined a sample composed solely of right-handers and found that the correlation between strength of right-handedness and corpus callosum size was −0.69, meaning that almost half of the inter-individual variation in callosal size was associated with degree of handedness. Similar findings have been reported by Clarke and Zaidel (1994), Denenberg, Kertesz, and Cowell (1991), and Habib, Gayraud, Oliva, Regis, Salamon, and Khalal (1991). The smaller callosal size in consistent right-handers is consistent with decreased interhemispheric interaction in such individuals.

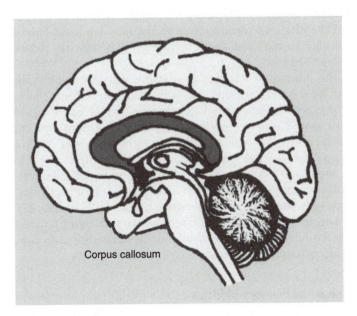

Corpus callosum

Figure 8.1 The corpus callosum.

From a behavioral perspective, there is growing evidence that cognitive processes known to be functionally lateralized to opposite hemispheres show decreased interaction in consistent right-handers. Studies have shown decreased interaction in consistent right-handers between left-hemisphere (LH) and right-hemisphere (RH) motor processes (Christman, 1993), LH-based word reading and RH-based color naming (Christman, 2001), LH-based processing of local form and RH-based processing of global form (Christman, 2001), and LH-based belief maintenance processes and RH-based belief updating processes (Christman, Bentle, & Niebauer, 2007a; Christman, Henning, Geers, Propper, & Niebauer, 2008a; Jasper & Christman, 2005; Niebauer, Aselage, & Schutte, 2002; Niebauer, Christman, Reid, & Garvey, 2004). In addition, evidence indicates that consistent right-handedness is associated with decreased access to RH-based processing of risk (Christman, Jasper, Sontam, & Cooil, 2007b). This decreased interaction between the LH and RH and decreased access to RH processing in consistent right-handers is hypothesized to reflect decreased interhemispheric inter-action in consistent right-handers.

Before discussing the implications of these findings for individual differences in memory, a few words about how handedness is measured and classified are in order. The handedness inventory (Oldfield, 1971) used in our studies asks about hand preference for ten common activities, with scores ranging from −100 (perfectly left-handed) to +100 (perfectly right-handed). The median score on this handedness inventory is used to define the cut-off point between classification as inconsistent- versus consistent-handed. The median score on the handedness inventory is typically +80. By this criterion, simply doing one or two of the activities consistently with the non-dominant hand (and the remaining eight or nine with the dominant hand) is sufficient to be classified as inconsistent-handed.

While this practice of referring to someone who does nine things always with their right hand and only one with their left as being "inconsistent-handed" may seem counter-intuitive, we argue that the use of a median split divides the sample into two natural, non-arbitrary groups: one comprising people who perform *all* actions with their right hand, and one comprising people who display *any* degree of inconsistent hand preference. Finally, the current chapter will have little to say about consistent left-handedness. Individuals who consistently use their left hand for most or all activities are rare, comprising only about 2% of the population (Lansky, Feinstein, & Peterson, 1988). Owing to logistic difficulties associated with obtaining large samples of consistent left-handers, studies reviewed in this chapter focus on comparisons between inconsistent- and consistent-right-handed groups.

Handedness and memory abilities

The fact that consistent handedness is associated with decreased interhemispheric interaction and decreased functional access to RH processing has important implications for Tulving's HERA model of episodic memory: to the extent that the retrieval of episodic memories relies on the RH, then consistent handedness should be associated with poorer episodic retrieval arising from consistent handers' relative lack of interhemispheric access to RH-based retrieval processes. This hypothesis has been confirmed across a variety of memory tasks (see Table 8.1 for a summary of the handedness studies reviewed below).

Propper, Christman, and Phaneuf (2005) examined handedness differences in the retrieval of episodic memories. Experiment 1 used a standard laboratory-based memory procedure directly adapted from Tulving, Schacter, and Stark (1982). Participants viewed a total of 36 words on a computer screen, one at a time for 5 seconds each. Then, after a retention interval, they were given a blank sheet of paper and asked to recall as many of those 36 words as they could. Consistent right-handers performed significantly worse on this recall task than inconsistent-handers. In particular, consistent right-handers made almost twice as many false alarms (incorrect guesses) as did inconsistent-handers, suggesting that consistent right-handedness is associated with poorer source memory. Similar findings were reported by Lyle, Logan, and Roediger (2008a). Using a similar paradigm, they reported a marginal trend toward better correct recall in inconsistent-handers, as well as a significantly lower false alarm rate in inconsistent-handers.

Importantly, Propper et al. (2005) reported no handedness differences in a control task in which another set of participants performed a word fragment completion task after the retention interval. The overall number of fragments

Table 8.1 Summary of research on handedness differences in memory

Task	Findings	Effect size (d)	Citation
Free recall of words	Inconsistent-handed advantage	.63	Propper, Christman, & Phaneuf, 2005
Free recall of words	Inconsistent-handed advantage	.41	Lyle, Logan, & Roediger, 2008a
Free recall of words	Inconsistent-handed advantage	.68	Christman & Butler, 2007
Free recall of events from own life	Inconsistent-handed advantage	.73	Propper, Christman, & Phaneuf, 2005
Recall of early childhood memories	Inconsistent-handed advantage	.58	Christman, Propper, & Brown. 2006
Paired-associate recall	Inconsistent-handed advantage	.33	Lyle, McCabe, & Roediger, 2008b
Source memory (DRM paradigm)	Inconsistent-handed advantage	.58	Christman, Propper, & Dion, 2004
Source memory (sensory modality)	Inconsistent-handed advantage	.64	Lyle, McCabe, & Roediger, 2008b
Self-reported memory abilities in everyday life	Inconsistent-handed advantage	.47	Christman & Propper, 2008
Self-reported recall of dreams	Inconsistent-handed advantage	.41	Christman, 2007
Incidental memory for deeply processed words	Inconsistent-handed advantage	.90	Christman & Butler, 2007
Incidental memory for shallowly processed words	No handedness difference	.15	Christman & Butler, 2007
Know vs. remember judgments	Inconsistent: Rem > Know	1.63	Propper & Christman, 2004
	Consistent: Rem = Know	.38	
Word recognition	No handedness difference	.18	Propper & Christman, 2004
Word recognition	No handedness difference	.22	Lyle, Logan, & Roediger, 2008a
Face recognition	No handedness difference	.07	Lyle, McCabe, & Roediger, 2008b
Implicit memory	No handedness difference	.28	Propper, Christman, & Phaneuf, 2005
Semantic memory	No handedness difference	.10	Propper, Christman, & Phaneuf 2005

completed is a measure of semantic memory, while the number of completed fragments for previously studied words minus the number for new words is an implicit test of memory; thus, performance on this task does not require the explicit retrieval of episodic memories. The lack of handedness differences on this task rules out the possibility that the inconsistent-handed advantage on the retrieval task was due to overall greater effort.

In Experiment 2 of Propper et al. (2005), memory for real-world events was studied. Participants kept a daily journal for a week in which they wrote down a couple of notable events each day. They were instructed to *not* write down common, everyday events (e.g., "I woke up and got dressed"), but instead to record distinctive events (e.g., "I stubbed my toe really bad" and "I went to the park with my cousin and had ice cream"). Participants were not informed of the purpose of the journals, and turned them in at the end of the week. A week later, they were asked to recall the gist of all the previous journal entries that they could remember. Consistent right-handers recalled fewer of the journal entries and made more false alarms. Thus, the inferior memory of consistent right-handers was observed for both lab-based and real-world memories.

The notion that the poorer memory among consistent right-handers is due, at least in part, to problems with source memory was confirmed in a study by Christman, Propper, and Dion (2004). In this study, participants engaged in the false memory task popularized by Roediger and McDermott (1995), the so-called Deese–Roediger–McDermott paradigm. In this task, subjects listen to lists of words composed of verbal associates to a critical lure item that is *not* included in the list. For example, participants would hear a list of words like "thread," "eye," "sewing," "sharp," "thimble," "haystack," "syringe," etc., all of which are close associates of the word "needle," which did not appear in the list. Once again, consistent right-handedness was associated with an increased number of false alarms, with consistent right-handers falsely recalling the critical lures at a rate 50% higher than that for inconsistent-handers.

Similar findings were reported by Lyle, McCabe, and Roediger (2008b). In their study, subjects were presented with words to remember: Half of the words were presented visually on a computer and the other half were presented via headphones. During a subsequent recognition test, inconsistent handedness was associated with superior ability to attribute correctly recognized items to the correct source. Interestingly, this effect was limited to younger adults; older adults (aged 60–90) did not exhibit handedness differences. Lyle et al. (2008b) also reported an inconsistent-handed advantage in paired-associate recall, another standard test of episodic memory. Importantly, they did not find handedness differences in non-episodic memory tasks, ruling out the possibility that inconsistent handedness was associated with superior performance regardless of the task.

One other aspect of the Lyle et al. (2008b) study bears comment. They also looked at a face recognition task, in which subjects first studied a set of faces and were later presented with faces which they had to judge as being "old" or "new." While this task also taps into episodic memory, no handedness differences were observed. There are two possible bases for this finding. First, our work has shown that handedness differences are observed only for recall tasks, not recognition (e.g., Christman & Propper, 2001; Propper & Christman, 2004), as recognition memory can be based on non-episodic judgments of familiarity (e.g., Gardiner, 1988). Second, it is possible that the handedness differences in episodic memory are confined to verbal material, as Propper and Christman (1999) reported that interhemispheric interaction was not associated with enhanced memory for pictorial stimuli.

Further support for the existence of poorer source memory in consistent right-handers comes from a study of handedness differences in "know–remember" judgments (Propper & Christman, 2004). In this task, participants were given a recognition task, again using the procedure and materials from Tulving et al. (1982); for each item they indicated that they recognized, participants were asked to indicate whether (i) they explicitly remembered that item, (ii) they simply knew that they saw it before, even though they did not explicitly remember it, or (iii) they were merely guessing.

Prior research indicates that "remember" judgments are based on episodic memory, while "know" judgments reflect semantic memory (Gardiner, 1988). Although there were no handedness differences in overall recognition memory, correct recognitions for inconsistent-handers were more likely to be based on "remember" judgments; in contrast, correct recognitions of consistent right-handers were roughly equally divided among "know" and "remember" judgments. Again, the abundance of "know" judgments by consistent right-handers presumably reflects their inability to explicitly remember the source of those recognized items.

We have extended these findings to other memory tasks. In a study of the offset of childhood amnesia (the inability to explicitly remember events from the first years of life), we found that the average age for earliest memory was 6.1 years for consistent right-handers versus 5.5 years for inconsistent-handers (Christman, Propper, & Brown, 2006). It is important to note that this handedness difference appears to arise at the retrieval, not encoding, stage, as consistent right-handers in an eye-movement condition that is hypothesized to enhance interhemispheric interaction (described below) had an average age for earliest memory of 5.5 years, equaling the performance of inconsistent-handers in the absence of eye movements.

We have also explored handedness differences in incidental learning as a function of the depth of processing (Christman & Butler, 2007). Employing materials and procedures developed by Craik and Tulving (1975), we presented participants with lists of 24 words, one at a time on a computer screen. There were four between-subjects conditions: (i) judgments of whether each word was printed in upper- or lower-case letters, a very shallow processing condition, (ii) judgments of whether or not each word rhymed with a target word, a moderately shallow processing condition, (iii) judgments of whether or not each word fit a specified sentence frame, a deep processing condition, and (iv) an intentional learning condition, in which participants were told to study the words as their memory would be subsequently tested. The first three conditions constituted incidental learning conditions, as participants did not know at the time of study that their memory for the words would later be tested.

Replicating prior findings, consistent right-handedness was associated with poorer recall in the intentional learning condition. In the incidental learning conditions, no handedness differences were observed in correct recall in the two shallow encoding conditions, but consistent right-handers performed significantly worse in the deep processing condition, suggesting that part of the basis of the inconsistent-handed advantage in episodic memory arises from greater semantic elaboration at encoding, consistent with reports of greater semantic fluency among inconsistent-handers (Sontam & Christman, 2007; Sontam, Christman, & Jasper, 2006). We also found that consistent right-handers made more false alarms across all four conditions, again consistent with the presence of poorer source memory in consistent right-handers.

We have also studied self-report, non-performance-based measures of memory, finding that consistent right-handers report fewer déjà vu experiences and decreased dream recall (Christman, 2007), and report poorer memory ability in everyday situations (Christman & Propper, 2008). It is also worth noting that another recent study indicates that consistent right-handers may be better able to feign symptoms of memory impairment, a phenomenon known as malingering (Christman, Hoelzle, & Meyer, 2008b). In this study, participants were administered a memory test (Tombaugh, 1996) that produces ceiling levels of performance in both normal and patient populations; the poorer performance of inconsistent-handers under conditions of simulated malingering is therefore not due to actual poorer memory. Instead, these results may reflect the fact that inconsistent-handers were too zealous in their simulation of memory impairment, perhaps related to inconsistent-handers' increased openness to persuasion (Christman et al., 2008a).

Finally, these effects extend beyond personal handedness. Christman and Propper (2001) reported superior episodic memory among individuals with left-handed relatives in their immediate family, relative to individuals without any immediate left-handed relatives. Similarly, Christman, Garvey, Propper, and Phaneuf (2003) reported a marginal trend toward superior episodic memory among individuals with left-handed relatives.

In conclusion, individual differences in episodic memory as a function of degree of handedness have been found for a wide variety of tasks assessing both lab-based and real-world memories. From a neural perspective, these handedness differences have been interpreted as arising from the presence of decreased interaction between left-hemisphere-based encoding and right-hemisphere-based retrieval processes in consistent right-handers. From a functional perspective, our studies suggest that consistent right-handers have poorer source memory/monitoring, a finding with implications for eyewitness testimony. In the next section, we will switch focus from handedness, a trait variable associated with increased interhemispheric interaction, to the effects of bilateral eye movements, a state variable also associated with increased interhemispheric interaction.

BILATERAL EYE MOVEMENTS

Behavioral and neural foundations

The notion that bilateral eye movements (leftward–rightward alternating eye movements) might (a) increase episodic memory and (b) do so via interhemispheric interaction originally came from research on post-traumatic stress disorder (PTSD). Symptoms of PTSD are variable, but one hallmark of the disorder is memory disturbance. In addition to the intrusive, uncontrollable recall of the traumatic event diagnostic of PTSD, research demonstrates other evidence of episodic impairment. For example, individuals may have difficulty recalling specific memories that are unrelated to the trauma. When asked to report a specific memory that demonstrates the word "relax," individuals with PTSD may state a general memory, such as "when I go for walks in the park." This is in contrast to specific, time-dated memories reported by untraumatized individuals, such as "when I went for a walk in the park last Tuesday with my wife." Individuals with PTSD persist in reporting over-general memories even when repeatedly prompted for specific information (McNally, Lasko, Macklin, & Pitman, 1995).

We reasoned that if one aspect of PTSD is a dysfunction of episodic memory, then treatments that relieve PTSD symptoms may offer clues to memory function even in the absence of trauma. One such treatment is eye movement desensitization and reprocessing (EMDR; Shapiro, 1989). EMDR traditionally involves the rapid reorienting of attention via bilateral stimulation (alternating left–right fist clenching, finger tapping, or, most frequently, eye movements) at the rate of approximately two movements per second, while a therapist guides the PTSD sufferer in the verbal replay of the traumatic event.

There is considerable controversy surrounding EMDR's efficacy (e.g., Senior, 2001), in large part stemming from the fact that the neural mechanisms underlying its alleged efficacy remain largely unexplored. As one review noted, "a direct link between the theoretical basis of the therapy and observable psychological and neurobiological changes has yet to be established" (Spector & Read, 1999, p. 165). There is also controversy regarding whether bilateral stimulation is a necessary component of EMDR (e.g., Van Duesen, 2004). However, regardless of the ultimate findings concerning the clinical efficacy of EMDR, our research suggests that the bilateral eye movements often used in EMDR have robust and systematic effects in normal subjects on patterns of cortical activation and on the recall of episodic memories and hence are of potential interest to non-clinical researchers.

We have proposed that the bilateral stimulation component of EMDR facilitates episodic memory access via corpus-callosum-mediated interhemispheric interaction. Specifically, there is evidence that leftward versus rightward eye movements selectively activate the contralateral hemisphere (Bakan & Svorad, 1969). Thus, repeated bilateral eye movements should result in simultaneous activation of both hemispheres.

This was confirmed by Christman and Garvey (2001), who reported that engaging in bilateral eye movements reduced pre-existing asymmetries in hemispheric activation, as indexed by perceptual asymmetries on a free-vision chimeric faces task (Levy, Heller, Banich, & Burton, 1983). Bilateral saccadic eye movements also increased Stroop interference, relative to pre-eye movement baseline measures (Christman & Garvey, 2003), and such interference has been shown to arise at least in part from increased interhemispheric interaction (Christman, 2001).

Since one hemisphere is typically more activated than the other (Klein & Armitage, 1979), we hypothesized that the bilateral cortical activation induced by bilateral eye movements may induce a special neurological state. In turn, we hypothesized that bilateral cortical activation should enhance interhemispheric interaction, since, if the two hemispheres possess different levels of activation, it may be difficult for the less activated hemisphere to "keep pace" and interact efficiently with the more active hemisphere.

Direct evidence linking bilateral eye movements and facilitation of interhemispheric interaction can be found in studies of brain activity during rapid eye movement (REM) sleep. Evidence indicates that interhemispheric electroencephalographic (EEG) coherence increases significantly during REM sleep (e.g., Dumermuth & Lehman, 1981). Furthermore, the increase in interhemispheric EEG coherence has been specifically linked to the presence of eye movements (Dionne, 1986). Since the majority of eye movements during REM sleep are horizontal (Hansotia et al., 1990), this evidence suggests that bilateral eye movements are associated with increased interhemispheric interaction and coordination.

Finally, a recent study looked directly at the effects of bilateral eye movements on electrophysiological activity in the brain (Propper, Pierce, Bellorado, Geisler, & Christman, 2007). The results indicated that the no eye-movement control condition used in previous studies by Christman and colleagues had no effect on interhemispheric EEG coherence, while the bilateral eye movements resulted in significant changes in interhemispheric EEG coherence in the gamma band. Contrary to predictions, eye movements were associated with decreased, not increased, coherence.

However, a decrease in interhemispheric EEG coherence does not necessarily indicate a decrease in functional interhemispheric interaction. As noted by Uttal (2001), changes in measures of brain activity do not always map directly onto changes in cognitive function (e.g., increases in activation of a brain region associated with a specific task do not necessarily indicate that that region is primarily responsible for that task). To illustrate, decreases in gamma-band interhemispheric EEG coherence have been reported as subjects become better at a bimanual motor task in which the movements of the left and right hand, and hence right and left hemisphere processing, need to be coordinated (Gerloff & Andres, 2002). Thus, the current results should be interpreted as reflecting EM-induced *changes* in interhemispheric interaction, not necessarily EM-induced *decreases* in interhemispheric interaction. For example, increased interhemispheric EEG coherence implies that the two hemispheres are doing similar things, while increased interhemispheric interaction implies that the two hemispheres are doing coordinated, but not necessarily similar, things.

Bilateral eye movements and memory abilities

With regard to bilateral stimulation increasing access to episodic memories, we have published a series of papers demonstrating superior episodic memory following eye movements (see Table 8.2 for a summary of the eye movement studies reviewed below). In these studies, we used stimulation similar to that used in EMDR: bilateral visual stimulation with left–right alternating information, presented at the rate of two stimuli per second. Participants watched a dot appear alternately on the left and right sides of a computer screen for 30 seconds, with dots alternating left–right position every 500 ms. This "moving dot" condition was contrasted with a "central fixation" control condition, in which participants viewed a central dot that changed color twice a second; thus, the control condition involved periodic visual stimulation but in the absence of eye movements.

Our results have been surprising, but robust; following bilateral eye movements, participants experience superior episodic memory relative to the central fixation control condition for both laboratory-based and real-world information. Specifically, this superior memory takes the form of (i) increased recognition for words from a list (Christman *et al.*, 2003); (ii) increased recall of words (Christman, 2004); (iii) decreased false memories (Christman et al., 2004); (iv) younger age at which one's first childhood memory is recalled (Christman et al., 2006); and (v) increased recall for personal, real-world, autobiographical memories (Christman et al., 2003).

Similar results have been found by other laboratories. Lyle et al. (2008a) reported that engaging in bilateral eye movements enhanced both recall and recognition performance. Parker and Dagnall (2009) reported that bilateral eye movements reduced the number of false memories in the DRM paradigm. Parker, Relph, and Dagnall (2008) reported that bilateral eye movements enhanced free recall and paired associate recall. Finally, Parker, Buckley, and Dagnall (2009) found that bilateral eye movements enhanced picture recognition as well as reducing the misinformation effect (in which misleading post-event information is mistakenly incorporated into one's recall).

Direct support for the hypothesis that the effects of eye movements reflect hemispheric interaction was provided by Christman et al. (2003). Their

Table 8.2 Summary of research on the effects of bilateral saccadic eye movements (EMs) on memory retrieval (all studies involve EMs immediately prior to retrieval except where noted)

Task	Findings	Effect size (d)	Citation
Free recall of words	EMs beneficial for consistent-handers, detrimental for inconsistent-handers	.33 −.02	Lyle, Logan, & Roediger, 2008a
Free recall of words	EMs beneficial	.53	Christman & Butler, 2005
Free recall of events from own life	EMs beneficial	.66	Christman, Garvey, Propper, & Phaneuf, 2003
Recall of early childhood memories	EMs beneficial	.55	Christman, Propper, & Brown, 2006
Misinformation effect	EMs reduce effect	.80	Parker, Buckley, & Dagnall, 2009
Source memory	EMs beneficial	.87	Christman, Propper, & Dion, 2004
Source memory	EMs beneficial	.57	Parker & Dagnall, 2007
Recognition of words	EMs beneficial	.53	Christman, Garvey, Propper, & Phaneuf, 2003
Recognition of words	EMs beneficial for consistent-handers, detrimental for inconsistent-handers	.46 −.21	Lyle, Logan, & Roediger, 2008a
Recogition of words	EMs beneficial	.63	Parker, Relph, & Dagnall, 2008
Associative recognition	EMs beneficial	.86	Parker, Relph, & Dagnall, 2008
Recognition of pictures	EMs beneficial	.58	Parker, Buckley & Dagnall, 2009
Know vs. remember judgments	Horizontal EMs lead to more "remember" judgments than no EMs	.81	Parker, Buckley & Dagnall, 2009
Color memory	EMs beneficial	.69	Parker, Relph, & Dagnall, 2008
Spatial location memory	EMs beneficial	.72	Parker, Relph, & Dagnall, 2008
EMs at encoding	EMs detrimental	.69	Christman & Butler, 2005
Implicit memory	EMs have no effect	.12	Christman, Garvey, Propper, & Phaneuf, 2003
Semantic memory	EMs have no effect	.22	Christman, Garvey, Propper, & Phaneuf, 2003

study compared four different eye movement conditions, yielded by the factorial combination of horizontal versus vertical eye movements and saccadic versus pursuit eye movements. As noted above, leftward versus rightward eye movements result in selective activation of the contralateral hemisphere (Bakan & Svorad, 1969); thus, bilateral horizontal eye movements are hypothesized to induce bilateral hemispheric activation, which in turn is hypothesized to enhance interhemispheric interaction. In contrast, vertical eye movements presumably do not selectively activate a specific hemisphere. In line with this reasoning, Christman et al. (2003) found that vertical eye movements had no effects on memory. Similarly, Parker et al. (2008) also reported that horizontal eye movements led to better memory than vertical eye movements or no eye movements (which were not different from each other).

With regard to saccadic versus pursuit eye movements, voluntary saccadic eye movements generate greater activity in the frontal lobes than do pursuit eye movements, which are largely controlled by subcortical structures (O'Driscoll, et al., 1998). Thus, we reasoned that only the combination of horizontal *and* saccadic eye movements would enhance episodic memory, which is what we found: vertical and pursuit eye movements had no significant effects on memory performance, although there was a non-significant trend for saccadic eye movements (horizontal or vertical) to lead to better memory performance than pursuit eye movements.

Interestingly, in contrast to the findings of Christman et al. (2003) and of Parker et al. (2008), Lyle et al. (2008a) reported that both vertical *and* horizontal saccadic eye movements led to enhanced episodic memory. It is possible that saccadic eye movements may benefit memory in two independent ways. One is the presumed increase in interhemispheric interaction discussed previously.

Stickgold (2002) has proposed an alternative account, arguing that "the repetitive redirecting of attention in EMDR induces a neurobiological state, similar to that of REM sleep, which is optimally configured to support the cortical integration of traumatic memories into general semantic frameworks" (p. 61). That is, any procedure that induces repetitive redirecting of attention, be it left/right (as with horizontal eye movements) or up/down (as with vertical eye movements), may benefit the consolidation of memory traces. The "interhemispheric interaction" and "redirecting of attention" accounts are not mutually exclusive, and the combined results from the studies by Christman et al. (2003), Parker et al. (2008), and Lyle et al. (2008a) suggest that both accounts may have merit.

Three other findings on the effects of eye movements on memory deserve comment. First, Christman et al. (2003) reported that bilateral saccadic eye movements tended to induce more conservative response biases (i.e., a decreased likelihood to respond to "new" items as "old"). Thus, the eye movements appear to enhance episodic retrieval primarily by reducing the number of "false alarms" (as opposed to increasing the number of "hits"). However, the reliability of this effect is questionable, as Parker et al. (2009) reported no effects of eye movements on response bias.

Second, the studies reviewed above focused solely on consistent right-handers. However, Lyle, et al. (2008a) reported that engaging in bilateral eye movements prior to retrieval had no effect on recognition and actually impaired recall for inconsistent-handers. They hypothesized that the relation between interhemispheric interaction and episodic retrieval may be character-ized by an inverted-U-shaped function: up to some point, an increase in interhemispheric interaction is beneficial, but past that point, it becomes detrimental. Thus, for consistent-handers, who display less baseline interhemi-spheric interaction, eye movements may be beneficial, but for inconsistent-handers, who already display higher levels of interhemispheric interaction, increases in interaction induced by eye movements push them over the top of the inverted-U function and lead to impairment of memory, perhaps due to increased access to related but non-presented semantic information in the right hemisphere.

Finally, Christman and Butler (2005) examined the effects of eye move-ments on the encoding versus retrieval of episodic memories. In terms of retrieval, they replicated prior work: eye movements prior to testing improved recall. However, they found that engaging in eye movements immediately prior to encoding led to impairments in subsequent recall. Although the basis for this finding remains unclear, a potential explanation is that one effect of increased interhemispheric interaction is to increase functional access to right-hemisphere-based processing. If so, then, according to the HERA model, increased access to the right hemisphere would be beneficial for retrieval but detrimental to encoding.

In summary, engaging in bilateral saccadic eye movements immediately prior to the retrieval of episodic memories has a beneficial effect, at least in consistent-handers, across a wide variety of memory tasks. The effects of vertical saccadic eye movements remain unclear, with two studies reporting no effects of vertical eye movements (Christman et al., 2003; Parker et al., 2008) and a third study reporting that vertical eye movements were beneficial for memory (Lyle et al., 2008a). Finally, the beneficial effects of eye move-ments appear to be restricted to consistent-handers, as such eye movements may impair some forms of memory retrieval in inconsistent-handers (Lyle et al., 2008a).

IMPLICATIONS FOR APPLIED MEMORY RESEARCH

Episodic memory plays a critical role in many applied memory contexts, from eyewitness testimony to the false/recovered memory debate. Although sys-tematic individual differences in episodic memory performance as a function of strength of handedness have been repeatedly reported, they are not of sufficient magnitude to allow for global pronouncements, such as "only inconsistent-handers make reliable eyewitnesses." There is considerable overlap in the memory abilities of consistent- and inconsistent-handers, making strength of handedness a relatively crude diagnostic for predicting memory accuracy. However, we do think that our findings have great utility for researchers investigating applied memory phenomena, especially the fact that inconsistent-handedness is associated with superior source memory, a critical issue in eyewitness memory. Moreover, our emphasis on contrasting consistent- versus inconsistent-handers provides a major logistical advantage over the traditional approach of comparing right- and left-handers, as, by our operational definition of using a median split on handedness scores, any sample will consist of roughly equal numbers of consistent- and inconsistent-handers, eliminating the need to specifically recruit left-handers.

At the very least, even if one is not explicitly interested in individual differences, including strength of handedness as an explicit variable in analyses should help move variability out of the error term and into an effect term, thereby allowing greater precision and power in the testing of general models and theories. At best, explicit inclusion of handedness as an individual difference variable of interest in models of memory could help shed further light on our current knowledge of individual differences in memory, which focus primarily on sex and age.

Indeed, the existing literature on sex and age differences in memory may be incomplete and misleading, as there is good reason to think that both sex and age are at least partly confounded with handedness. For example, unpublished demographic data from our lab indicates that females are more likely to be consistent-handed (left or right), while males are more likely to be inconsistent-handed. Thus, an observed sex difference could be due to sex *per se*, or could reflect a confounded effect of strength of handedness, or both.

Similarly, with regard to aging, there is evidence that corpus-callosum-mediated interhemispheric interaction has a complex developmental trajectory. First, the corpus callosum is one of the last major brain structures to become fully myelinated and mature (e.g., Giedd, et al., 1996). Second, there is also evidence that the corpus callosum may age more quickly than other brain structures (e.g., Persson et al., 2006). This implies that handedness differences in callosally mediated interhemispheric interaction and memory may not be found in very young children and older adults. In fact, Lyle et al. (2008b) reported that the inconsistent-handed advantage was more robust in middle-aged adults than in older adults. Thus, it may be the case that handedness, sex, and age all interact in complex ways in determining the nature of individual differences in episodic memory.

Other individual differences in applied memory are likely related to our findings of an inconsistent-handed advantage in episodic memory. For example, individuals with increased predisposition to dissociation are poorer at source monitoring and are more susceptible to misinformation effects (e.g., Cann & Katz, 2005; Eisen, Morgan, & Mickes, 2002). In turn, consistent-handers (both left *and* right) are more prone to dissociative experiences than inconsistent-handers (Christman & Ammann, 1995). Our view is that the decreased interhemispheric interaction observed in consistent-handers is responsible both for their increased tendency to dissociate and their poorer episodic memory performance.

Similarly, there is evidence that increased susceptibility to misinformation is also related to poorer spatial imagery ability (Tomes & Katz, 1997). This may be related to reports that consistent-handedness is also associated with poorer spatial visualization ability (e.g., McGee, 1978; Snyder & Harris, 1993). Finally, a recent paper reported that individuals with lower working memory capacity are more susceptible to the misinformation effect (Gerrie & Garry, 2007). In this light, it is interesting to note that consistent-handedness in males is associated with decreased working memory capacity (Kempe, Brooks, & Christman, 2006). It is possible that the disparate dimensions of individual difference in susceptibility to the misinformation effect (e.g., dissociation, spatial visualization, working memory capacity) are, in fact, all manifestations of a more fundamental dimension of individual differences in consistency of handedness.

Research on the beneficial effects of bilateral eye movements on episodic retrieval may offer more immediate benefit to applied memory researchers. Although one obviously has no control over an individual's handedness, it appears that one can at least temporarily induce a state of greater interhemispheric interaction and, in turn, enhanced retrieval of episodic memories, by having subjects engage in bilateral eye movements immediately prior to recall.

Much research has been done on finding ways to enhance memory retrieval in applied contexts. For example, hypnosis has been extensively investigated (e.g., Dywan & Bowers, 1983; Kebbel & Wagstaff, 1998). However, hypnosis suffers from such problems as the fact that not all individuals are susceptible to hypnosis and the fact that hypnosis leads to increased suggestibility, leading to the possibility of false memories being incorporated into recall. Context reinstatement is another, more cognitive, technique that has been studied (e.g., Hammond, Wagstaff, & Cole, 2006; Krafka & Penrod, 1985). Given that (i) the right hemisphere is more sensitive to contextual information (e.g., Ornstein, 1997), and (ii) bilateral eye movements appear to increase functional access to right hemisphere processing, the use of bilateral eye movements may prove to be a powerful adjunct to context reinstatement techniques. An added potential benefit of eye movements is the tentative evidence that, in addition to enhancing overall recall, they also lead to more conservative response biases, thus sharply decreasing the likelihood of reporting false memories.

On the other hand, a direct examination of any relationship between bilateral eye movements and suggestibility has not been conducted, although previous research suggests that increased interhemispheric interaction is associated with increased suggestibility (Christman et al., 2008a). Thus, future applied work might examine the effects of bilateral eye movements on persuasion in contexts such as the misinformation effect and advertising.

CONCLUSION

The primary motivation behind the current chapter is to bring recent basic research on the relation between interhemispheric interaction and the retrieval of episodic memories to the attention of applied memory researchers. The fact that both trait-like (i.e., consistency of handedness) and state-like (i.e., bilateral eye movement-induced changes in hemispheric activation) variables have been shown to have systematic relations with memory performance across a wide variety of tasks offers researchers new tools to study the limitations of human memory ability and ways to enhance memory retrieval in applied contexts.

References

Bakan, P., & Svorad, D. (1969). Resting EEG alpha asymmetry of reflective lateral eye movements. *Nature, 223*, 975–976.

Cann, D. R., & Katz, A. N. (2005). Habitual acceptance of misinformation: Examination of individual differences and source attributions. *Memory and Cognition, 33*, 405–417.

Christman, S. (1993). Handedness in musicians: Bimanual constraints on performance. *Brain and Cognition, 22*, 266–272.

Christman, S. D. (2001). Individual differences in Stroop and local-global processing: A possible role of interhemispheric interaction. *Brain and Cognition, 45*, 97–118.

Christman, S. D. (2004). Strong right-handers exhibit decreased Stroop interference and poorer explicit memory: Interhemispheric mechanisms. Presented at the 45th Annual Meeting of the Psychonomic Society, Minneapolis.

Christman, S. D. (2007). Individual differences in *déjà vu* and *jamais vu* experiences: Degree of handedness and access to the right hemisphere. Presented at the 19th Annual Meeting of the Association for Psychological Science, Washington, DC.

Christman, S., & Ammann, D. (1995). Dissociative experiences and handedness. Presented at the Annual Meeting of the Midwestern Psychological Association, Chicago.

Christman, S. D., Bentle, M., & Niebauer, C. L. (2007a). Handedness differences in body image distortion and eating disorder symptomatology. *International Journal of Eating Disorders, 40*, 247–256.

Christman, S. D., & Butler, M. (2005). Bilateral eye movements impair the encoding and enhance the retrieval of episodic memories. Presented at the 46th Annual Meeting of the Psychonomic Society, Toronto.

Christman, S., & Butler, M. (2007). Individual differences in intentional versus incidental learning: Effects of handedness and interhemispheric interaction. Presented at the 48th Annual Meeting of the Psychonomic Society, Long Beach.

Christman, S., & Garvey, K. (2001). Bilateral eye movements reduce asymmetries in hemispheric activation. Presented at the 2001 EMDR International Association Conference, Austin, TX.

Christman, S., & Garvey, K. (2003). Bilateral eye movements increase Stroop interference: A role of interhemispheric interaction. Presented at the 31st Annual Meeting of the International Neuropsychological Society, Honolulu.

Christman, S. S., Garvey, J. K., Propper, R. E., & Phaneuf, K. (2003). Bilateral eye movements enhance the retrieval of episodic memories. *Neuropsychology*, *17*, 221–229.

Christman, S. D., Henning, B., Geers, A. L., Propper, R. E., & Niebauer, C. L. (2008a). Mixed-handed persons are more easily persuaded and are more gullible: Interhemispheric interaction and belief updating. *Laterality*, *13*, 403–426.

Christman, S., Hoelzle, J., & Meyer, G. (2008b). Individual differences in the ability to simulate malingering. Presented at the 37th Annual Meeting of the International Neuropsychological Society, Waikoloa, Hawaii.

Christman, S. D., Jasper, J. D., Sontam, V., & Cooil, B. (2007b). Individual differences in risk perception versus risk taking: Handedness and interhemispheric interaction. *Brain and Cognition*, *63*, 51–58.

Christman, S. D., & Propper, R. E. (2001). Superior episodic memory is associated with interhemispheric processing. *Neuropsychology*, *15*, 607–616.

Christman, S., & Propper, R. (2008). Individual differences in performance on the Everyday Memory Questionnaire: Effects of degree of handedness. Presented at the 37th Annual Meeting of the International Neuropsychological Society, Waikoloa, Hawaii.

Christman, S. D., Propper, R. E., & Brown, T. J. (2006). Increased interhemispheric interaction is associated with earlier offset of childhood amnesia. *Neuropsychology*, *20*, 336–345.

Christman, S. D., Propper, R. E., & Dion, A. (2004). Increased interhemispheric interaction is associated with decreased false memories in a verbal converging semantic associates paradigm. *Brain and Cognition*, *56*, 313–319.

Clarke, J. M., & Zaidel, E. (1994). Anatomical–behavioral relationships: Corpus callosum morphometry and hemispheric specialization. *Behavioural Brain Research*, *64*, 185–202.

Craik, F. I. M., & Tulving, E. (1975). Depth of processing and the retention of words in episodic memory. *Journal of Experimental Psychology*, 104, 268–294.

Denenberg, V. H., Kertesz, A., & Cowell, P. E. (1991). A factor analysis of the human's corpus callosum. *Brain Research*, *548*, 126–132.

Dionne, H. (1986). Protocole d'analyse de la cohérence interhémisphérique cérébrale durant le sommeil paradoxal. Mémoire de Maître ès Sciences Appliquées, Université de Montréal.

Dumermuth, G., & Lehman, D. (1981). EEG power and coherence during non-REM and REM phases in humans in all-night sleep analyses. *European Neurology*, *22*, 322–339.

Dywan, J., & Bowers, K. (1983). The use of hypnosis to enhance recall. *Science*, *22*, 184–185.

Eisen, M. L., Morgan, D. Y., & Mickes, L. (2002). Individual differences in eyewitness memory and suggestibility: Examining relations between acquiescence, dissociation and resistance to misleading information. *Personality and Individual Differences*, *33*, 553–572.

Gardiner, J. M. (1988). Functional aspects of recollective experience. *Memory and Cognition*, *16*, 309–313.

Gerloff, C., & Andres, F. G. (2002). Bimanual coordination and interhemispheric interaction. *Acta Psychologica*, *110*, 161–186.

Gerrie, M. P., & Garry, M. (2007). Individual differences in working memory capacity affect false memories for missing aspects of events. *Memory*, *15*, 561–571.

Giedd, J. N., Rumsey, J. M., Castellanos, F. X., Rajapakse, J. C., Kaysen, D., Vaituzis, A. C., et al. (1996). A quantitative MRI study of the corpus callosum in children and adolescents. *Developmental Brain Research, 91*, 274–280.

Habib, M., Gayraud, D., Oliva, A., Regis, J., Salamon, G., & Khalal, R. (1991). Effects of handedness and sex on the morphology of the corpus callosum: A study with brain magnetic resonance imaging. *Brain and Cognition, 16*, 41–61.

Habib, R., Nyberg, L., & Tulving, E. (2003). Hemispheric asymmetries of memory: The HERA model revisited. *Trends in Cognitive Sciences, 7*, 241–245.

Hammond, L., Wagstaff, G. F., & Cole, J. (2006). Facilitating eyewitness memory in adults and children with context reinstatement and focused meditation. *Journal of Investigative Psychology and Offender Profiling, 3*, 117–130.

Hansotia, P., Broste, S., So, E., Ruggles, K., Wall, R., & Friske, M. (1990). Eye movement patterns in REM sleep. *Electroencephalography and Clinical Neurophysiology, 76*, 388–399.

Jasper, J. D., & Christman, S. D. (2005). A neuropsychological dimension for anchoring effects. *Journal of Behavioral Decision Making, 18*, 343–369.

Kebbell, M. R., & Wagstaff, G. F. (1998). Hypnotic interviewing: The best way to interview eyewitnesses? *Behavioral Sciences and the Law, 16*, 115–129.

Kempe, V., Brooks, P. J., & Christman, S. D. (2006). Gender modulates effects of hemispheric connectivity on verbal episodic memory. Presented at the 47th Annual Meeting of the Psychonomic Society, Houston.

Klein, R., & Armitage, R. (1979). Rhythms in human performance: 1½-hour oscillations in cognitive style. *Science, 204*, 1326–1328.

Krafka, L., & Penrod, S. (1985). Reinstatement of context in a field experiment on eyewitness identification. *Journal of Personality and Social Psychology, 49*, 59–69.

Lansky, L. M., Feinstein, H., & Peterson, J. M. (1988) Demography of handedness in two samples of randomly selected adults ($N = 2083$). *Neuropsychologia, 26*, 465–477.

Levy, J., Heller, W., Banich, M., & Burton, L. (1983). Are variations among right-handed individuals in perceptual asymmetries caused by characteristic arousal differences between the hemispheres? *Journal of Experimental Psychology: Human Perception and Performance, 9*, 329–359.

Lewin, C., Wolgers, G., & Herlitz, A. (2001). Sex differences favoring women in verbal but not in visuospatial episodic memory. *Neuropsychology, 15*, 165–173.

Lyle, K. B., Logan, J., & Roediger, H. L. (2008a). Eye movements enhance memory for individuals who are strongly right-handed and harm it for individuals who are not. *Psychonomic Bulletin and Review, 15*, 515–520.

Lyle, K. B., McCabe, D. P., & Roediger, H. L. (2008b). Handedness is related to memory via interhemispheric interaction: Evidence from paired associate recall and source memory tasks. *Neuropsychology, 22*, 525–530.

McGee, M. G. (1978). Handedness and mental rotation. *Perceptual and Motor Skills, 47*, 641–642.

McNally, R. J., Lasko, N. B., Macklin, M. L., & Pitman, R. K. (1995). Autobiographical memory disturbance in combat-related posttraumatic stress disorder. *Behaviour Research and Therapy, 33*, 619–630.

Niebauer, C. L., Aselage, J., & Schutte, C. (2002). Interhemispheric interaction and consciousness: Degree of handedness predicts the intensity of a sensory illusion. *Laterality, 7*, 85–96.

Niebauer, C. L., Christman, S. D., Reid, S. A., & Garvey, K. (2004). Interhemispheric interaction and beliefs on our origin: Degree of handedness predicts beliefs in creationism versus evolution. *Laterality, 9*, 433–447.

O'Driscoll, G. A., Strakowski, S. M., Alpert, N. M., Matthysse, S. W., Rauch, S. L., Levy, D. L., & Holzman, P. S. (1998). Differences in cerebral activation during smooth pursuit and saccadic eye movements using positron-emission tomography. *Biological Psychiatry, 44*, 685–689.

Oldfield, R. (1971). The assessment and analysis of handedness: The Edinburgh Inventory. *Neuropsychologia, 9*, 97–113.

Ornstein, R. (1997). *The right mind.* New York: Harcourt Brace.

Parker, A., Buckley, S., & Dagnall, N. (2009). Reduced misinformation effects following bilateral saccadic eye movements. *Brain and Cognition, 69*, 89–97.

Parker, A., & Dagnall, N. (2007). Effects of bilateral eye movements on gist based false recognition in the DRM paradigm. *Brain and Cognition, 63*, 221–225.

Parker, A., Relph, S., & Dagnall, N. (2008). Effects of bilateral eye movements on the retrieval of item, associative, and contextual information. *Neuropsychology, 22*, 136–145.

Persson, J., Nyberg, L., Lind, J., Larsson, A., Nilsson, L.-G., Ingvar, M., & Buckner, R. L. (2006). Structure–function correlates of cognitive decline in aging. *Cerebral Cortex, 16*, 907–915.

Propper, R. E., & Christman, S. (1999). A test of the HERA model II: Objects as stimuli. *Brain and Cognition, 40*, 227–229.

Propper, R. E., & Christman, S. D. (2004). Mixed- versus strong-handedness is associated with biases toward "Remember" versus "Know" judgments in recognition memory: Role of interhemispheric interaction. *Memory, 12*, 707–714.

Propper, R. E., Christman, S. D., & Phaneuf, K. A. (2005). A mixed-handed advantage in episodic memory: A possible role of interhemispheric interaction. *Memory and Cognition, 33*, 751–757.

Propper, R. E., Pierce, J., Bellorado, N., Geisler, M. W., & Christman, S. D. (2007). Effects of bilateral eye movements on interhemispheric gamma EEG coherence: Implications for EMDR therapy. *Journal of Nervous and Mental Disease, 95*, 785–788.

Rehnman, J., & Herlitz, A. (2007). Women remember more faces than men do. *Acta Psychologica, 124*, 344–355.

Roberts, K. P. & Blades, M. (2000). *Children's source monitoring.* Mahwah, NJ: Lawrence Erlbaum Associates, Inc.

Roediger, H. L., & Geraci, L. (2007). Aging and the misinformation effect: A neuropsychological analysis. *Journal of Experimental Psychology: Learning, Memory, and Cognition, 33*, 321–334.

Roediger, H. L., & McDermott, K. B. (1995). Creating false memories: Remembering words not presented on lists. *Journal of Experimental Psychology: Learning, Memory, and Cognition, 21*, 803–814.

Schacter, S. C. (1994). Ambilaterality: Definition from handedness preference questionnaires and potential significance. *International Journal of Neuroscience, 77*, 47–51.

Senior, J. (2001). Eye movement desensitisation and reprocessing: A matter for serious consideration? *Psychologist, 14*, 361–363.

Shapiro, F. (1989). Efficacy of the eye movement desensitization procedure in the treatment of traumatic memories. *Journal of Traumatic Stress, 2*, 199–223.

Snyder, P. J., & Harris, L. J. (1993). Handedness, sex, and familial sinistrality effects on spatial tasks. *Cortex, 29*, 115–134.

Sontam, V., & Christman, S. D. (2007). Semantic organization: Possible individual differences based on handedness. Presented at the 48th Annual Meeting of the Psychonomic Society, Long Beach.

Sontam, V., Christman, S. D., & Jasper, J. D. (2006). Semantic flexibility. Presented at the 47th Annual Meeting of the Psychonomic Society, Houston.

Spector, J., & Read, J. (1999). The current status of eye movement desensitization and reprocessing (EMDR). *Clinical Psychology and Psychotherapy, 6*, 165–174.

Stickgold, R. (2002). EMDR: A putative neurobiological mechanism of action. *Journal of Clinical Psychology, 58*, 61–75.

Tombaugh, T. N. (1996). *The Test of Memory Malingering*. Toronto: Multi-Health Systems.

Tomes, J. L, & Katz, A. N. (1997). Habitual susceptibility to misinformation and individual differences in eyewitness memory. *Applied Cognitive Psychology, 11*, 233–251.

Tulving, E., Kapur, S., Craik, F. I. M., Moscovitch, M., & Houle, S. (1994). Hemispheric encoding/retrieval asymmetry in episodic memory: Positron emission tomography findings. *Proceedings from the National Academy of Science, USA, 91*, 2016–2020.

Tulving, E., Schacter, D. L., & Stark, H. A. (1982). Priming effects in word-fragment completion are independent of recognition memory. *Journal of Experimental Psychology: Learning, Memory, and Cognition, 8*, 336–342.

Uttal, W. (2001). *The new phrenology: The limits of localizing cognitive processes in the brain*. Cambridge, MA: MIT Press-Bradford Books.

Van Deusen, K. M. (2004). Bilateral stimulation in EMDR: A replicated single-subject component analysis. *The Behavior Therapist, 27*, 79–86.

Voyer, D., Postma, A., Brake, B., & Imperato-McGinley, J. (2007). Gender differences in object location memory: A meta-analysis. *Psychonomic Bulletin and Review, 14*, 23–38.

Witelson, S. F., & Goldsmith, C. H. (1991). The relationship of hand preference to anatomy of the corpus callosum in men. *Brain Research, 545*, 175–182.

9 Déjà vu

Insights from the dreamy state and the neuropsychology of memory

Chris J. A. Moulin and
Patrick Chauvel

> There is a curious experience which everyone seems to have had – the feeling
> that the present moment in its completeness has been experienced before – we
> were saying just this thing, in just this place, to just these people.
>
> (James, 1890, p. 675)

Research suggests that déjà vu is a fairly common experience, and that
around 70% of the population have experienced it (Brown, 2003). People
are sometimes unsure of whether or not they have had it, as it is such a
subjective experience. Many people will have, at some point in their life, trav-
elled to a new city or country and have a fleeting feeling that they have been
there before, even though they know they have not. Such an experience is one
example of the déjà vu experience. As you will see, psychologists tend to
define it as a sensation of familiarity for something that you *know* to be
unfamiliar. Most interestingly, it seems that the experience of déjà vu is,
amongst other things, experienced more frequently when we are tired,
stressed or intoxicated, experienced more by younger people, and is related
positively to education and intelligence. (For a full account of factors associated with déjà vu experience, see Brown, 2004.) As such then, it is a topic
that should resonate with psychologists of all ages and stages who are reading
this book.

Two aspects of déjà vu research continually surprise those who research it.
First, it is continually presented in the media, and stories about déjà vu and
those who suffer from it pathologically are recycled over and over. Second, in
the absence of an established account of the phenomenon, it is amazing
how steadfast personal folk-beliefs about the experience are. We believe that
these two factors are related and that they both spring from the fact that
contemporary cognitive psychology is only now being able to understand and
interpret déjà vu and its cause in the healthy – and unhealthy – brain.

As an example of the first aspect of this work consider Nobel prize-
winning neuroscientist Tonegawa's comments to the media about déjà vu
which he made to the international press in 2007 (Halber, 2007):

Déjà vu is a memory problem, Tonegawa explained, occurring when our brains struggle to tell the difference between two extremely similar situations. As people age, Tonegawa said, déjà-vu-like confusion happens more often—and it also happens in people suffering from brain diseases like Alzheimer's. "It's not surprising," he said, "when you consider the fact that there's a loss of or damage to cells in the dentate gyrus."

The paper by Tonegawa and colleagues (McHugh et al., 2007) makes an undoubted contribution to the field of memory, and in particular, memory disorders such as Alzheimer's disease. In short, it considers a very fundamental aspect of memory – that we might match 'patterns' of activation in the brain. The reason we recognize something is because it makes a pattern of activation in the brain that we can match to existing representations in the brain. Tonegawa looked at this process in mice. But the paper does not mention déjà vu; déjà vu is merely a useful tag by which to promote the work to the media. There is much more public interest in déjà vu than there is in basic neuroscience on mice!

Presumably, this interest in the sensation of déjà vu is because it is a relatively striking and intensely personal experience. Indeed, religious education teachers tend to use déjà vu as an example of a religious experience, citing its very subjective nature and how mysterious it is. In fact, even fellow academic psychologists, at least at the University of Leeds, suggest that researching déjà vu is a bit like researching the existence of ghosts, since the experience of having déjà vu is arguably as personal, subjective and without explanation as seeing a ghost. It is amazing how aggressively people can be opposed to a memory-based explanation of déjà vu. Take for instance this posting to one of our websites about our research looking at people who, as a result of brain damage, have constant and debilitating sensations of déjà vu:

> I'm an experienced and functioning [person who experiences déjà vu] living longer with my 'peculiar' perception of time than Chris Moulin's been alive. You might want to factor 'precognition' into your studies, as well as the temporal research being done by physicists. Time itself is not solely linear. Our brains can, under certain conditions, serve as interfaces with 'higher dimensions'. . . . Expand the horizons of your work, and you will benefit humanity. Continue to portray to the media that continual déjà vu is merely an illness, and you will destroy many people who otherwise would survive. You choose. The glaciers are melting.

This chapter, then, aims to give an overview of research into déjà vu. The main aim is to put forward the idea that déjà vu is nothing more sensational than an infrequent and esoteric memory error. In this respect, Tonegawa's comments are correct: déjà vu is caused by a memory error. The brain is set up in a particular way to deal with memory function and a natural consequence of that set-up is that it is susceptible to a variety of errors, one of which is the sensation of déjà vu. In reviewing the area, we will give a flavour of the history of déjà vu research, but to illustrate our theory, we will need to give an overview of contemporary neuropsychology of memory. In presenting this work we aim to show how the very subjective nature of déjà vu places it at the forefront of research into memory, and how this research into subjective experience leads memory theory forward. To foreshadow our argument: déjà vu is caused by higher-order malfunctions in the brain. The déjà vu sensation itself, then, should be able to illuminate our understanding of the complexity and subjectivity of memory.

HISTORICAL PERSPECTIVES: DÉJÀ VU AS AN ANOMALOUS EXPERIENCE

> 'Supernature abhors a vacuum,' and any vacuum in scientific psychology will inevitably be filled by parapsychology.
>
> (Walsh, 2004, p. 284)

Déjà vu is a French term and literally translates as 'already seen'. In fact, in French the more complete 'phénomène de déjà vu' is usually used. It is somewhat contentious as to who first used the term, and as early as 1896, Arnaud was debating what the scientific definition of the term should be and how it differed from false memory and other strange memory sensations (Arnaud, 1896). The term is certainly in use in English in the first half of the nineteenth century although there is a great deal of imprecision about its use. Sometimes it seems to be used for strange, false sensations of memory, as we tend to use it now, but it is also used to describe normal functioning memory processes, such as used by Claperede in 1907 (translated by Nicolas, 1996), to describe the lack of recognition memory in a famous case of Korsakoff's amnesia.

One hundred years later, and the web of science search engine returns 807 papers purportedly on the topic of déjà vu. Not one-tenth of these papers consider memory, psychology or even the brain. For the popularization of the term déjà vu, we probably have to thank the celebrated baseball player and manager-turned-commentator Yogi Berra, whose famous tautology 'it's like déjà vu all over again' is quoted *ad nauseam*. In fact, 181 articles use the phrase 'déjà vu all over again' in the title, and only one of those is about psychology, a review of our work in the *New Scientist* in 2009. As many articles about engineering, business and economics use the term déjà vu in the title as do psychological studies. 'Deja vu all over again: Rapid enumeration of *Legionella pneumophila* in water' (Edelstein, 2006) is just one example. As the usage of the term increases, this has knock-on effects. Gallup and Newport (1991) reported that from 1978 to 1990 people who had experienced déjà vu increased from 30% of the population to 55%. This suggests that societal and media influences may alter the general public's understanding of the term, and, as a result, more people say that they experience it. Whether or not this increase is for 'genuine' déjà vu or not is a point of contention, since there is also a sense in which any repetition, whether erroneous or not, leads to the usage of the term, such as the Pepsi advertising in 2006, 'Déjà vu in every gulp'. If the specificity of the term slips, more people will say that they experience it, but we will be less sure whether people are referring to a common experience.

Long before the term entered common parlance, it was used technically by a variety of authors to explain either specific processes in recognition memory or errors related to that process. Much of the early work on déjà vu emphasizes the bizarre or supernatural in its genesis. For instance, the ancient Pythagoreans cited the experience as proof of the transmigration of one's soul, and it was a topic discussed by monks: Saint Augustine in the fifth century referred to it as 'falsae memoriae'. Other famous theories of déjà vu exist. For instance, Freud suggested that déjà vu was caused by re-experiencing issues and events that had at one point been repressed. The religious or supernatural emphasis has proved hard to shift. William James (1902) refers to déjà vu as a variety of religious experience, which he defines as: 'a kind of insight into which I cannot help ascribing some metaphysical significance'. His pioneering work is as often cited by philosophers of religion as it is by an experimental psychologist, but James's ideas were that by studying mystical and nebulous experiences such as déjà vu, we might better understand people. This focus has possibly been a little slow to develop in experimental psychology, but, as we will see, there are clear links between religious experience, déjà vu and the brain. In fact, an emerging topic in neuroscience and cognitive psychology is the understanding of religious experience and belief in general – for example work on the 'Folk psychology of souls' (Bering, 2006).

However, the clearest lineage between contemporary research on déjà vu and its history comes from the study of epilepsy. Epilepsy comes from the Greek, to seize or to grasp, and its core feature is seizures, which can vary in magnitude and form. A full description of the disease is not possible here. In short, it can be thought of as a cortical disorder: the surface of the brain, in one or many regions, has disturbed electrical activity. This typically manifests itself as a series of seizures which may or may not be triggered by events, and may affect limited or extended areas of the cerebral cortex in a more or less synchronized way. Epilepsy can be acquired following brain injury or disease or due to a developmental defect; it can also be of undetermined origin. Crucially, one of the common features of epilepsy, in varying forms, is of the disturbance of consciousness, and the prevalence of alternative experiential or behavioural states, with a paroxysmal occurrence (sudden, unexpected occurrences). Indeed, epilepsy was long thought of as a sacred disease, giving the sufferer unique insights into the spiritual and mystic aspects of life (Saver & Rabin, 1997).

The modern history of epilepsy research is dominated by Hughlings Jackson, a British neurologist working in the latter half of the nineteenth century (for an account of his contribution see Meares, 1999 and Dewhurst, 1982). Jackson coined the phrase 'dreamy state' which he used to refer to the 'vague and yet exceedingly elaborate mental states' that characterize certain seizures. These dreamy states often included nebulous sensations and feelings, but notably scenes and experiences from the past, like flashbacks. Jackson (1888), for instance, reports a 37-year-old man who as part of his seizures detected strange smells, then began (uncontrollably) to think of 'things from boyhood's days'. Jackson's contribution was to begin to understand that the workings of the epileptic mind, far from being an inexplicable or spiritual anomaly, were a window into healthy function of the brain and mind. His exploration of dreamy states opened up the neurological examination of consciousness, and he was able to make links between brain function/physiology and subjective experience. Jackson, for instance, noted that each case's intellectual aura usually took a consistent form. This was because each person's focus of epilepsy remained constant in the brain, and this part of the brain was consistently responsible for the same function. Jackson did not use the term, but it is now accepted that one feature of the dreamy state is déjà vu. Note that the official start date of Psychology is usually given as 1879, with Wundt studying subjects' introspections of the contents of consciousness. People were trained in how to report their subjective experience in order to illuminate the theories of psychologists. This method resonates with Hughlings Jackson's concept of 'self', which was similarly subjective, arising from the 'introspection of consciousness' (cited in Meares, 1999). Therefore, right at the birth of psychology, Hughlings Jackson was using parallel methods and theories to explore the subjective experience of people with epilepsy.

RESEARCHING SUBJECTIVE EXPERIENCE: COGNITIVE FEELINGS

One of the conceptual and historical issues that dominate the déjà vu literature is the subjective nature of the experience. A brief foray into the literature suggests that déjà vu was a prominent topic in the late nineteenth century. For example, Freud, Titchener and James all devote time to the topic in their texts. However, after that point, it was less discussed in mainstream psychology. In the main, this was probably due to shifts in emphasis in the study of psychology. Mainstream psychology began to consider behaviour as measured by experimentation and the observable actions of subjects in the laboratory. Much less researched were feelings and conscious states and people's 'introspections' about their thought processes. At this point, we might suggest that déjà vu became less a focus of study, since it could not be reproduced in the laboratory, and participants' responses or behaviours became more important than reports of their conscious experience.

Much later, Tulving (1989) directly attacked this prevalent 'behaviourist' view, describing it as the 'doctrine of concordance'. According to the behaviourist, behaviour, cognition and experience were one and the same: if you could measure one, you could infer processes about the others. The modern view, however, is that subjective experience plays an important part in memory function. Tulving's (1985) major contribution was to classify memory on the basis of experience, and suggest that without measuring experience you could not investigate cognition. His theory posits that memory retrieval is either self-knowing or not – and this judgement was something that only the participant in an experiment could report. Crudely speaking, it was the kind of issue that the behaviourists had overlooked in their experiments. 'Self-knowing' or 'autonoetic' memory describes a memory where the first-person experience was of 'remembering'. Memory without self-knowledge, 'noetic', is often described as 'just knowing'. According to Tulving, then, episodic memories are self-knowing – that is, some aspect of the memory includes its source, an awareness of its origin, a feeling of pastness, a conscious evaluation of itself. On the other hand semantic memories are not, they are just facts, or stored knowledge.

Tulving's classifications revitalized the exploration of conscious processes in memory. Using his concepts of *remembering* and *knowing*, many insights into memory dysfunction (e.g., Moulin, Conway, Thompson, James, & Jones, 2005), education (e.g., Conway, Gardiner, Perfect, Anderson, & Cohen, 1997) and the ageing process (e.g., Souchay, Moulin, Clarys, Taconnat, & Isingrini, 2007) have been made. For reviews of this topic, see O'Connor, Moulin and Cohen (2007) and Gardiner (2001). Interestingly, some scholars suggest that these experiential distinctions between remembering and knowing were anticipated by Hughlings Jackson's theories, which are widely described as being ahead of their time (e.g., Luria, 1973; Meares, 1999).

A critical point about remembering and knowing is that they are experiential states which allow us to experience our mental processing. They are feelings with a purpose: 'remembering' something signifies that you are retrieving something from your personal past, not daydreaming or inventing information. The feeling of knowing something tells you that information is stored and is readily available. These sensations, and others, we describe as 'cognitive feelings'. They signal to the experient what processing is going on and how to interpret it. Table 9.1 gives some common examples.

Measuring subjective experience

Cognitive psychology and, in particular, memory research within cognitive psychology grew from scientific approaches which sought to remove subjective feelings, and avoid the 'bias' of subjective report. How, then, should we measure subjective experience, and be confident that we are reflecting true internal processes, and not the idiosyncrasies of a few select participants? There are four general principles that underpin much research on subjective experience:

Subjective evaluations should relate to actual performance

People's feelings should relate to their behaviour: if you feel that something has been very well learned, then your performance for that item should be high. People *can* predict how well they will perform or how well they have performed, suggesting that their subjective reports are indicative of some access to mental operations. For instance, Lovelace (1984) showed that an individual's prediction of memory functioning for a to-be-remembered item was more accurate than an average of everyone's predictions for that item: the individual is conscious of their memory processing in a way not captured in a group aggregate of predictions.

Subjective evaluations should relate to objective characteristics of stimuli

We know that different types of materials are remembered differently, and that these appear to be processed in different ways. For instance, high-frequency words (such as 'jacket') and low-frequency words (such as 'epaulette') produce different levels of memory performance, but re-assuringly, they generate markedly different reports of subjective experience too. The low-frequency words are vivid, and usually bizarre, they tend to generate rich, evocative memories, whereas words like 'jacket' are difficult to differentiate, and tend to generate vague feelings. This type of difference has been explored with subjective reports of remembering and knowing by Gardiner and Java (1990); these stimuli yield very different types of subjective experience.

Participants should be able to justify their responses

Gardiner, one of the leaders in the field of memory and consciousness, put forward this approach (e.g., Gardiner, Ramponi, & Richardson-Klavehn, 1998) and the parallels to the early work of the introspectionists are clear. Simply, people's justification of responses should relate to their experience, and the way that they have responded to the test. We regularly collect

Table 9.1 Some examples of cognitive feelings

Cognitive feeling	What it signifies
Tip of the tongue	I know that I know this word!
Familiarity	I have encountered this before!
Recollection	I remember this!
Feeling of knowing	I know this!
Aha! (Eureka moment)	I solved it! (Insight)
Uncertainty	I am unsure!
Ease of processing	I can do this!

justifications from our participants, and they can effortlessly discriminate between feelings such as, '*It's vague – I think I saw it before*' and '*I made an association with Polka dot. It's a Polish word, it means woman.*' It is particularly persuasive if people spontaneously justify their experience, or draw parallels between what you have produced in the laboratory and what they feel in daily life.

There should be converging evidence from neuropsychology or neuroimaging

Brain damage and neuroimaging are powerful tools, often regarded as 'converging evidence' by cognitive psychologists. If we are measuring a verifiable subjective process, we would hope that we could see it in the brain, or that it might break down in a systematic manner in brain damage. (It is on this latter angle that we have produced much research; see below.) Work on the subjective nature of cognition has utilized ambiguous figures, such as Rubin's vase – a famous illusion, where you can see the figure either as two faces in profile looking at each other, or as a vase. Andrews, Schluppeck, Homfray, Matthews, and Blakemore (2002) showed that different areas of the brain were activated when seeing this as a face or a vase: people's subjective reports mapped onto activation within their brain (or vice versa). The same has been demonstrated for memory: the responses of different brain regions differ according to the phenomenology (Henson, Rugg, Shallice, Josephs, & Dolan, 1999). Even animals' memory seems to have two parallel systems divided into a more effortful, remembering-like process, and a faster more elemental simple familiarity system (Aggleton & Brown, 1999). (However, it is very unlikely that animals have any kind of cognitive feeling analogous to our own associated with these two separate systems.) In short, a different part of the brain seems to be responsible for *remembering* than for *knowing*.

This fourth and final category is critical for déjà vu. If we can find out what brain region or mechanism might contribute to this strange subjective experience, we are closer to finding something objective and tangible and a means of categorizing subjective experience. This is why the investigation of epilepsy, where there are clear disruptions to brain function, and often in quite specific areas of the brain, has proved so insightful in a range of cognitive theories, not just memory. In short, where we know there are neural networks in the brain responsible for cognitive feelings such as *remembering* or *knowing*, we know that a glitch in those areas of the brain might lead to a temporary inappropriate sensation: that is, the brain feels as if it finds something familiar, whereas all the available information suggests that this is not true. That is, déjà vu is a natural consequence of there being brain regions set up to interpret memory processing.

THEORIES OF DÉJÀ VU FORMATION

There are probably as many theories of déjà vu formation as there are déjà vu researchers; and not all researchers favour a memory-based account. O'Connor and Moulin (2008) suggest that scientific theories of déjà vu formation can be broadly divided into two classifications: bottom-up sensori-perceptual theories suggesting that the sensation of déjà vu arises from familiarity evoked by some element of the perceptual environment, and top-down higher-order theories suggesting that déjà vu results from an over-arching cognitive feeling that is applied to perceptual input. This chapter will predominantly demonstrate evidence for the second account; the brain, and a glitch in the working of the memory system, causes déjà vu. Parapsychological (non-scientific) accounts of déjà vu are covered in Brown (2004).

Of the bottom-up accounts, examples include Gestalt familiarity (Dashiell, 1937), single-element familiarity (Leeds, 1944) and optical pathway delay theory (Osborn, 1884). Gestalt theories suggest that configuration of perceptual elements, such as the arrangements of objects in a room, may parallel similar stored representations (not unlike Tonegawa's ideas above) and that this overlap in general configuration might lead to a sense of familiarity, and thus, déjà vu. Sno and Linszen (1990) provide a detailed technological analogy for the way in which aspects of the perceptual experience are degraded in their holographic model. Single element familiarity proposes that one item in the scene drives the feeling of familiarity which extends as a vague familiarity for the entire environment or situation. The final subset of these theories concerns a glitch slightly further along: there is a problem with how the perceptual world is communicated to the part of consciousness which is interpreting it. In this category are dual pathway theories such as optical pathway delay, which have intuitive appeal and a high public awareness. In these theories, the brain short-circuits in such a way that information arrives at one point before it arrives at another. A crude example of this is that déjà vu is caused by information arriving from one eye to the brain more quickly than the other. Support for these perceptual accounts is somewhat diminished by the fact that people who are congenitally blind still report normal sensations of déjà vu (O'Connor & Moulin, 2006). If déjà vu is formed by information in the environment triggering matches or mismatches in the brain, it certainly is not merely an optical mechanism.

The alternative to such theories is that the sensation of déjà vu is higher order, or driven by erroneous cognitive feelings usually used to successfully interpret cognitive processing. By our account, normal healthy cognitive feelings operate to raise to consciousness mental acts such as remembering, knowing, problem solving and temporary retrieval failure. Normally, cognitive processing is accompanied by appropriate cognitive feelings. A dissociation between the objective knowledge of memory and the subjective sensation of familiarity, removed from perceptual content altogether, is responsible for déjà vu. Such top-down accounts are likely to be linked to neuronal accounts of déjà vu formation, since a candidate mechanism has to be found which is both higher order, but essentially unpredictable – i.e., not driven by stimuli in the perceptual domain. In the following sections we shall characterize déjà vu as a top-down, brain-based error of memory, such as experienced by people with temporal lobe epilepsy.

DÉJÀ VU AND THE BRAIN: INSIGHTS FROM EPILEPSY

> He who is faithfully analyzing many different cases of epilepsy is doing far more than studying epilepsy.
>
> > (Hughlings Jackson, cited in Penfield and Perot, 1963, p. 596)

The modern contributions of epilepsy are two-fold, both of them stemming from Wilder Penfield's early work. First, it is possible to study the subjective experience of spontaneous dreamy states in people with temporal lobe epilepsy. Second, it is possible to provoke dreamy states by directly stimulating the cortex of the brain.

Spontaneous déjà vu

Let us first consider the contribution of examining first-person accounts of déjà vu in people with temporal lobe epilepsy. Consider this typical account of someone experiencing epilepsy-related changes to their conscious experience:

> I can be doing anything at all, either thinking about déjà vu or not. It doesn't make a difference where I am. It will start off with me hearing something e.g. someone talking or anything, actually. It will just be some information that I am taking in. I will briefly think that I have heard what is being said before. It almost feels like I am having a premonition. If it was just this then I could cope but it's what follows which is so disturbing and frightening to me. I will explain what happened the last time I had one which was today because they seem to be increasing with severity every time. I suddenly feel like all the happiness in me has been sucked out. I explain this to people like the dementors in Harry Potter. It's simply as though I have no happiness or hope or future. All I can think about is what the déjà vu was about. Nothing else. Everything else in my life has vanished totally from my mind. If I am somewhere I like, I will hate it and feel uncomfortable to be there. It feels different to how it feels normally. It's like the way you see things in your dreams; you know them but they're different in some ways and you feel disturbed by them. Now that they have increased in severity I totally forget where I am and when I start to come round I don't know where I am. It's like turning on the telly and suddenly seeing a scene played out in front of you which you didn't

know was going to be there before you turned it on. . . . As for the déjà vu [experiences] themselves; it feels like I have either heard it before or more frequently it feels as though it has been in a dream. I don't think it has though. I sort of create a whole alternative world in my head for those few moments and nothing else in the world exists. I don't feel at all comfortable with it and I would do anything to get away. At first it seemed as though I was only getting them when in traffic or somewhere busy. I seemed to get them when I looked at lights e.g. traffic lights.

This long account includes general descriptions of feelings and thoughts which are probably at all stages of the epileptic episode: before, during and after. There is a feeling of strangeness, and a mood change (the sense of sadness), associated with a sort of hallucination of scenes, and 'déjà entendu' (see Table 9.2). This full description, in its richness, would be termed a dreamy state, even though the experient focuses on the déjà vu sensation – i.e., déjà vu is just one facet of this larger passage of associated experiences. The relation to memory processes here seems complex; this account is not purely a feeling of familiarity. Interestingly, these feelings that events or episodes are repeating are mostly based on hearing, and déjà entendu rarely seems to evoke mere familiarity.

Through detailed first-person accounts like this, it is possible to draw parallels between healthy memory function and what happens when those sensations go awry. When we know about the focus of the epilepsy in someone's brain, we can use that information to triangulate on what areas of the brain are responsible for what areas of function. But we can also ask these people to participate in our research; because they experience more frequent and profound bouts of déjà vu, we can use them to help demystify the experience and consider theoretical points in their experience. For instance, patient MH (O'Connor & Moulin, 2008) helps us converge on the fact that déjà vu tends not to be triggered by events or stimuli in the environment. MH was a 39-year-old, right-handed, male software engineer, who had obtained a physics degree at Oxford and had no history of mental illness. Having recovered from encephalitis at the age of 33, MH suffered resultant temporal lobe

Table 9.2 Some proposed varieties of déjà vu experiences (top panel) and our broader, theoretical classification (lower panel)

Term	Description
Déjà senti	Already felt (for thoughts or emotions)
Déjà parlé	Already said/spoken (for conversational material)
Déjà visité	Already visited (for places and locations)
Déjà entendu	Already heard (for aural material)
Déjà vu	An inappropriate sensation of familiarity
Déjà vécu	An inappropriate sensation of recollection

epilepsy (TLE). Prior to contracting encephalitis, MH had never experienced déjà vu. In fact, when he first experienced it, he suspected that it was a spiritual event. At first, he found the experiences disturbing although he later appreciated that the sensation was a consequence of his brain injury. He reported that his déjà vu experiences lasted between 5 and 60 seconds and occurred from once a month to three times a day. He described a typical déjà vu in a very standard fashion: 'An event will occur and I will have the sensation of knowing that the event was going to happen at that time, and I will recognize every detail of it as it happens. It is as though it has already happened. It is as though I have lived through that period of time before.'

As MH was initially upset by the experience of déjà vu, he tried many different ways of stopping it. The illusion that he recognized every detail of the current event led MH to believe that he would be able to end the sensation if he diverted his attention to something else: 'I . . . went through a period of looking away from what I was recognizing, hoping that this would get rid of the déjà vu. I now know that looking away, or at other things doesn't help, because the déjà vu follows my line of vision and my hearing.' Thus, it does not matter what MH diverts his attention to; the sensation persists. Moreover, the length of the déjà vu experience, sometimes up to a minute long, means that MH has diverted attention to many events within the same episode and yet the sensation persists.

MH's experiences provide a valuable insight into the formation of déjà vu. Because his experiences arise more frequently and are often of longer duration than is reported in the general population, he was able to test data-driven theories of déjà vu formation by diverting his attention from any possible 'cause' of the déjà vu. In doing so, and noticing the persistence of the experience, sometimes over a number of different diversions, MH came to the conclusion that the sensation of familiarity he was experiencing was not brought about by stimuli, but by a persisting sensation of familiarity resulting from his TLE, which applied itself to whatever he was experiencing at the time. At least in this one case, this is inconsistent with data-driven accounts of déjà vu formation, and is consistent with a brain-based account which influences higher-order cognitive feelings, Penfield's 'interpretive illusion' (1955). If MH's experience is comparable to that of the healthy brain, then we are closer to understanding what déjà vu is.

However, our account is directly at odds with other theorists. In a line of reasoning similar to Tonegawa's comments to the press (above), Gloor (1990) proposed that erratic firing of temporal lobe neurons could result in erroneous matches with previous experiences, thus giving rise to the sensation of familiarity, and déjà vu. This doesn't seem to explain MH's experiences though, as it does not account for the persistence of déjà vu across several shifts in attention – unless each new perception is related to a new previous perceptual experience. Thus, it is simpler to suggest that erratic neuronal firing in areas responsible for familiarity (Spatt, 2002) may cause a generalized sense of familiarity which extends to all perceived experiences for the duration of the inappropriate neuronal firing.

Provoked déjà vu: cortical stimulation

Secondly, then, we can also stimulate the brain directly, and observe what memory and other experiences this produces. Stimulating the brain directly like this is an important part of clinical work: if a neurosurgeon wishes to remove part of the brain responsible for seizures in order to treat the epilepsy, it is important that they locate the focus of the epilepsy. This procedure occurs while the patient is conscious – they are able to report the sensations of what happens while the electrodes are applied to the brain. So, a consequence of this clinical approach is that we can gain information about which areas of the brain produce which sensations or feelings. Penfield and Perot (1963, p. 597) describe the results of their studies as follows:

> . . . gentle electrical stimulation of temporal lobe cortex also produced sudden "feelings" – sometimes the feeling of familiarity that clinicians had been in the habit of calling déjà vu, sometimes an alteration in the apparent meaning of things seen or heard. . . . These are signals of altered interpretation of present experience. When they occur during a seizure they come as illusions of interpretation.

Penfield's interpretative illusions in epileptic subjects parallel our own theories about cognitive feelings. The use of 'interpretative' in Penfield's work is key, because it suggests that these are not epiphenomena, but signals and sensations which are attributed meaning. We argue that the meaning part of these signals is the meaning usually gleaned from cognitive feelings. That is, interpretative illusions are what arise when erroneous processing or brain dysfunction (however momentary or benign) produces cognitive feelings that are removed from current experience. Penfield was able to produce a range of interpretative illusions by stimulating the temporal cortex, but here we shall focus on memory.

Penfield and Perot (1963) report directly stimulating the cortex of 1132 patients, 520 of whom received stimulation of the temporal lobe. Of these 520 patients, 7% experienced experiential responses and 10% had spontaneous experiential hallucinations following stimulation. As an example, Case 30 produced the following accounts, each line being a response following brief stimulation (p. 642):

> "Sounded like I was singing a song."
> "I seemed to hear a song, sort of familiar, like on the radio."
> "Yes, I felt just terrified for an instant." Stimulation was continued. She was asked if she still felt terrified and she said, "No." She explained it was the kind of terror she has with her attacks.

Patient said, "No." Then she said, "It reminded me of a song but I do not know what song it was."

In this case, the patient reports a sensation of overwhelming familiarity, and one can imagine it is the sort of sensation that we sometimes feel when information is on the 'tip of our tongue'. But note that none of the material is retrieved: this is an illusion – a feeling which is divorced from normal processes. It *feels* as if a memory is being retrieved and yet nothing comes to mind.

Few, if any, memory textbooks describe the work of Penfield. In fact, his ideas largely fell from view, since they did not neatly fit into emergent ideas. For instance, he believed that when full scenes and visual information were reproduced following stimulation, it was a direct stimulation of something that was stored in that location, whereas contemporary ideas favour an inter-connected network. Memory research became so concerned with the veracity of memory and of suggestibility that his work was overlooked. For instance, when Case 31 (p. 643) received stimulation she reported:

A true experience. This man, Mr Meerburger, he, oh well, he drinks. Twice his boy has run away. I went to the store once for an ice cream cone and I saw that he was back and I said 'Hmm, he is back,' and the lady asked me, 'What is the matter?' and I didn't know how to explain so I said, 'Well you know Mr Meerburger drinks.' I thought that was the easiest way but later my mother told me, no, and it made it a lot worse.

This mini-narrative is difficult to verify. In the 1950s and 1960s, at a point when memory research was concerned with the objective nature of the cognitive system, and of observing only concrete, measurable entities, these kinds of 'memories', whether true or not, were considered difficult to interpret. Note that, presumably, even the subject may not know whether this is a true memory. The nature by which this memory was produced is so artificial that even they might not know that it is false – it may simply *feel* like a memory.

However, the contemporary view is not so concerned with veracity. In fact, by studying patients who are known to fabricate memories (the so-called 'honest lies' produced by confabulators), we are able to understand a lot more about how memories are constructed (see Conway, 2005 for a neuro-psychological account of false memory and confabulation, and see also the concluding remarks of this chapter). In short, the contemporary view is that false memories and confabulations come about because they are accom-panied by a feeling that the memory is real. A cognitive feeling enables you to experience your confabulation as if it is a real memory (Marshall, Halligan, & Wade, 1995).

Another change in the field is that it is now widely accepted that false memories are a normal part of memory's nature. That is, false memories are not only experienced by people with brain damage or following direct stimulation of the brain. If you ask people about their memories for a vivid public event, such as where they were and what they were doing when they heard about the attacks of September 11th, 2001, their account is liable to change on subsequent occasions when you ask them. Even George Bush's account of how he heard changed (Greenburg, 2004). If these vivid memories change, then not *all* accounts can be correct, even though at each stage people feel that their memory is unaltered.

A further reason to revisit Penfield's pioneering work is the emergence of research into autobiographical memory as a major research theme. Autobiographical memory concerns how people retain memories of their life events (Conway & Pleydell-Pearce, 2000), and it is concerned with the kind of personal material that Penfield's subjects produced. All in all, Penfield's methods were so diligent, and his reports so full and detailed, that current theory suggests that revisiting his case reports and observations could continue to yield insights which can be incorporated into contemporary ideas.

Several researchers still continue to use stimulation in order to gain insights about the memory system, and, in particular, retrieval of memory. This recent work benefits from both technological and theoretical advances. The advantage of this more recent work is that it is now able to locate the precise area of stimulation of the brain, and that these findings can be incorporated back into memory theory. Chauvel and colleagues, for instance, have managed to differentiate the role of two separate cortical systems in déjà vu (i.e., feelings of familiarity) and the full retrieval of scenes (i.e., recollection) (e.g., Bartolomei et al., 2004). In this way, they were able to further fractionate the function of the temporal lobe. Feelings of familiarity akin to déjà vu are produced by stimulation of a small portion of this area called the entorhinal cortex (in 16.8% of cases), whereas reminiscence of scenes was produced by stimulation of the perirhinal cortex (7.9% of cases). These tiny regions are not more than a couple of centimetres apart, so you begin to understand the complexity and specificity of this memory system. The unique contribution of such technical work is that separate sub-areas of the temporal lobe are involved in separate experiences of the dreamy state.

More modern research continues to refine the definitions of various aspects of the dreamy state, including déjà vu, whilst still generating incredible first-person accounts of experience: 'I'm reliving something . . . but I can see you clearly . . . It's as if what is happening now has already happened to me, it's like an old memory that I am in the middle of living out' (Vignal, Maillard, McGonigal, & Chauvel, 2007, p. 92). Because the fragmentary memories that come to mind are usually visual, they are often described as 'hallucinations'. Vignal et al. suggest that when these hallucinations are experienced in conjunction with sensations of having lived through the present moment before, this results in a feeling of reminiscence, supporting the cognitive feeling theory above. The content (hallucination) and associated sensation (déjà vécu – see below for a description) combine to form a complete sensation of reminiscence. Although this is produced artificially, presumably it feels no different from how you or I normally experience our memories. The dreamy state is when these two, content and sensation, are produced individually.

The other contribution of this more recent work is a sophisticated understanding of the networks involved in memory retrieval. The above description of perirhinal and entorhinal accounts is necessarily crude, but bear in mind that all of the brain is interconnected in a complex network. As an example, Barbeau et al. (2005) investigated which areas of the brain were activated when patient FGA underwent stimulation of the cortex (see Figure 9.1). Like other cases, FGA reported sensations and images similar to memories when his temporal lobe was stimulated:

> The patient immediately said that something had materialized and that it was a neighbor going by in the street on a motorbike. He added: "I see him very often" and said that it was his brother's friend. Questioned later, he explained that he had seen a chromed part of a motor, then a black-leathered boot and that he had inferred from these "distinct signs" that the person he was seeing was his brother's friend.
>
> (Barbeau et al., 2005, pp. 1333–1334)

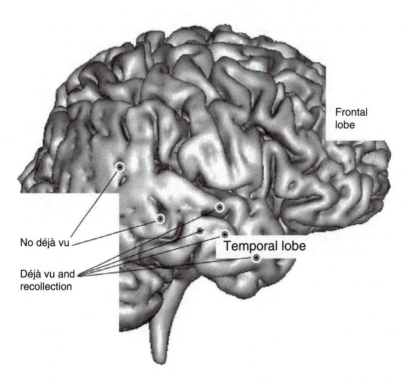

Figure 9.1 Sites of electrode stimulations eliciting déjà vu and recollection (from Barbeau et al., 2005).

The results indicated that recollection of vivid memories was based on acti-vation of wide networks of brain areas that 'transiently synchronize'. Experiential phenomena are rarely obtained after brain stimulation, as Penfield noted. Barbeau and colleagues indicate that it is necessary for a wide range of brain areas to fire together in order to get these complex and bizarre sensations, hence it does not merely occur when one zone of the brain is activated. Thus a contemporary view of the neuropsychology of memory has to see it as a complex network of interconnected areas, and not any one region.

Thus Chauvel and colleagues have shown that stimulation of the temporal lobe extends into other areas – into the hippocampus and amygdala in par-ticular (Bancaud, Brunet-Bourgin, Chauvel, & Halgren, 1994; Bartolomei et al., 2004; Vignal et al., 2007). The hippocampus has long been known to be critical for memory function and conscious recall (see patient HM, below), but the amygdala can be crudely thought of as being the emotion centre of the brain, so that when activation extends to this region from the temporal lobe, you might expect that the sensation becomes emotionally valenced, explaining why many epileptics' experience of déjà vu includes intense emo-tions such as terror. Many TLE patients report a sensation of fear before seizure and before any sensation of déjà vu or recollection of scenes.

Research into the dreamy state is important in confirming the importance of large networks responsible for memory of past events. The classical view is that it is the hippocampus (see patient HM, below) which is important for memory function. However, the hippocampus is part of a network which involves the amygdala and other areas of the temporal lobe. Vignal et al. (2007) found that 45% of dreamy states were produced by stimulation of the amygdala, and many of these stimulations resulted in recollection of scenes. When stimulation extends to the amygdala it has the effect of causing physio-logical response, including facial expressions and uneasy sensations in the stomach (Bancaud et al., 1994). This is one area where there is a large dis-crepancy between healthy and unhealthy experiences of déjà vu. Temporal lobe epileptics tend to have emotive déjà vu sensations coupled to physiological and taste abnormalities, whereas people experiencing déjà vu in healthy mental life do not seem to consistently have marked sensations of fear or report strange tastes.

Chauvel and colleagues (Vignal et al., 2007) have also incorporated these sensations into contemporary views of autobiographical memory. An important feature of autobiographical memory is that it is organized around lifetime periods, such that you may recall your personal memories with reference to particular periods, such as, 'when I lived in Bristol', 'the year Manchester United won the Champions League' and 'whilst I was dating Tess' (Conway & Pleydell-Pearce, 2000). When activation is sufficient to retrieve full images and memories following stimulation, it is rare that the same electrode produces the same memory on each occasion. However, Vignal et al. showed that these flashes of memory do come from the same lifetime period. The organization of memory gathered from psychology experiments is possibly borne out in the physical structure of memories as represented in the brain.

To summarize this section: it has long been known that there was an association between epileptic activity in the temporal lobe and illusions and experiences such as déjà vu. For the mainstream memory researcher, there are two main contributions from this field. First, the network of regions activated in these patients, either spontaneously or in stimulation studies, converges on a network of temporal regions incorporating the hippocampus and extending to the amygdala. Second, given the current focus on subjective experience, these studies demonstrate that, however artificially, it is possible to have sensations of memory functioning (feelings of remembering and familiarity) which are devoid of content – usually these feelings are described as déjà vu. Equally, it is possible to have content devoid of the normal feelings of processing and initiation: fragments and flashbacks can just appear in the mind without reason. Only when the content and the sensation are working in unison do these patients probably feel anything like a 'normal' retrieval of information from memory.

PATHOLOGY AND DÉJÀ VU: CONTRIBUTIONS FROM NEUROPSYCHOLOGY

In this section, we consider processes other than epilepsy and how they influence the brain. Modern theories of memory formation are indebted to neuropsychology – learning from damaged brains about how healthy brains function – and the rationale for déjà vu is no different from forgetfulness, except that the concepts are a little more subjective. No undergraduate psychologist can escape hearing about the fundamental contribution of patient HM to the understanding of human memory.

HM had severe epilepsy as a boy in the 1940s, and did not respond well to treatment. In 1953, he had a bilateral temporal lobectomy, removing part of his temporal lobe – the area around and including the hippocampus. This procedure reduced epileptic symptoms; Jasper and Penfield had recently published the 'Montreal Procedure' (in 1951, see Jasper & Penfield, 1954), which, as well as describing direct stimulation of the brain, also described how removing the part of the brain involved in epileptic seizures reduced symptoms. HM's epileptic symptoms were reduced but he was left with a profound memory disorder, and subsequently became a one-man focus for memory research. This is because he had a well-defined area of damage within the brain linked to a clear memory deficit, but it must also partly be due to the fact that HM was prepared to patiently endure so many memory tests. HM was intensively researched by Brenda Milner, one of Penfield's PhD students; Penfield's contribution to the field is immense. For more about HM, see Hilts (1995).

HM had, for the most part, anterograde amnesia, in that he could not acquire new memories, even though he could remember events prior to his surgery (Scoville & Milner, 1957). He was not intellectually impaired generally: language and intellectual function were actually better after surgery than before. HM could not recall instances of previous test sessions, but he could 'learn' skills like mirror drawing, without being aware of it. Thus, he showed intact procedural memory, but impaired declarative memory, supporting the notion of two distinct memory systems, one available for conscious report (memory with awareness) and the other not (memory without awareness). Tulving's theory of remembering and knowing was an extension of this, having memory without awareness ('anoetic') and memory with awareness being split into self-aware (autonoetic – 'remembering') and (noetic – knowing). HM's contribution was to refine the theories of memory in existence at the time, and to demonstrate the role of the hippocampus in bringing memory to conscious awareness (Corkin, 2002). This idea has proved very robust, and data from HM still contribute a lot to this notion; the hippocampus is important for memory, and the experience of 'remembering'.

We can try to evaluate the déjà vu experience in a similar fashion, hoping to learn from the brain in order to refine our understanding of the experience. That is, having arrived at an explanation of déjà vu that is brain-based, one would expect that with damage to the brain, or by interfering with its delicate chemical balance, we might see changes in déjà vu incidence. As well as epileptic changes, other aspects of brain physiology should lead to sensations of déjà vu. The chapter started by stating that déjà vu experience was related to intoxication, tiredness and stress. As well as having clear psychological effects, we also know that these have clear impacts on brain physiology, so it seems unsurprising that they may affect déjà vu prevalence. Migraine is also noted as a cause of intense déjà vu in some people (Sacks, 1970). We have also already seen how elegant and simple questions provide sound answers: the mere fact that someone who is blind has déjà vu means that it is not essentially a visual experience; there must be more to it than just optical pathway delay. Here we present a series of cases that suggest that disruptions to the brain chemistry through pharmacology influence déjà vu, and finish up with some more pronounced cases, where brain damage leads to a particularly debilitating form of déjà vu.

Déjà vu and psychopathology

Adachi et al. (2007) administered a questionnaire on déjà vu to 113 schizophrenics and 386 controls. People with schizophrenia actually experienced déjà vu less frequently than controls. Additionally, the déjà vu characteristics as assessed by the questionnaire were no different from controls, although the schizophrenics reported being more distressed by the experience. Adachi and colleagues suggest that the low level of déjà vu reported, and its similarity to healthy experiences of déjà vu, means that déjà vu is not a pathological experience. Additionally, recent work from this group shows no relation between a key concept in psychopathology – dissociation – and déjà vu occurrence (Adachi et al., 2008). Not only might we conclude that déjà vu is not a spiritual experience, it is apparently not a psychopathological one, either.

Déjà vu and psychopharmacology

Three separately reported cases illustrate the effect of an imbalance in brain chemistry on the memory system. First, Taiminen and Jääskeläinen (2001) report a case who they suggest suffers from déjà vu as a result of disruptions to the dopaminergic brain system. Their brief report is of an otherwise healthy male taking amantadine and phenylpropanolamine together to relieve flu symptoms. This resulted in his having intense and prolonged sensations of déjà vu. This was apparently not a nasty experience, since the paper reports that the subject experiencing déjà vu completed the course, describing it is a pleasant sensation. Kalra, Chancellor, and Zeman (2007), on the other hand, report the case of a 42-year-old woman whose persistent déjà vu was so severe that she shut herself in a darkened room:

> Everything that had happened on Tuesday happened again. This time I went to my room, switched off TV, turned off the phone and asked to be left alone. I had the same feeling of having seen and done all of this before . . . The funny thing with all of this was that if you asked me what was going to happen I didn't know, I just felt that as things were happening I had done it all before and it felt natural for me to know all of this.
>
> (Kalra et al., 2007, p. 312)

Kalra et al. speculate a serotoninergic mechanism: this otherwise healthy woman had received 5-hydroxytryptophan, in combination with carbidopa, as treatment for palatal tremor (distressing, repetitive and involuntary movements of the soft palate), on two separate occasions. Each time, she experienced intense, protracted déjà vu, lasting for several hours. Finally, Singh (2007) reports the case of a 15-year-old boy who was hospitalized with paranoia, déjà vu and mental slowing after taking salvia, a hallucinogen. He complained frequently of déjà vu without concurrent hallucinations, but became paranoid towards those who tried to reassure him that events or conversations had not occurred before. Although likely to be very rare, Singh suggests that this drug may be associated with long-term effects, one of which could be déjà vu. Normally, one would only consider that salvia has short-term effects on brain chemistry and cognition.

Déjà vécu: Cases of recollective confabulation

Thus far, this chapter has drawn on contemporary conceptions of episodic and semantic memory, as defined by Tulving (1985). Déjà vu seems to be based on a sensation of erroneous familiarity, and Chauvel and colleagues are able to differentiate between stimulations which produce such sensations of familiarity, experienced as déjà vu, and stimulations which produce more full recollections, based on episodic remembering. Our contribution is to suggest that just as there must be an erroneous feeling of familiarity, there must also be a comparable experience, where one erroneously believes oneself to be *remembering* information. We distinguish these as déjà vu and déjà vécu respectively, based on earlier terminology used by Funkhouser (1995). To illustrate this theory we originally presented two cases who, as a result of dementia causing damage to temporal and frontal regions, have false sensations of remembering, which cause them to confabulate previous episodes of encoding information. It is not that these patients find things falsely familiar, but that they feel that they are remembering previous events and fabricate 'evidence' that they have encountered such events before.

AKP was an 80-year-old man who initially presented to his family doctor with memory problems and frequent sensations of déjà vu. MA was a 70-year-old woman who presented to her doctor, convinced that things had happened before, as evidenced by her memory for them happening as they happened. AKP's and MA's erroneous sensations of memory were so compelling that the patients were unwilling to engage in activities such as watching television and reading the newspaper as they felt they had already carried them out. Note that healthy déjà experiences do not lead to behavioural changes: one is able to challenge and resist the sensation that one has encountered something before, whereas these patients act on their beliefs.

In order to establish the recollective nature of déjà vécu, we administered a recollective experience-based recognition task to AKP and MA. Using this standard memory task, we were able to ascertain a typical response pattern. AKP and MA were required to try to memorize a list of words, and then later select those words from a set of distracters. If they felt that they had seen the word before, they then reported their experiential state (see Gardiner, 2001, for a full account of this method). When we compared the déjà vécu patients' responses to those of age-matched controls, the déjà vécu patient responses were characterized by a greater number of false positives – that is, they said that they had seen words that in fact they hadn't. When asked to report whether this was because they found each word familiar or they remembered something about it, the patients were most likely to report that they *remembered* seeing the item, and to justify this experience they 'invented' evidence to support this view (i.e., they reported experiences and thoughts from the non-existent study phases for non-presented items).

In fact, this *recollective confabulation* is a critical feature of this condition. Since recollection is associated with the retrieval of contextual information and experiences at study, it is perhaps unsurprising that these patients with high levels of déjà vécu also generate high levels of incorrect contextual information for items which, in fact, they have not encountered before. AKP made such reports spontaneously, for instance confabulating secret early morning trips to the newsagents to read the newspaper as it was unloaded from the lorry whilst his wife was asleep in bed. This tendency was also noted in Mr K, a 92-year-old man who started experiencing memory difficulties in his eighties. Mr K's déjà vécu became apparent to his son when they took a family holiday to France, a country Mr K had never previously visited. His son reported an episode of recollective confabulation (O'Connor, Lever, & Moulin, in press):

> When we travelled round France, my father saw a hospital and said, "I have been here before, I visited this hospital to see my friend." He then told the story of his previous visit to confirm his memory. When he was asked how this could be possible when he had never visited France before, my father said, "I know that I have never been here when I consider my personal history seriously and logically, but I still strongly feel that I have been here before." We thought he was over-tired so we took a two-day break from sightseeing. Unfortunately, when we resumed sightseeing his memory situation had not changed.

The dissociation between Mr K's feelings of recollection and his awareness that he could 'logically' not have been to the hospital in France illustrates the conflict caused by Mr K's déjà vécu: it was only when challenged that Mr K would concede that his sense of recollection could be false. However, such was the strength of his memory sensation that, unless he was forced to consider the consistency of his memories with what he knew about his past experience, Mr K would believe that his memories were accurate.

The déjà vécu cases also make a contribution to the brain-based account of déjà vu. While not as specific or precise as the direct stimulation of the cortex described above, images from neuroimaging of the brain with MRI technologies suggest that these patients have damage to the frontal lobes as well as the regions of the brain thought normally to be responsible for déjà vu. Perhaps this is why these cases cannot help but act on the sensations of déjà vécu; the frontal lobes are crudely speaking responsible for controlling and monitoring the rest of cognitive function (see Stuss & Levine, 2002). Certainly, our view is that the frontal lobes are part of the system responsible for making decisions and initiating actions based on the sensations derived from the temporal lobe.

THE ULTIMATE TEST: PRODUCING DÉJÀ VU IN THE LABORATORY

So where are we now with déjà vu research? Thus far we have demonstrated that the topic is far from being an inexplicable paranormal experience. It is quite clear that déjà vu, at least when experienced as part of brain injury, or disease, has quite clear origins in the brain – almost certainly the medial temporal lobe and portions of the frontal lobe, regions that are known to be used in healthy memory function. Given that these brain systems are set up to experience and interpret our rich, complex memory systems, when they have temporary or permanent malfunctions, they should result in strange, yet predictable sensations. In this manner, déjà vu is an illusion of memory which can help us understand better the human memory system. Interestingly, memory researchers have been somewhat slow to use such illusions to illuminate their understanding. In comparison, the vision scientists looking at the psychology of perception have long used visual illusions in order to better understand how that system works in everyday situations and in the healthy brain (Gregory, 1968).

We have also outlined the contemporary classification of memory, which is as much based on how it feels to retrieve a memory as it is on the content of the memory. At this stage in the field, researchers are busy investigating the parallels between healthy subjective experience and the various forms of déjà vu and the pathologies that can cause it. One idea that needs further support is on our distinction between déjà vu and déjà vécu. Because the memory system is such that it can either re-experience events with a sense of familiarity or a sense of recollection, we think that it makes sense that there are different varieties of the déjà experience based on either of these two systems (Moulin et al., 2005). These two subtly different experiences can be felt by healthy people.

We turn back to the classification and description of 'healthy' déjà experiences. Previous classifications have centred on which modality of perception, or for what material the déjà vu has occurred with. Such terms read like a revision list of past participles in a French exam (for examples see Table 9.2, and for a full list, see Brown, 2004). Our classification hinges on the state of the art in memory research. A sensation of déjà vu is a fleeting sensation of inappropriate *familiarity*, of finding something familiar but knowing that you have not encountered it before. A sensation of déjà vécu, on the other hand, is an error based on falsely feeling as though you *remember* something that you know you might have encountered before. Because remembering is usually more effortful, longer lasting and evocative than memory retrieval based on familiarity, we suggest that this experience might be longer lasting, more emotive and a more complete sensation. Indeed, remembering is an experience normally associated with the reintegration of memories from different stores in the brain, and in particular, emotional material. Thus, we might expect déjà vécu experiences to be more emotive than déjà vu experiences. Our line of argument is largely based on the hypothesis that there are two parallel memory systems, based on remembering and knowing, and our experience of working with people with memory impairment. More research is needed to test this theory – especially in healthy populations.

It is important to try to differentiate déjà vu and other memory errors, in particular, false memories (for an account of false memory see Schacter, 2001). Much research shows that a feature of healthy memory is that it will occasionally remember events that did not actually occur. Within patient groups, the terminology for such memories is varied. Some authors use *false memory*, some *delusional memory*, and others the term *confabulation* (as above). In healthy and brain-damaged individuals the idea is the same: these memories are experienced as *real* – the person does not appreciate that they are for events that did not happen. For the healthy person, these false memories tend to be mundane over-generalizations, such as 'remembering' that you have been given the word 'sleep' in a memory test, whereas you have in fact only been asked to remember 'doze', 'bed', 'rest', 'snore', 'snooze' and a whole list of words related to the critical, non-presented word, 'sleep'. See Roediger and McDermott (1995) for an overview of this procedure.

Critically, for false memories of any description, the experient does not know that the memories are not true, even though in patient groups they can be fantastic and implausible. The main difference between healthy and pathological false memories is the scale and vividness of the memories. Healthy false memories tend to involve misremembered details and situations, reconstructed to form plausible but incorrect memories. Pathological false memories, on the other hand, can involve fantastic beliefs about implausible events and happenings. As outlined above, one theory stemming from the subjective approach advocated by Tulving is that it is a dysfunctional sensation of recollection that lets us re-experience false memories as if they are true: they are experienced as if they are memories, not daydreams, or random thoughts. Similarly, as above, when participants 'recognize' having seen 'sleep' before in a memory test, when in fact they have not – it is based on a feeling of 'remembering' (Roediger & McDermott, 1995).

Déjà vu is clearly not merely the same as false memory, since it requires two opposing sensations or evaluations. We can quite readily produce memories based on the gist of a previous encounter, such as 'remembering' 'sleep', but this does not produce déjà vu. For déjà vu to occur, there needs to be the sensation of retrieving something from memory combined with the knowledge that you have, in fact, not encountered it before. To continue with this example – we would have to simultaneously produce the sensation that they had encountered 'sleep' before whilst somehow making the participant certain that they had not encountered the word before.

In clinical groups the difference between déjà vu and false memory is harder to pin down but still rests on the person feeling two opposing sensations or at least a general sense of confusion combined with the knowledge that what they are experiencing is not normal, as described in the example above: 'It feels different to how it feels normally. It's like the way you see things in your dreams; you know them but they're different in some ways and you feel disturbed by them. . . . I sort of create a whole alternative world in my head for those few moments and nothing else in the world exists.' The key issue here is that the patient is aware of this clash in evaluations. If we simply feel that something has occurred before, to all intents and purposes it has. A false memory occurs when we unwittingly accept the evaluation that an event or item has been experienced before, when in fact it has not. A déjà vu requires awareness of the error, and an opposing mental evaluation. In truth, without verification we might never know how many subjectively 'true' false memories we may be experiencing.

The final challenge is to produce déjà vu and déjà vécu in the laboratory in healthy participants to test these ideas. Certainly, work on déjà vu in this regard is in its infancy. O'Connor, Barnier, and Cox (2008) have successfully produced déjà vu in the laboratory, drawing on early work by Banister and Zangwill (1941), who observed that people hypnotized to forget material, on re-encountering that material, had sensations similar to déjà vu: there was a clash between how the material felt (familiar) and the knowledge (imposed under hypnosis) that they had not encountered the material before. O'Connor et al. gave participants a task in which they had to solve a children's puzzle. This task involved moving pieces, shaped like trains, waggons and carriages, around a board. O'Connor et al. gave their participants the suggestion that they would find the aspects of the task familiar:

> After you wake up, I will give you a puzzle task to do. You will feel as though you have done the task before but you will not understand why you are having this feeling. As you lean forward to look at the task, you will have an overwhelming and surprising sense of familiarity – of having done this exact action before. When you notice the little red engine and the exit gate, you will believe that you have seen them before.

This suggestion resulted in 67% of participants having a strong sense of familiarity for the puzzle and 83% of participants feeling a 'strong' sense of déjà vu. Participants spontaneously likened this sensation to déjà vu, even though no reference to it was made in the suggestion:

Participant:　I think I've done something like this before. I dunno . . . I was just looking at what had to go where and how it could be manipulated. Actually, when I first looked at it I thought I wouldn't expect to finish it but once I started doing it, it made sense. It was just a bit odd.

Hypnotist:　So you told me that you felt as though you had done it before. Tell me a bit about that.

Participant:　It was pretty déjà vu. It seems like a real childhood toy kind of thing. I think I've done something similar to it before.

Hypnotist:　Can you tell me when you might have done that?

Participant:　I'm not sure. Probably when I was a kid or something.

Hypnotist:　Were there any particular aspects of the task that seemed familiar?

Participant:　Like the engine . . . how it feels and how it slides on the board. It just seems familiar.

Brown and Marsh (2008) have also produced an illusion comparable to déjà vu in the laboratory. In their study, in a first phase, participants briefly processed pictures of locations where they had never been, whilst concentrating on another task. At a later session, participants viewed the pictures again, this time saying whether or not they thought they had been to those places. Brown and Marsh found that participants who were exposed to pictures without processing them deeply were more likely to report that they had visited that location. If this simple finding were extended to the real world, where you may arrive at a location and find it familiar, but not know why, it may feel something like déjà vu. In fact, Cleary (2008) reviews experimental work on familiarity-based recognition and concludes that it could be the basis of déjà vu formation, but does not offer any empirical support. In general, the field of déjà vu research needs a lot less theorizing, and a lot more work in the laboratory.

CONCLUSION

These lines of experimentation are of critical importance to understanding déjà vu, since once we have successfully produced this state in the laboratory, we can produce it in the neuroimaging scanner. This would enable us to re-converge on the issue of what brain regions are responsible for this strange sensation, finally building a bridge between healthy and pathological experiences of déjà vu. In doing so, we will have demonstrated that one of the most esoteric, mysterious and intensely human experiences is just a by-product of the set-up of the normal memory system, and along the way we may understand much more about the experience of memory, research that will filter its way back into helping care for and understand people with memory problems, and open up new fields of understanding of consciousness and the human condition. It won't solve the problem with the glaciers, though.

Acknowledgements

This work stems directly from an ESRC-CNRS collaborative workshops programme awarded to Moulin, where Chauvel presented as an invited speaker, Leeds, UK, June 2007 (Recollection, Remembering and the Complex Nature of the Self RES-170-25-0008). We are very grateful for the insightful contribution of Fiadhnaith O'Grady Sindall and several others who have emailed us their experiences. This overview would not have been possible without the diligent work of Akira O'Connor, whose work at undergraduate, postgraduate and postdoctoral level has illuminated this field. Such advances in understanding still derive from such bright students asking difficult questions.

References

Adachi, N., Adachi, T., Akanuma, N., Matsubara, R., Ito, M., Takekawa, Y., et al. (2007). Déjà vu experiences in schizophrenia: Relations with psychopathology and antipsychotic medication. *Comprehensive Psychiatry*, *48*, 592–596.

Adachi, N., Akanu, N., Adachi, T., Takekawa, Y., Adachi, Y., Ito, M., & Ikeda, H. (2008). Déjà vu experiences are rarely associated with pathological dissociation. *Journal of Nervous and Mental Disorders*, *196*, 417–419.

Aggleton, J. P., & Brown, M. W. (1999). Episodic memory, amnesia and the hippocampal–anterior thalamic axis. *Behavioral and Brain Sciences*, *22*, 425–498.

Andrews, T. J., Schluppeck, D., Homfray, D., Matthews, P., & Blakemore, C. (2002). Activity in the fusiform gyrus predicts conscious perception of Rubin's vase–face illusion. *Neuroimage*, *17*, 890–901.

Arnaud, F. L. (1896). Un cas d'illusion du 'déjà vu' ou de 'fausse mémoire'. *Annales Médico-Psychologiques*, *3*, 455–471.

Bancaud, J., Brunet-Bourgin, F., Chauvel, P., & Halgren, E. (1994). Anatomical origin of déjà vu and vivid 'memories' in human temporal lobe epilepsy. *Brain*, *117*, 71–90.

Banister, H., & Zangwill, O. L. (1941). Experimentally induced visual paramnesias. *British Journal of Psychology*, *32*, 30–51.

Barbeau, E., Wendling, F., Regis, J., Duncan, R., Poncet, M., Chauvel, P., & Bartolomei, F. (2005). Recollection of vivid memories after perirhinal region stimulations: Synchronization in the theta range of spatially distributed brain areas. *Neuropsychologia*, *43*, 1329–1337.

Bartolomei, F., Barbeau, E., Gavaret, M., Guye, M., McGonigal, A., Regis, J., & Chauvel, P. (2004). Cortical stimulation study of the role of rhinal cortex in déjà vu and reminiscence of memories. *Neurology*, *63*, 858–864.

Bering, J. M. (2006). The folk psychology of souls. *Behavioural and Brain Sciences*, *29*, 453–498.

Brown, A. S. (2003). A review of the déjà vu experience. *Psychological Bulletin*, *129*, 394–413.

Brown, A. S. (2004). *The déjà vu experience*. Hove: Psychology Press.

Brown, A. S., & Marsh, E. J. (2008). Evoking false beliefs about autobiographical experience. *Psychonomic Bulletin and Review*, *15*, 186–190.

Cleary, A. M. (2008). Recognition memory, familiarity, and déjà vu experiences. *Current Directions in Psychological Science*, *17*, 353–357.

Conway, M. A. (2005). Memory and the self. *Journal of Memory and Language*, *53*, 594–628.

Conway, M. A., Gardiner, J. M., Perfect, T. J., Anderson, S. J., & Cohen, G. M. (1997). Changes in memory awareness during learning: The acquisition of knowledge by psychology undergraduates. *Journal of Experimental Psychology: General*, *126*, 393–413.

Conway, M. A., & Pleydell-Pearce, C. W. (2000). The construction of autobiographical memories in the self memory system. *Psychological Review*, *107*, 261–288.

Corkin, S. (2002). What's new with the amnesic patient H.M.? *Nature Reviews Neuroscience*, *3*, 153–160.

Dashiell, J. F. (1937). *Fundamentals of objective psychology*. Boston: Houghton Mifflin Company.

Dewhurst, K. (1982). *Hughlings Jackson on psychiatry*. Oxford: Sandford Publications.

Edelstein, P. H. (2006). Déjà vu all over again: Rapid enumeration of *Legionella pneumophila* in water. *Applied Environmental Microbiology, 72*, 980.

Funkhouser, A. (1995). Three types of déjà vu. *Scientific and Medical Network Review, 57*, 20–22.

Gallup, G. H., & Newport, F. (1991) Belief in paranormal phenomena among adult Americans. *Skeptical Inquirer, 15*, 137–146.

Gardiner, J. M. (2001). Episodic memory and autonoetic consciousness: A first-person approach. *Philosophical Transactions of the Royal Society of London, B: Biological Sciences, 356*, 1351–1361.

Gardiner, J. M., & Java, R. I. (1990). Recollective experience in word and nonword recognition. *Memory and Cognition, 18*, 23–30.

Gardiner, J. M., Ramponi, C., & Richardson-Klavehn, A. (1998). Experiences of remembering, knowing and guessing. *Consciousness and Cognition, 7*, 1–26.

Gloor, O. (1990). Experiential phenomena of temporal lobe epilepsy: Facts and hypotheses. *Brain, 113*, 1673–1694.

Greenburg, D. L. (2004). President Bush's false [flashbulb] memory of 9/11/01. *Applied Cognitive Psychology, 18*, 363–370.

Gregory, R. L. (1968). Perceptual illusions and brain models. *Proceedings of the Royal Society of London. Series B, Biological Sciences, 1024*, 279–296.

Halber, D. (2007). Research deciphers 'déjà vu' brain mechanics. Retrieved 27 March 2008 from: http://web.mit.edu/newsoffice/2007/deja-vu-0607.html.

Henson, R. N., Rugg, M. D., Shallice, T., Josephs, O., & Dolan, R. J. (1999). Recollection and familiarity in recognition memory: An event-related functional magnetic resonance imaging study. *Journal of Neuroscience, 19*, 3962–3972.

Hilts, P. J. (1995). *Memory's ghost: The strange tale of Mr M. and the nature of memory*. New York: Simon and Schuster.

Jackson, J. H. (1888). 'Intellectual aura', one case with symptoms of organic brain disease. *Brain, 11*, 179–207.

James, W. (1890). *The principles of psychology*. New York: Henry Holt and Company.

James, W. (1902). *The varieties of religious experience*. New York: Longmans, Green, and Co.

Jasper, H., & Penfield, W. (1954). *Epilepsy and the functional anatomy of the human brain* (2nd ed.). New York: Little, Brown and Co.

Kalra, S., Chancellor, A., & Zeman, A. (2007). Recurring déjà vu associated with 5-hydroxytryptophan. *Acta Neuropsychiatrica, 19*, 311–313.

Leeds, M. (1944). One form of paramnesia: The illusion of déjà vu. *Journal of the American Society for Psychical Research, 38*, 24–42.

Lovelace, E. A. (1984). Metamemory: Monitoring future recall ability during study. *Journal of Experimental Psychology: Learning, Memory, and Cognition, 10*, 756–766.

Luria, A. R. (1973). *The working brain*. Harmondsworth, UK: Penguin.

McHugh, T. J., Jones, M. W., Quinn, J. J., Balthasar, N., Coppari, R., Elmquist, J. K., et al. (2007). Dentate gyrus NMDA receptors mediate rapid pattern separation in the hippocampal network. *Science, 317*, 50–51.

Marshall, J. C., Halligan, P. W., & Wade, D. T. (1995). Reduplication of an event after head-injury: A cautionary case-report. *Cortex, 31*, 183–190.

Meares, R. (1999). The contribution of Hughlings Jackson to an understanding of dissociation. *American Journal of Psychiatry, 156*, 1850–1855.

Moulin, C. J. A., Conway, M. A., Thompson, R. G., James, N., & Jones, R. W. (2005).

Disordered memory awareness: Recollective confabulation in two cases of persistent déjà vecu. *Neuropsychologia, 43,* 1362–1378.

Nicolas, S. (1996). Experiments on implicit memory in a Korsakoff patient by Claparede (1907). *Cognitive Neuropsychology, 13,* 1193–1199.

O'Connor, A. R., Barnier, A. J. & Cox, R. E. (2008). Déjà vu in the laboratory: A behavioral and experiential comparison of posthypnotic amnesia and posthypnotic familiarity. *International Journal of Clinical and Experimental Hypnosis, 56*(4), 425–450.

O'Connor, A. R., Lever, C. & Moulin, C. J. A. (in press). Novel insights into remembering: Cases of déjà vécu and recollective confabulation. *Cognitive Neuropsychiatry.*

O'Connor, A. R., & Moulin, C. J. A. (2006). Normal patterns of déjà experience in a healthy, blind male: Challenging optical pathway delay theory. *Brain and Cognition, 62,* 246–249.

O'Connor, A. R. & Moulin, C. J. A. (2008). The persistence of erroneous familiarity in an epileptic male: Challenging perceptual theories of déjà vu activation. *Brain and Cognition, 68,* 144–147.

O'Connor, A. R., Moulin, C. J. A., & Cohen, G. (2007). Memory and consciousness. In G. Cohen & M. A. Conway (Eds.), *Memory in the real world* (3rd ed., pp. 327–356). Hove, UK: Psychology Press.

Osborn, H. F. (1884). Illusions of memory. *North American Review, 138,* 476–486.

Penfield, W. (1955). The twenty-ninth Maudsley lecture: The role of the temporal cortex in certain psychical phenomena. *Journal of Mental Science, 101,* 451–465.

Penfield, W., & Perot, P. (1963). The brain's record of auditory and visual experience. *Brain, 86,* 596–696.

Roediger, H. L., III, & McDermott, K. B. (1995). Creating false memories: Remembering words not presented on lists. *Journal of Experimental Psychology: Learning, Memory, and Cognition, 21,* 803–814.

Sacks, O. (1970). *Migraine.* London: Faber and Faber.

Saver, J. L., & Rabin, J. (1997). The neural substrates of religious experience. *Journal of Neuropsychiatry and Clinical Neuroscience, 9,* 498–510.

Schacter, D. L. (2001). *The seven sins of memory: How the mind forgets and remembers.* New York: Houghton Mifflin.

Scoville, W. B., & Milner, B. (1957). Loss of recent memory after bilateral hippocampal lesions. *Journal of Neurology, Neurosurgery and Psychiatry, 20,* 11–21.

Singh, S. (2007). Adolescent salvia substance abuse. *Addiction, 102,* 823–824.

Sno, H. N., & Linszen, D. H. (1990). The déjà vu experience: Remembrance of things past? *American Journal of Psychiatry, 147,* 1587–1595.

Souchay, C., Moulin, C. J. A., Clarys, D., Taconnat, L., & Isingrini, M. (2007). Diminished episodic memory awareness in older adults: Evidence from feeling of knowing and recollection. *Consciousness and Cognition, 16,* 769–784.

Spatt, J. (2002). Déjà vu: Possible parahippocampal mechanisms. *Journal of Neuropsychiatry and Clinical Neurosciences, 14,* 6–10.

Stuss, D. T. & Levine, B. (2002). Adult clinical neuropsychology: Lessons from studies of the frontal lobes. *Annual Review of Psychology, 43,* 401–433.

Taiminen, T., & Jääskeläinen, S. K. (2001). Intense and recurrent déjà vu experiences related to amantadine and phenylpropanolamine in a healthy male. *Journal of Clinical Neuroscience, 8,* 460–462.

Tulving, E. (1985). Memory and consciousness. *Canadian Psychologist, 26,* 1–12.

Tulving, E. (1989). Memory: Performance, knowledge, and experience. *European Journal of Cognitive Psychology*, *1*, 3–26.

Vignal, J. P., Maillard, L., McGonigal, A., & Chauvel, P. (2007). The dreamy state: Hallucinations of autobiographic memory evoked by temporal lobe stimulations and seizures. *Brain*, *130*, 88–99.

Walsh, V. (2004) Here we go again . . . [Review of the book *The déjà vu experience*]. *Trends in Cognitive Sciences*, *8*, 483–484.

Discussion

A future for applied memory research

Daniel B. Wright and Graham M. Davies

In the introduction we talked about the success of Neisser's (1978, p. 4) battle cry: "If X is an interesting or socially significant aspect of memory, then psychologists have hardly ever studied X." It helped to bolster the number of people conducting applied memory research, but angered many traditional laboratory memory researchers. It led to the inevitable backlash that was most poignant in Banaji and Crowder's (1989) paper where they state: "the movement to develop an ecologically valid psychology of memory has proven itself largely bankrupt and, moreover, that it carries the potential danger of compromising genuine accomplishments of our young endeavor" (p. 1185). At the beginning of the 1990s the applied and basic memory researchers were at loggerheads. Like the Jets and the Sharks from *West Side Story*, each performed carefully choreographed arrangements around each other in committee meetings and departmental corridors before returning to their separate enclaves at SARMAC and Psychonomics.[1]

The tone of both Neisser's battle cry and Banaji and Crowder's counteroffensive was hostile, but rhetoric aside they both made good points. In 1978 there was some work on applied memory, but not as much as Neisser would have liked, and since 1978 it has increased. And the increase has included both good and bad research. Banaji and Crowder rightly pointed out that it was important to think about methodological rigour regardless of how interesting the research topic is. So what has happened since the early 1990s? Are there still warring factions and are we likely to suffer the same tragic fate as Tony in *West Side Story* (Tony died)? What does the future hold?

First, it is clear that there is excellent applied memory research being conducted which is of the utmost quality by both applicability and methodological standards. The contributions in this book show this. We chose these authors because they conduct research that satisfies both applied and basic research goals. Authors could have been chosen who fitted more into the applied memory group or the basic memory group. There remain differences between these groups. There still are journals which tend to publish applied research and others which tend to publish basic research. The ambience of SARMAC and Psychonomics conferences differs and, while any individual talk could appear at either, thumbing through their programmes will leave the reader with a different view of the current state of memory research. These institutional differences do reflect different approaches to memory. We think having different approaches is positive. The area of memory is vast and it is important that different methods are used to explore it and different theories to account for it. It is important that these groups communicate with each other to share knowledge, to prevent repeating others' successes and failures, and to criticize each other.

In this chapter we describe some ways to differentiate types of memory research. We describe how the most successful topics in applied memory have research projects which satisfy all the different types. We finish by justifying our choices of topics for the book as some of the key large problems facing today's memory researchers and by speculating what societal-large problems applied memory researchers may be addressing tomorrow.

TYPES OF MEMORY RESEARCH

A goal of any intellectual enterprise is to classify things. This is probably most evident in biology where species are classified into a complex hierarchy, but it exists in all the sciences (e.g., the importance of the periodic table in chemistry) and in all the humanities (e.g., *West Side Story* is categorized with *Romeo and Juliet*). Academics also turn this need to classify onto themselves. Sometimes this is reflected bureaucratically, so that we have departmental structures, but even within memory research there are subdivisions. The concentration here is on methodological divisions, but it is worth first stressing that some divisions are based on subject matter. Memory is a topic that is studied in many disciplines (literature, computer science, neuroscience, anthropology, etc.). Those of us within the cognitive psychology tradition are often blinkered from these other developments because our methods are very different from their methods, we do not read their journals, and we work in different buildings. Even within cognitive psychology, most memory people work either on short-term memory or on long-term memory. Of course there are important relationships between these (Baddeley, 2000), but memory has become such a vast topic that most of us cannot even pretend to keep up to date on both.

When memory researchers talk about SARMAC and Psychonomics, different images come to mind. SARMAC conferences are small gatherings usually on lush green campuses during the summer break. Dress is informal. Psychonomics occurs in dark cold November in monolithic edifices to corporate America. People wear suits! One of us has a lasting memory from a Psychonomics conference that summed up this difference. When Jonathan Schooler presented six case studies of people who reported not having remembered a traumatic event and then later *discovering* a memory for it (Schooler & Fiore, 1995), one member of the audience proclaimed (from memory with some help from Schooler): "Six studies a Psychonomics talk does not make." The Yoda-like grammatical structure made the person sound like a wise elder of an ancient and traditional society. The person wanted to distance Psychonomics conferences from those where this kind of methodology was acceptable.

There are three features that seem to differentiate the typical talks at Psychonomics from those at SARMAC:

- experimental (causal hypotheses) versus non-experimental (associative hypotheses);
- artificial (sometimes simple) versus non-artificial (sometimes complex) stimuli;
- basic versus applied.

These are the typical attributes, but chapters in this book show how successful research programmes often cross boundaries.

The first distinction is between studies where participants are randomly allocated to conditions (or some variation of this) and quasi-experimental/ correlational studies. The choice of which design to use depends primarily on whether the researcher is evaluating a causal or an associative hypothesis (Wright, 2006). These types of hypothesis are often complementary. Consider Christman and Propper's chapter on interhemispheric interaction and memory. They reviewed two sets of studies. One set looked at the causal effects of having people make eye movements on memory and therefore most of these studies used experimental designs. The other set looked at the association between handedness and memory. Because you cannot randomly allocate people into being left-, mixed-, or right-handed, these studies could not look directly at causal hypotheses. The distinction between experimental and non-experimental is usually fairly easy to make for any given study, but within any topic area there is often interest in the causal mechanisms, the conditions in which they occur, and existing associations.

The second distinction is a continuum from the highly artificial CVCs of Ebbinghaus to complex stimuli like real events and video footage. Most memory research within cognitive psychology is not at either of these extremes. The problem with using meaningless CVCs is that we know some of the memory processes are dependent on the meaning of stimuli. The problem with using complex natural stimuli is that, because memory processes are dependent on many aspects that make the stimuli complex, it is difficult to know whether the results generalize to other stimuli. This problem is compounded because researchers often do not know all aspects of the stimuli they are observing. Within a typical study researchers often rely on one type of stimuli, but when integrating data on any topic it is best to examine research using simple and complex stimuli. Reporting of child sexual abuse is an important topic within applied memory research. London and Kulkofsky's chapter described research showing that often people fail to report actual child sexual abuse. This is critical to establish that there is a large problem. However, the data they examine are complex, making it difficult to pinpoint the reasons for why some people do and do not disclose abuse. They also then discuss research using simpler stimuli. Geraerts, Raymaekers and Merckelbach's chapter uses a similar approach in order to identify some of the processes and conditions associated with accurate and inaccurate disclosure of abuse.

The third way that differentiates the stereotypes of SARMAC and Psychonomics is the applied versus basic distinction. This is a difficult distinction because it depends on how the research is used. A classic example from the history of science is the development of calculus by Leibniz and Newton. In one sense this was a pulling together of centuries of work on the theoretical mathematics of small changes, but it is also applicable to countless real-world problems. Is their work theoretical when taught in a mathematics course but applied when taught in a physics course? Moving forward from Leibniz and Newton, consider Moulin and Chauvel's work on déjà vu. This work is not halfway between applied and basic, it is applied *and* basic. There are people who experience déjà vu whose difficulties are being addressed by this research *and* the research impinges on some fundamental questions about cognition and neuropsychology. This is not to say that all research is both applied and basic, but that research can be both of these.

HOW TOPICS ARISE IN APPLIED MEMORY RESEARCH

How much interaction is there between applied and basic research? In the introduction we described how drawing a distinction between applied and basic memory research in the UK is difficult. We mentioned the lineage of Bartlett–Broadbent–Baddeley at Cambridge, but other UK research hotspots were also not in the grip of behaviourism as much as in the US. The breakthroughs for US applied memory research were led both by theoretical breakthroughs and by application. The theoretical breakthroughs (Neisser's *Cognitive psychology*, 1967; Minsky's *frames*, 1975; Schank and Abelson's *scripts*, 1977) meant that much of the exciting work was on the complexity of the events to be remembered. The largest application breakthrough within memory research was eyewitness testimony research.

Defence attorneys had long argued that eyewitness testimony was fallible, but during the behaviourist years there was little US psychology research that they could use to support their belief. The research by Elizabeth Loftus and others in the 1970s, and the strides to get this research into courts (since prosecuting attorneys did not want this research admitted), established eyewitness testimony as one of the main topics in the recent history of applied memory research. Much of this research has been on what has become known as the misinformation effect. This is because it is also important for memory theories. This research showed the reconstructive nature of memory and for memory applications this has been influential for interviewing adults and children.

Eyewitness testimony research transcends the three ways, listed above, for distinguishing the typical Psychonomics and SARMAC talks. It is basic (e.g., we know more about the reconstructive nature of memory, about the effect of emotional stimuli) *and* applied (e.g., many jurisdictions use the cognitive interview and sequential line-up). It is about causation (e.g., presenting misinformation lowers accuracy) *and* association (e.g., White people are better at identifying other White people than people of other races). And the stimuli range from the simple (the rapid display of faces on a computer screen) to the complex (archival analysis of actual cases). Indeed, the research on eyewitness testimony is at such a high level that when the US Attorney General saw that eyewitness testimony was the main cause of errant convictions in cases overturned on the basis of DNA evidence, the American Psychology-Law Society was ready with a set of recommendations (Wells et al., 2000). The reason why the American Psychology-Law Society could help was that there was applicable basic scientific research.

Another topic which brought the applied and the basic memory researchers together in the 1990s was the recovered memory debate. There was a fundamental argument about memory, and yet initially memory researchers were not that involved. Initially it was difficult for memory researchers to say much about people recovering memories of trauma from decades before because it had not been studied as a phenomenon. Normally, memory researchers expose people to an event, do something, and then test their memory. For recovered memories, one of the main questions was whether the event existed or not. When the likes of Loftus, Roediger, Schacter, etc., became involved it was clear that a multi-pronged approach to the phenomenon would be taken. The line between SARMAC and Psychonomics became blurry because now there was a different group that could be criticized: the clinical psychologists who traditionally eschew experimental methods in favour of case studies. As we noted in the introduction, an uneasy calm now reigns, but it is easy to imagine that this conflict in research cultures will arise again.

Education is another topic of great interest to psychologists in general but one which until recently had been rather neglected by memory researchers. The branches of educational psychology and developmental psychology have long applied theories to education. The prime example is the work by Piaget. There is a difference between the education-related chapters in this book and the other chapters. Applied memory researchers are explicitly taking theories of memory and applying them to education. The purpose is to complement not supplement research from other perspectives. Memory is a critical facet of education and a topic that applied memory researchers could do more to address. President Lyndon Johnson wasn't explicitly referring just to memory researchers when he said: "Education is not a problem. Education is an opportunity," but his word "opportunity" is appropriate.

The final topic we chose for this book was memory research related to neuroscience and neuropsychology. People with neuropsychological detriments have always been of interest to psychologists, and throughout the last

100 years many memory detriments have shown how theoretical insight can also help treatment. This line of research has been particularly active recently thanks to the advent of modern brain imaging techniques that can locate processes temporally and spatially. There was also a great increase in research funding following Presidential Proclamation 6158 declaring the 1990s the Decade of the Brain. The themes explored in this book represent just a few of many topics which memory researchers have recently explored in this field, but have been selected because of the link they demonstrate between theory and method.

WHAT TOPICS ARE GOING TO BE HOT?

Gazing into a crystal ball to decide what will be major areas of applied memory research over the next decade is risky. Looking at the past is always a good start:

- Children will still need to learn.
- Eyewitnesses will still be errant.
- The brain will continue to be a fallible but increasingly transparent seat of cognition.

So these three broad areas should continue to fill the pages of Applied Memory books and journals. The specific research questions will change. Education in much of the world is now interlinked with computer technology, and projects like "One Laptop Per Child" (OLPC http://laptop.org/) are making this linkage more widespread. How will education work when children can rely not only on their own human memory but also on their computer's memory in the classroom? How will they survive cognitively when they are away from their computers?

Eyewitnesses will still make errors, but technologies like CCTV surveillance and DNA profiling are changing policing. Many of these advances have specific (sometimes disputed) error rates associated with them. This will mean, for instance, combining evidence from line-ups with other evidence that has specific quantitative estimates of its reliability. Does this mean that eyewitness researchers need to design studies to estimate error rates (as suggested in the US Supreme Court ruling in *Daubert*) rather then just detecting the presence of an effect? These are just some of the issues which will challenge the next generation of eyewitness researchers.

Speculating about neuroscience is more difficult. Much of what already goes on seems like science fiction, but then there are still the basic, millennium-old questions about the relation between brain and mental activities that are unanswered. As editors, we can speculate. With imaging techniques becoming more available, much of the "noise" of past studies will be systematically analysed and over the next ten years a major area of memory-neuroscience research will be individual differences. This will complement genome research, which also has as one of its goals highlighting individual differences.

What other areas will be hot? To decide this we must direct our crystal ball at society. Three areas seem to be of particular importance: changes in health, the environment, and shared belief systems.

First let us look at health and how changing demographics affect health needs. In the rich developed countries, people are living longer. Work on Alzheimer's and other age-related deficits is already an important area of applied memory research, but other areas are also equally in need of research attention. The memory needs of an ageing population will gain in importance. There are other health needs that will also need to be addressed. People in the developed countries are gaining in weight, and with that there is an increased risk of diabetes (with adverse consequences like blindness) and strokes (and their associated cognitive deficits). Outside the wealthy countries, television images, particularly from Africa, show that large portions of society face very different health problems: famine and epidemic. Research on memory applied to the health problems of the rich and poor countries is still at an early stage.

The second major concern today is the environment and scientists of all persuasions need to ask themselves how they can help. It would be naïve to assume that a memory researcher can design a way of making people remember to turn off light switches to aid the return of the arctic ice pack, but small steps like that would be useful. In the not too distant future, we might be facing a situation where the industrialized world is forced drastically to reduce energy consumption (with all the consequent economic problems) and where, according to most models, the non-industrialized world (plus the south of Florida, where this sentence is being typed) would undergo vast environmental change. How can memory researchers help with this? One way will be to develop techniques to convince and remind people to change their habits and to learn and remember to adapt.

The final topic is shared belief systems; by this we mean systems not based on evidence, but based on faith. In some cases this is not problematic, but in recent years faith has been used to justify war and terrorism, and has changed global politics. It has led many to argue that particular theories about nature should be fast-tracked into scientific acceptance. Faith has always had positive and negative consequences. Arguments can be made about which aspects are good and which are bad, but it is undeniably an important topic to which psychology in general and memory researchers in particular have made precious few contemporary contributions. Applied memory researchers have only just begun to look at faith-based belief systems. For instance, in some of the recovered memory cases, people were convinced that they were royalty in a satanic cult. Understanding belief systems as large and complex as a developed religion or the dynamics of a cult are the type of stimuli that would not fit well within an Ebbinghaus study. But the methodologies of modern cognitive psychology can be used alongside those of anthropology, religious studies, social psychology, and other sciences to better understand these processes at a societal level.

CONCLUSION

We began this book by saying that applied memory research is one of the most exciting areas in cognitive psychology. It is. It has been successful and that feels good, but it is important to stress that much of this success was built on the work of basic memory researchers and input from practitioners in a variety of fields. It is also a challenging field. Journal editors argue that strict methodological control must be followed but then practitioners question whether our research is applicable precisely because of that control. This is a good challenge. If we are going to be among the scientists who address the problems of justice, education, the environment, health, and terrorism we need to face such criticisms and address them.

Note

1 SARMAC (Society for Applied Research in Memory And Cognition) is most associated with the applied/everyday form of memory research. Although the Practical Aspects of Memory (PAM) conferences predate SARMAC as an organization they also define this genre. The annual Psychonomics conference is the venue most associated with experimental memory research.

References

Baddeley, A. (2000). The episodic buffer: A new component of working memory? *Trends in Cognitive Sciences, 4*, 417–423.

Banaji, M. R., & Crowder, R. G. (1989). The bankruptcy of everyday memory. *American Psychologist, 44*, 1185–1193.

Minsky, M. (1975). A framework for representing knowledge. In P. H. Winston (Ed.), *The psychology of computer vision* (pp. 211–277). New York: McGraw-Hill.

Neisser, U. (1967). *Cognitive psychology*. New York: Appleton Century.

Neisser, U. (1978). Memory: What are the important questions? In M. M. Gruneberg, P. E. Morris, & R. N. Sykes (Eds.), *Practical aspects of memory* (pp. 3–24). London: Academic Press.

Schank, R. C., & Abelson, R. P. (1977). *Scripts, plans, goals, and understanding: An inquiry into human knowledge*. Hillsdale, NJ: Lawrence Erlbaum Associates, Inc.

Schooler, J. W., & Fiore, S. M. (1995). Toeing the middle line: Evidence for both recovered and fabricated memories of abuse. Paper presented at the meeting of the Psychonomic Society, Los Angeles, CA.

Wells, G. L., Malpass, R. S., Lindsay, R. C. L., Fisher, R. P., Turtle, J. W., & Fulero, S. (2000). From the lab to the police station: A successful application of eyewitness research. *American Psychologist, 55*, 581–598.

Wright, D. B. (2006). Causal and associative hypotheses in psychology: Examples from eyewitness testimony research. *Psychology, Public Policy, and Law, 12*, 190–213.

Author index

Subject index